Habent sua fata libelli

Habent sua fata libelli

HAVE
BOOKS THEIR DESTINY
OWN

Essays
in honor of
Robert V. Schnucker

EDITORS
Robin B. Barnes,
Robert A. Kolb, and
Paula L. Presley,
and a Dedication by
Robert M. Kingdon

VOLUME L
SIXTEENTH CENTURY ESSAYS & STUDIES

*The editors gratefully acknowledge the generous support of Truman State University
at Kirksville, Missouri, in the production of this book.*

Library of Congress Cataloging-in-Publication Data

Habent sua fata libelli, or, Books have their own destiny : essays in honor
of Robert V. Schnucker / edited by Robin B. Barnes, Robert A.
Kolb, and Paula L. Presley with dedication by Robert M. Kingdon.
    p.   cm. — (Sixteenth century essays & studies ; v. 50) Includes
bibliographical references and index.
    ISBN 0-940474-59-X. (alk. paper). — ISBN 0-940474-60-3
(pbk. : alk. paper).
    1. Book industries and trade—Europe—History—16th century.
2. Europe—Intellectual life—16th century. I. Barnes, Robin Bruce,
1951–. II. Kolb, Robert A., 1941–. III. Presley, Paula Lumpkin,
1938–. IV. Schnucker, Robert V. Series.
Z291.3.H33   1998
381'.45002'09409031—dc2198–35348

                                            CIP

CONTENTS

Foreword

I HAVE KNOWN DR. ROBERT SCHNUCKER for more than four decades as a child-hood acquaintance, neighbor, pastor, teacher, scholar, and colleague; most importantly, however, I have known him as a friend in the highest sense of the word. I recall that when I first assumed the presidency of Truman State University, he immediately expressed concern about my health. In fact, for several weeks he appeared on my front porch at seven o'clock in the morning and invited me to walk briskly with him. My family was really impressed and grateful. My feelings were somewhat mixed! Seriously, I gladly join in honoring Bob, whose dedication, vision, and years of service have made such a positive difference in the lives of so many.

Dr. Schnucker can easily be described as a leader and an innovator. He has utilized his skills for the betterment of the Kirksville community, the Truman State University community, and the worldwide community of higher education. However, he does not focus on only the macro; he impacts very positively the life of each individual with whom he comes in contact.

As the state's liberal arts and sciences university, Truman State University is dedicated to student development, which includes instilling in each student the importance of lifelong learning. What a fit Dr. Schnucker is with this fine institution! He embraces this philosophy wholeheartedly. He has written: "I am convinced that it is now imperative for education to meet new challenges and new needs with imagination, experimentation, and courage.... The teacher must become one who stresses the position of being the consultant or stimulator for the learning process of the student. The output should be a person who is in the process of achieving intellectual independency and who possesses a zest for self-education throughout life."

Bob's former students describe him as highly effective, but certainly not easy. They praise him for his unwavering commitment to student development. His effectiveness can be measured partially by the numbers of students he inspired to pursue advanced degrees. They are now historians, clergy, faculty members, lawyers and other professionals who readily attest to his positive influence on their lives and career choices.

Bob's dedication to learning led him into the realm of publishing in the early 1970s. Since then, he has become an expert in this field. He oversaw the creation and the success of the Thomas Jefferson University Press at Truman State University. Over the years, his expertise in the management of a small press has been recognized by the American Council of Learned Societies, the

Organization of American Historians, the Conference of Historical Journals, and other professional organizations. Bob has brought great honor to this University, as well as to himself, through his many years of dedicated service to scholarly publication.

Now that I have talked about the educator and publisher, I would like to tell you a little more about the man, Bob Schnucker. I could always count on Bob to give me honest and well-thought-out advice when I needed assistance (and sometimes even when I didn't need it!). Rarely did I have to wonder about his opinion on a topic. I like that kind of forthrightness.

Bob's work ethic will long be discussed on our campus. He was the first to arrive at work in the morning, and frequently he could be seen on campus on holidays and weekends. He put in the hours to please his toughest critic, himself. He set very high standards for himself and for others.

As this book honors the life and contributions of an amazing individual, I wish to thank him for the many years of friendship he has given me personally and for the selfless dedication he has bestowed upon Truman State University. He has enhanced our institutional success and greatly enriched our lives. The entire University community joins me in wishing Bob, Anna Mae, and their family an abundance of blessings. We shall eagerly watch as Bob begins another stage of an already incredible life.

Jack Magruder
President

Truman State University
Kirksville, Missouri

Robert V. Schnucker

An Appreciation

Robert M. Kingdon

THIS BOOK CELEBRATES the remarkable career of a remarkable man. Robert V. Schnucker has carved for himself a unique place as an organizer and publisher of scholarship in the considerable variety of disciplines dealing with the period of the sixteenth century.

Schnucker was born in Iowa in 1932, in a family that had been active for generations in the Reformed faith. It thus came as no surprise that after earning an A.B. from Northeast Missouri State University (now Truman State University) and a B.D. from the University of Dubuque, in 1956 he became the minister of the United Presbyterian Church in Springville, Iowa. He soon developed a thirst for more intellectual stimulation than he could find in a parish, however, and enrolled in the graduate program in the School of Religion at the University of Iowa. That was where I first met him. I had just arrived, in 1957, from my first teaching position at the University of Massachusetts in Amherst, lured in good part by the prospect of teaching graduate students for the first time. Although my teaching appointment was in the Department of History, many of my students were from the School of Religion, drawn by my special interests in the history of the Reformation. One of the first was Bob Schnucker. I still remember what a pleasure it was for me to have him in class. I still treasure the compliments he paid me on a lecture I delivered on the Calvinist doctrine of predestination, compliments that meant a great deal to me as a scholar without any formal training in theology coming from a student who had already studied theology for several years. He then asked me to act as supervisor of an M.A. thesis he was planning on "English Intervention in the Scottish Reformation." That turned out to be a mistake. I simply did not know enough about English history of the period to supply the kind of guidance he needed. He was awarded his degree, but then switched over for his Ph.D. to James Spalding of the School of Religion, a fellow Presbyterian and eminent specialist on ecumenical initiatives designed to bring Christian churches back together in seventeenth-century England. The dissertation with which Schnucker won that Ph.D., in 1969, was on "Views of Selected Puritans on Marriage and Human Sexuality, 1550–1635." It reflected a growing concern he had developed as a working minister, dealing with teenagers grappling with problems of sexuality in a period when American standards in this field were shifting swiftly, asking him as their pastor for information on subjects like birth control.

A few years later, Schnucker published as a spin-off of his dissertation an important article on the early Puritan views of adultery. It appeared in what was then the most distinguished scholarly periodical in the world in the relatively new field of "total" history, the French *Annales*. In the same issue of that periodical appeared articles by Delumeau, de Certeau, and Flandrin, as well as Genicot and Trexler, and yet others, many destined to become leading stars in the firmament of great historians of the twentieth century. Bob was in distinguished company indeed. He had already begun teaching with a joint appointment in both history and religion at his alma mater, then Northeast Missouri State University. All the signs pointed to a distinguished career of a traditional type for him as both teacher and publishing scholar.

But Schnucker's interests were already veering off in another direction. He became very concerned about scholarly publication, about the preparation of published materials that could be used in classrooms. He became deeply involved in the Forum Press, a corporation created to publish books for historians written by historians. And he came to the attention of Carl S. Meyer, a professor of Church History at Concordia Seminary in St. Louis. Meyer was one of a group of ecumenically minded scholars at this flagship institution of the Lutheran Church–Missouri Synod determined to cultivate contacts among scholars of many confessional backgrounds. Meyer organized several scholarly conferences on the campus of his seminary; he was one of the driving forces behind the creation of the Foundation (now Center) for Reformation Research, located very near to the seminary, and became its director; he helped organize a new scholarly society designed to bring together scholars of many disciplines and backgrounds interested not just in the Reformation but in the entire period in which it had emerged, accordingly named the Sixteenth Century Studies Conference; he was determined to launch a program of publication that would give scholars with these interests the wider attention they deserved. In Schnucker, Meyer detected a young scholar with precisely the kinds of energy and vision necessary to realize these ambitions.

In a few years, however, Carl Meyer died suddenly and unexpectedly. He was succeeded at the Foundation for Reformation Research by an erudite colleague in Church History at the Concordia Seminary, Arthur Carl Piepkorn, who within another year also died suddenly and unexpectedly. And the seminary began to be ravaged by the schism within the Lutheran Church–Missouri Synod which shook that generation of Lutherans to their roots. The work of the Foundation remained in the hands of Robert A. Kolb, who had been hired right out of graduate school as an assistant to the director. He had been trained within the educational system of the Lutheran Church–Missouri Synod, up through its seminary in St. Louis, and then had come to the University of Wisconsin–Madison to earn degrees in history with me. Kolb and Schnucker together faced the problem of what to do with the Sixteenth Century Studies Conference and with the publication program it had planned to sponsor. A few issues of a journal had already been published, made up largely of papers read at the annual meetings of the Conference, but it had only a handful of subscribers and depended financially on subsidies from a Foundation with very few resources of its own.

Schnucker at that point took charge. He organized both the Sixteenth Century Studies Conference and *The Sixteenth Century Journal* as not-for-profit independent corporations in the state of Missouri, separate from the Foundation for Reformation Research with its shaky finances and the Concordia Seminary with all its problems. He and Kolb turned to me, as a former teacher of them both, to become the chief editor of *The Sixteenth Century Journal*. For more than twenty years, from 1973 to 1997, we worked together as a team, sometimes referred to as The Three Bobs. For most of that time, I made the final decisions on what would appear in the *Journal,* and Kolb served as associate editor, supervising the process of receiving and soliciting the opinions of specialists on manuscripts. For all of that time, Schnucker served as both book review editor and managing editor. He made himself an expert on the publishing business and on the printers allied to it. He took over supervision of both composition and distribution of every issue of the journal. He found ways of doing this at costs far lower than most other scholarly journals, in good part because he and his wife and other associates in Kirksville did so much of the work themselves. The end result was a journal far more successful than most of us had believed possible, with a subscription list growing from the low hundreds into nearly three thousand, submissions coming from both promising and established scholars all over the world, and a growing international reputation.

Not content with managing a successful scholarly journal, Schnucker then turned to editing scholarly books. In 1982, he set up a series titled Sixteenth Century Essays and Studies. We recruited Charles Nauert to be the first general editor of this series of monographs. With this book that series now totals fifty volumes. This particular book may well be the first for which Schnucker did not assume personally most of the managerial functions of arranging for composition, advertisement, and distribution. The series has turned into a considerable success, with several of these books winning prizes, many winning favorable reviews, most selling in gratifying numbers. The publishing acumen Schnucker displayed in building up this series was also tapped by his home institution in building up a university press, the Thomas Jefferson University Press. Schnucker became its director. That made it possible for scholars in yet other disciplines to benefit from his formidable managerial skills in the field of publication.

Meanwhile for a dozen years Schnucker also supervised the compilation and distribution of an annual newsletter, the *Scholars of Early Modern Studies,* designed to circulate informal information on scholars from all over the world interested in this period. This newsletter had been created by De Lamar Jensen of Brigham Young University, who, after a few years, wanted to pass it on to someone else. Schnucker with his usual energy made it ever larger and wide-reaching, and yoked it usefully to the programs of the Sixteenth Century Studies Conference.

That Conference, indeed, was closely tied at many points to this program of publication. From the beginning the annual meetings of the Conference have generated much of the scholarship published by the *Journal* and in the Essays and Studies series. In its beginnings, the Sixteenth Century Studies Conference was a modest regional meeting, held on the campus of the Concordia Seminary in St. Louis, drawing the participation of only a few dozen scholars from the immediate vicinity, most of them historians and theologians. It increasingly attracted scholars from other disciplines interested in the sixteenth century, notably from a considerable variety of literary disciplines, also from the histories of art and science. Its meetings have grown considerably and move about the continent from city to city. They are among the largest in the relevant fields in all of North America. Every year the Conference now draws together hundreds of scholars of every generational cohort from all over this continent, and increasingly from Europe as well, to read research papers, to comment on papers, and to exchange ideas in less formal ways. Most of this spectacular growth has been organized and directed by Schnucker as executive secretary of the Conference.

Schnucker has even won respect for the Conference well beyond its own membership. He personally drafted an application for membership on behalf of the Conference in the American Council of Learned Societies, an umbrella organization coordinating the activities of all sorts of scholarly organizations in this country. The former president of the American Council of Learned Societies, Stanley Katz, told me that he found the application presented for the Sixteenth Century Studies Conference to be a real model of the genre, very likely the best application he had ever seen, describing every activity of the Conference with an impressive clarity, setting it with admirable precision in the spectrum of organizations represented in the Council. That application helps explain Schnucker's rise to a position of eminence within the governing circles of this Council for years thereafter.

Meanwhile despite all these managerial and executive activities, Schnucker continued to teach a heavy load of courses at the university that now calls itself Truman State University. He also remained a minister, serving the Labelle Methodist–Presbyterian Church for more than thirty years. He also managed to help raise a large and flourishing family, and to support his devoted wife, Anna Mae, through a series of illnesses that would have daunted many.

It seemed to us obvious that the best way to celebrate the career of this specialist in producing books on the sixteenth century would be to produce a book about sixteenth-century publishing. That is precisely what this is. It contains chapters by thirteen of Schnucker's friends and associates. Many of these chapters grow out of projects in which he was himself closely associated. They cover every part of Europe and range from overviews of selected types of publishing to microstudies of particularly interesting individual publications.

We find it difficult to imagine Bob Schnucker in retirement—and on an Iowa farm—raising vegetables and spoiling grandchildren. We find it impossible to imagine him without books. We hope this particular book will give him pleasure and win a place of honor in his own personal library. We trust the general community also finds that it supplies fitting evidence of the immense respect and admiration an entire profession holds for him.

THE STORY TOLD BY PRINTERS' MARKS

From Offense to Defense: The Nature of Reformed Theology in Its First Century

Brian G. Armstrong

OUR DEBT TO BOB SCHNUCKER for his oversight of the affairs of the Sixteenth Century Studies Conference is massive, touching every aspect of the Conference. His use of illustrative materials in its publications, often sixteenth-century woodcuts or portraits, alerted me to the importance of printers' marks on sixteenth- and seventeenth-century works. So this essay attempts, by referencing printers' marks, to support the argument that Calvinist theology underwent significant change from Calvin to later generations. I will focus on some common printers' marks in Calvin's works and compare them with printers' marks used by the main spokesman of French Calvinism of the seventeenth century.[1] In a society where literacy was uncommon, printers' marks conveyed, symbolically, the ideology and basic message of the author.

For a long time scholarship on Calvin and Calvinism has been the privileged playground of dogmaticians or academic theologians. Indeed, it almost seems it has been held hostage to a theological agenda, as Calvin has been seen in the light of disciplinary interest. While understandable on the part of those who teach and represent a continuing Reformed tradition, it also is a problem. First, as Francis Higmkan had noted, "At no stage in his life was Calvin an academic theologian, concerned only with the definition and exposition of the truth of the Gospel."[2]

---

[1] I am also indebted to Francis Higman's stimulating address at the meeting of the International Congress on Calvin Research (ICCR) in Edinburgh in 1994. Thanks to Robert Schnucker, Paula Presley, and staff, this essay is now published; see, "I Came Not to Send Peace, but a Sword," in *Calvinus Sincerioris Religionis Vindex*, Sixteenth Century Essays & Studies, 36, ed. W. H. Neuser and B. G. Armstrong (Kirksville, MO: Sixteenth Century Journal Publishers, Inc., 1997), 123–137.

[2] *Calvinus Sincerioris,* ed. Neuser and Armstrong, 123.

This is not to imply that such scholarship lacks importance, or that it has not produced solid scholarly analyses. But apart from debates such as that provoked by the Weber thesis, discussions of Calvin and Calvinism have continued to be dominated by traditional theological approaches and concerns.. Recently, control by the academic theologian has been loosened by the appearance of careful, historical studies in the traditional mode, and augmented by the so-called new Reformation history (social history, family and gender history, history of popular religion, and history of print and print culture, for example). Yet, until recently these new emphases have had scant application to Calvin himself, or to his followers. There is no study on Calvin similar to that on Luther; for example, the work by Erik Erickson.[3] Though there are social history studies on Calvin and Calvinism, these are more sporadic than steady. Still, pioneering studies of these genres are beginning to appear. William Bouwsma's biography of Calvin has been a watershed event in Calvin studies for the historical as well as, to a degree, the psychological approach, and the recognition that Calvin does not follow the program of an academic theologian. Bouwsma's contribution, as I see it, is to position Calvin, with considerable nuance, in his historical context, showing him to be a product of a very agitated age and shaped in personality and program by the events of his time. Moreover, Bouwsma undertakes to establish and demonstrate the radical principle that when "assessing his [Calvin's] intention, ... he was a rhetorician, less concerned with the objective truth of the message than with its effect on his audience."[4] If true, then clearly the dominating role of dogmatic interpretations of Calvin is challenged.[5]

Indeed, many recent studies signal the swing of the pendulum away from academic, theological analysis. We now have, for example, studies of Calvin's rhetoric, such as the brilliant study by Olivier Millet, works by Serene Jones, William Bouwsma, and the earlier studies of Quirinus Breen.[6]

---

[3]See Erik Erickson, *Young Man Luther: A Study in Psychoanalysis and History* (New York: W. W. Norton, 1958).

[4]William J. Bouwsma, *John Calvin: A Sixteenth Century Portrait* (New York: Oxford University Press, 1988), 141.

[5]One of the more impressive recent works of this genre is the very thorough study by David Steinmetz, *Calvin in Context* (New York: Oxford University Press, 1995). If a case can be made for the centrality of theological interest and tradition in Calvin's work, Steinmetz has surely done it. And he has shown that Calvin's writings can fruitfully be compared with, and analyzed from, his connections with the theological tradition. But that this represents the basic, essential Calvin is certainly open to debate.

[6]Olivier Millet, *Calvin et le dynamique de la parole: Étude de rhétorique réformée* (Paris: H. Champion, 1992). Cf. also idem, "*Docere/Movere*: Les catégories rhétoriques et leurs sources

Secondly, there is the recent flood of historical literature on the nature and influence of Calvinism in Europe. Among these are: *International Calvinism, 1541–1715,* edited by Menna Prestwich; *Calviniana: Ideas and Influence of Jean Calvin,* edited by Robert V. Schnucker; *Later Calvinism: International Perspectives,* edited by W. Fred Graham; *Sin and the Calvinists,* edited by Raymond A. Mentzer; and *Calvinism in Europe: 1540–1620,* edited by Andrew Pettegree, Alistair Duke, and Gillian Lewis—impressive collections of historical articles.[7]

Also worthy of special notice is the pioneering work of Robert Kingdon and colleagues in publishing the records of the Consistory of Geneva,[8] especially important since it is particularly the role and activity of the Consistory that confessional, theological, and personal biases have dominated in the literature.[9] As Kingdon has shown, the previous focus on the sensational cases has resulted in a distortion of both the role of the body itself and the image of Calvin.[10]

Now for a brief outline of the nature of the reform movement in Geneva and France from 1550 to ca. 1630, focusing on France. I will argue that

---

humanistes dans la doctrine calvinienne de la foi," in *Calvinus Sincerioris Religionis Vindex,* ed. Neuser and Armstrong, 35–51. Serene Jones, *Calvin and the Rhetoric of Piety,* Columbia Series in Reformed Theology (Louisville, KY, Westminster John Knox Press, 1995). William J. Bouwsma, *Calvinism as 'Rhetorica theologica': Protocol of the 54th Colloquy, 28 Sept. 1986* (Berkeley: Center for Hermeneutical Studies in Hellenistic and Modern Culture, 1987). "John Calvin and the Rhetorical Tradition," in *Christianity and Humanism: Studies in the History of Ideas,* with foreword by Paul Oskar Kristeller and preface by Heiko A. Oberman, ed. Nelson Peter Ross (Grand Rapids: Eerdmans, 1968).

[7]*International Calvinism 1541–1715,* ed. Menna Prestwich (Oxford: Clarendon Press, 1985); *Calviniana: Ideas and Influence of Jean Calvin,* ed. Robert V. Schnucker, Sixteenth Century Essays & Studies, 10 (Kirksville, Mo.: Sixteenth Century Journal Publishers, Inc., 1988); *Later Calvinism: International Perspectives,* ed. W. Fred Graham, Sixteenth Century Essays & Studies, 22 (Kirksville, Mo.: Sixteenth Century Journal Publishers, Inc., 1994); *Sin and the Calvinists: Morals Control and the Consistory in the Reformed Tradition,* ed. Raymond A. Mentzer, Sixteenth Century Essays & Studies, 32 (Kirksville, Mo.: Sixteenth Century Journal Publishers, Inc., 1994); and *Calvinism in Europe: 1540–1620,* ed. Andrew Pettegree, Alistair Duke, and Gillian Lewis (Cambridge: Cambridge University Press, 1994).

[8]Robert M. Kingdon, "A New View of Calvin in the Light of the Registers of the Geneva Consistory," in, *Calvinus Sincerioris Religionis Vindex,* ed. Neuser and Armstrong, 21–33.

[9]The best known of the studies of Calvin and the Consistory is doubtless W. Köhler, *Zürcher Ehegericht und Genfer Konsistorium,* vol. 2 (Leipzig, 1942). But as Kingdon and his team have shown, Köhler's information was based on extracts collected by F.-A. Cramer, and this of the sensational cases only.

[10]Kingdon, "New View of Calvin," 23.

important changes occurred in the content, method, mood, and purpose of the writings of the Reformed in this period, and that these were changes necessitated by the changed milieu to which these individuals were responding. That is, I hope to describe some of the evidence which supports the argument that significant change occurred in the nature of the Calvinist message. Among this evidence will be printers' marks found on Calvin's works and those of the main spokesman for seventeenth-century Calvinism in France, one Pierre du Moulin (1568–1658).[11]

In 1550 the euphoric optimism and idealism of the proponents for reform in Geneva and France were still in place, though this spirit had begun to be sobered by recent events; for example, failed union attempts, such as that at Regensberg (1540–41), Luther's death (1546), the defeat of the German Protestant armies in the late 1540s, the considerable success of the Catholic/Counter-Reformation (and especially the rise to prominence of the program of the Jesuits), developing animosities within the Lutheran and Reformed camps, and divisions amongst the French-speaking and German-speaking Calvinist churches. But the appearance of new reform movements in England, Emden, and many German principalities, along with the more moderate leadership of Melanchthon in North Germany, supported the belief that God's truth was marching on. So the reformers, with their deep faith in the God of history, still clung to the belief that the unity of the church would be restored under a reformed banner.

In Geneva, though still beleaguered by stiff opposition, Calvin had hopes of complete success. There was a steady flow of supportive emigrés into Geneva, many with leadership abilities. Calvin had managed a consensus with Heinrich Bullinger of Zurich to bring unity of the Genevan church with the Swiss churches, at least on the important matter of the Eucharist. This brought Calvin much more into favor with the German-speaking Swiss, especially the church of Berne with its serious reservations about his teaching and ideas of

---

[11]On du Moulin see L. Rimbault, *Pierre du Moulin, 1568–1658: Un Pasteur Classique à l'age Classique. Etude de théologie pastorale sur des documents inédits.* (Paris: Vrin, 1966). See also Brian G. Armstrong, "The Changing Face of French Protestantism: The Influence of Pierre du Moulin," in *Calviniana*, ed. Schnucker, 131 ff.; idem, "Pierre du Moulin and James I: The Anglo-French Dream," in *Melanges Elisabeth Labrousse, ed.* A. McKenna, et al., (Paris, 1994), 17 ff.; and Armstrong, *Bibliographia Molinaei: An Alphabetical, Chronological and Descriptive Bibliography of the Works of Pierre du Moulin* ...(Geneva: Droz, 1997), 734 pp.

church organization.[12] It may be true also, as Alistair Duke has suggested, that this led the Hungarian reformers to look to Geneva for training and ecclesiastical models, and this must certainly have triggered optimism.[13] These successes fueled the lingering hope that rapprochement with a reformed Roman Church might still be possible. They knew that truth would triumph!

In France, in spite of growing opposition, by 1550 there was still a steady increase of reform groups, if but "freestanding clandestine congregations...."[14] Mark Greengrass' estimate that some five thousand to eight thousand heresy cases had been brought before the courts by 1559[15] shows the growth of reform and the belief in its eventual success—which connects with the astonishing development of established, official churches as early as 1555—as well as the willingness of the great nobility to throw in their lot with these reformers.

But the decade of the 1550s turned sour for the reform. In Geneva the opposition to Calvin that had formed over the past few years boiled over into open disdain. Though Calvin emerged victorious from the bitter contests which eventuated, a great psychological toll was taken, a toll which I believe led Calvin to reshape somewhat his theoretical program.

Opposition to reform in France was also growing, with the Sorbonne issuing regular condemnations of its teachings, especially Calvin's, and Henry II issuing the violently antireform Edict of Châteaubriant, with a rejuvenated *chambre ardente.* These and other moves began to wrest the initiative from Calvin and fellow reformers in France; indeed, had begun to place them on the defensive. The onset of the wars of religion in 1562, and then the Dutch conflict in 1567, quickly solidified the move of the outnumbered reform groups from an offensive to a defensive strategy, both militarily and ideologically.

Yet the main factor which led to the reformers' need for a strategy of defense on the doctrinal front came from the Catholic counteroffensive, powerfully supported by the marvelous educational programs of the Jesuit order. And the Council of Trent, under the great Cardinal Morone, finally got its act together and ushered in a militant reform in theology and practice. This cut off all hope on the part of the reformers for rapprochement with the Roman Church. Secondly, this hard-line position was followed by an all-out counter-reform offensive, forcing the reform groups into a defensive posture to protect

---

[12]However, one should also take into account the renewed friction which resulted from the celebrated Bolsec affair.

[13]Cf. *Calvinism in Europe: 1540–1620,* ed. Pettegree, et al., 4.

[14]Cf. *Calvinism in Europe: 1540–1620,* ed. Pettegree, et al., 7.

[15]See *The Reformation in National Context,* ed. Bob Scribner, Roy Porter, and Mikulas Teich (Cambridge, Cambridge University Press, 1994), 52.

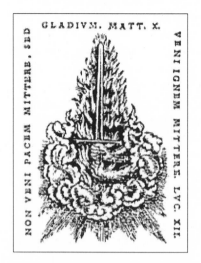

Flaming Sword title page image used by Calvin.

Shield title page image used by later Reformers.

their gains. So the positive presentation of their message, with its offensive imagery, was slowly exchanged for the language and imagery of defense.

This transition from offense to defense is seen on title pages, both in the verbiage of the title and in the printers' marks, as Francis Higman has shown in the case of Calvin's title pages, and is now easily seen from photocopy reproductions of the title pages in the magnificent Calvin bibliography of R. Peter and J. F. Gilmont.[16] A common title page image for Calvin's works is the sword, often the flaming sword, with the accompanying quotation from Jesus that "I came not to bring peace, but a sword."[17] This mark, which apparently appeared for the first time on Calvin's *Exposition sur ... Sainct Iudas ...* in 1542, is then used indiscriminately on title pages of commentaries (to both Old and New Testaments), sermons, the *Institutes,* a treatise against astrology, and so forth. While this universal usage indicates that it is not chosen as the appropriate mark for any particular title, it solidifies the impression of a general positive and offensive strategy.

[16]R. Peter and J. G. Gilmont, *Bibliotheca Calviniana: Les Oeuvres de Jean Calvin publiées au XVIe siècle,* 2 vols. (Geneva: Droz, 1991–).

[17]In the first volume alone of the aforementioned *Bibliotheca Calviniana,* more than forty editions of Calvin's works by the printer Jean Girard bear this mark in various forms; see, e.g., 126, 147, 149, 151, 158, 162, 168, 174, 176, 178, and others.

This sword imagery should be compared to the use of the shield as common imagery on title pages of the works of the later reformers. As is well known, both military and intellectual contests between Protestants and Catholics had developed in the later sixteenth century, with the changes on the intellectual battlefield having a most far-reaching effect on the nature of the Protestant movement.

Three important examples illustrate this shift. The first is the extensive editorial additions, notations, and emendations to Calvin's *Institutes*. Second is the call of the powerful Huguenot theologian and nobleman Antoine de la Roche Chandieu (1534–91) for the creation and implementation of a scholastic theology on the part of the reformers. And third, the energetic acceptance of Chandieu's call for the creation of a scholastic theology by the most important and popular Huguenot philosopher/theologian and minister of the seventeenth century in France, Pierre du Moulin (1568–1658).

ADDITIONS, NOTATIONS AND EMENDATIONS TO CALVIN'S *INSTITUTES*

At the outset it must be noted that Calvin, in spite of the four expanded editions of his original manual of 1536, which resulted in a quite formidable text, provided no apparatus for its easy use as a source for theological disputation.[18] In the light of the change to a strategy of defense, it was obviously felt by his friends and successors that a convenient, shortcut method and interpretation was needed to highlight the material and make it handy for disputation. Thus Nicolas Colladon, who wrote a biography of Calvin, provided two alphabetized "*indices des matières*," one for the French text and one for the Latin. The one for the French text was considerably more ample than the one for the Latin text, and if he can be believed, even modifications of the structure and organization of the text itself were effectuated. The larger index is described as "A Table ... *disposed in forme of common places,* wherein is briefly rehearsed the summe of the Doctrine concerning every point taught in the booke...."[19] The index comprises more than thirty-two oversize quarto pages of closely set type in two columns, and thus is a veritable handbook of quotations from the text,

---

[18]One may well wonder why this would be if he thought such was appropriate. As is evident by the many editions, it is certainly clear that he labored continuously to put the text into the shape with which he felt most comfortable, and had it, in his mind, needed a set of "common places," it seems logical that he would have provided it. It is well known that he pronounced himself satisfied with the final text of 1559. Overall, it seems clear to me that Calvin did not intend nor envision the *Institutes* as a manual to be used in a defensive theological arena.

[19]I cite the London edition of "A Table ... disposed in forme of common places, wherein is briefly rehearsed the summe of the Doctrine concerning every point taught in the booke ...," by Anne Griffin for Joyce Norton (1634), sig. Sss4,v°). In the rendition of Marolat's preface (of

conveniently arranged alphabetically according to theological topic; it also includes Colladon's brief—and handy-for-disputation—synopsis of the chapters referenced. By 1562 another of Calvin's colleagues at Geneva, Augustin Marolat, had added an index of debated topics. By 1576 Colladon added marginal summaries of each section with references to similar material elsewhere in the *Institutes*, to various of Calvin's commentaries, to similar passages in contemporary works by other authors. Colladon's work also has notations of objections to Reformed doctrine and their solutions. Also in 1576 the Englishman Edmund Bunny provided a compendium of the *Institutes* to serve as a handbook for disputation, and a veritable flood of such compendia followed, one of the more important by William de Laune (Launeus), whose brief one-volume summary turns Calvin's material into a polemical format for disputational use.[20] Finally, by 1585, editions of the *Institutes* included not only this material but also Caspar Olevian's "method and disposition, or argument of the entire work" to be followed in the next years by Olevian's own one-volume summary, by David Paraeus' one hundred aphorisms, and by others' similar works.

Thus we see transformation of the *Institutes*, with its rhetorical style, from a manual which served for the proclamation of evangelical teaching into a manual for polemical purposes based on the program of formal logic. It seems clear that these additions and adaptations were to make the work more serviceable for scholastic disputation.[21]

ANTOINE DE LA ROCHE CHANDIEU'S CALL FOR A SCHOLASTIC THEOLOGY

A fine article by Donald Sinnema has sketched Chandieu's call for a Reformed Scholastic Theology.[22] With Chandieu we see the gleeful adoption of Aristotelian philosophy, especially its logic, an enthusiasm also shared by Theodore Beza at Geneva and Claude Aubery at Lausanne. In 1580 Chandieu published

---

1562) in this edition, the "defense of the faith" fixation is already present in the statement "forasmuch as all the principall points of religion are in the Booke copiously and faithfully expounded, *we may easily refute the false opinions of the Adversaries*"; sig. [Yyy3], verso (emphasis added). I am indebted to the fine presentation on this topic by Olivier Fatio at the ICCR meeting in Amsterdam, and Richard Muller's recent revisitation of the topic.

[20]Cf. esp. the above-mentioned address by Professor Fatio.

[21]I wish to acknowledge my debt to Olivier Fatio and Richard Muller for articles showing this transformation of Calvin's text. See Fatio, "Présence de Calvin à l'époque de l'orthodoxie réformée" in W. H. Neuser, ed., *Calvinus Ecclesiae Doctor* (Kampen: Kok, 1979), 1711.

[22]Cf. Donald Sinnema, "Antoine De Chandieu's Call for a Scholastic Reformed Theology (1580)," in *Later Calvinism*, ed. Graham, 159–190. I wish to acknowledge with gratitude Dr. Sinnema's kindness in sharing with me even some of his unpublished papers on the scholastic theology of Chandieu.

his *De verbo dei scripto*. Its preface, "The Proper Method of Theological and Scholastical Argumentation," posits that Roman Catholic doctors do not follow properly the rules of logic and the syllogism, and stresses that the Reformed need to develop the proper method. He does not entirely reject the rhetorical style of Calvin's treatises, but posits that it is the analytical style of Aristotelian logic which presents matters such that "the very truth of things can be gazed upon with our eyes and nearly felt with our fingers."[23] As for this "new method," it is important to note that, as Sinnema says, "In calling for a scholastic approach to Reformed theology Chandieu sees himself as charting a new course."[24]

THE SCHOLASTIC THEOLOGY OF PIERRE DU MOULIN

By the time Du Moulin arrived in France in the wake of the issuance of the *Edit de Nantes* in 1598, the scholastic, defensive theology adopted by the Huguenots was well advanced.[25] As master of the horse for Henry IV, personal chaplain to Henry's sister Catherine, and pastor of the great Huguenot church at Paris, Du Moulin immediately established his role, which he believed was his by position and birthright (he was related to the royal house of both France and England), alongside Daniel Chamier, as the leading voice of French Protestantism. He had already established himself as a devotee of Aristotelian philosophy through publication of a handbook on logic, titled *Elementa logica ...,* a handbook which became the most popular of many such handbooks, going through nearly fifty editions in his lifetime alone, in at least six languages.[26] Thus Du Moulin was all too happy to come to the defense of the Reformed teaching and praxis. Though a man of great gifts on many fronts, his great love was the fray, especially the pamphlet warfare and public disputations that permitted him to carry on his noble penchant for the duel, using pen rather than sword. In these he became known as the Huguenot "defender of the faith." His success led to his fleeing for his life from France in 1620.

[23]Cf. Sinnema, "Antoine De Chandieu's Call," 171.

[24]Sinnema, "Antoine De Chandieu's Call," 187.

[25]Perhaps by this time its leading proponent and practitioner was Daniel Chamier (1565–1621) of the University of Montauban. It is therefore no surprise that one of Du Moulin's closest friends in spirit and in flesh was Chamier. A Roman Catholic pamphlet of the period, referring to the Huguenot leadership, speaks disparagingly of their "Pontif Chamier et son nonce du Moulin." A full-fledged, up-to-date study of Chamier is badly needed. The best to date is the study by Charles Read of 1853 titled simply *Daniel Chamier*. Cf. also Michel Nicolas, *Histoire de l'ancienne Académie Protestante de Montauban (1598–1659)* (Montauban: E. Forestié, 1885).

[26]There are, minimally, seventeen printings in Latin, twenty-two in French, two in Dutch, and two in English, and, I am told, two in Coptic.

In the writings of Du Moulin a defensive mentality and strategy to defend Protestantism are clearly evident. While this feature is found in nearly all of his writings, it is his book *Bouclier de la foy*,[27] perhaps the most popular of his very popular writings, through which the symbol of the shield was established as a common symbol for French Protestants of the seventeenth century. Yet, the titles of his writings are alone are proof enough of his commitment to the genre of defense-oriented productions. The following are just a few of the examples which might be adduced. In 1610, for example, Du Moulin published his *Defense de la Foy Catholique ...*, of which there are a dozen or so editions.[28] He also wrote, or coauthored, a work titled *Defense de la Confession des Eglises Reformees de France ...* (1617), which went through some twenty-three separate printings.[29] The list could easily be extended since the larger share of his writings is devoted to the defense of Reformed theology and practice.

Du Moulin represents in full flower the scholastic methodology adopted by the Protestants for use in the defense of their faith. He cites as his inspiration and source the theologians of the sixteenth century who most evidently adopted Aristotelian logic and the syllogism; namely, Theodore Beza, Peter Martyr Vermigli, Jerome Zanchi, and of course and especially, Antoine de la Roche Chandieu, from whom he borrows shamelessly. It is also important to note that he explicitly avoids the use of Calvin as a model.

In sum, the Renaissance-based rhetorical style and content of Calvin and colleagues in their religious writings has been replaced by a strict Aristotelian, logical system by the so-called Calvinists of the late sixteenth and the seventeenth centuries, changing the emphasis on proclamation, symbolized by the imagery of the sword, to that of defense, symbolized by the imagery of the shield. That is, the emphasis of the earlier reformers on the sword of the Spirit has been overtaken and overshadowed by an emphasis on the imagery of defense and protection, the shield of faith.

---

[27]There are some twenty-two different printings in French, two in Dutch, four in English, five in German, and, if I am correctly informed, at least one in Coptic and perhaps one in Polish.

[28]There are eleven French-language printings, one in English, and it would seem one in Italian. I have been told there is a Welsh edition but I have not found evidence of such a copy.

[29]For the details, see Brian G. Armstrong, *Bibliographia Molinari* (Geneva: Droz, 1997), 168–177, and the illustrations therein..

Astrology and Popular Print in Germany, c. 1470–1520

Robin B. Barnes

EVERY STUDENT OF EARLY MODERN COMMUNICATIONS knows that in the half-century or so before 1520, German towns witnessed a tremendous boom in the new industry of printing. Within the last generation, traditional attention to the humanistic, devotional, and theological publications of this era has been productively expanded through broad and systematic studies of popular vernacular literature, especially of *flugschriften* or pamphlets. The pamphlet studies have done much to enhance our understanding of lay interests and attitudes in the pre-Reformation and early Reformation decades. One drawback, however, is that these studies have been largely based on a definition of the pamphlet that all but excludes certain popular printed genres.[1] Such genres include two of the cheapest and most common of all published forms, namely annual astrological calendars and prognostications. By fixing attention on these highly ephemeral popular works, this essay seeks to revive older claims—now too often neglected—regarding the enormous weight of astrology in the emerging print culture of pre-Reformation Germany.[2]

Astrological publications for an urban lay market were a staple of the printing business from the very beginning. Like every other genre that came from the early presses, however, printed astrological works developed out of

---

[1]For the most influential definition of the pamphlet, see Hans Joachim Köhler, ed., *Flugschriften als Massenmedium der Reformationszeit: Beiträge zum Tübinger Symposium 1980* (Stuttgart: Klett-Cotta, 1981), introductory essay by Köhler.

[2]Nineteenth- and early-twentieth-century cultural historians such as Friedrich von Bezold, Will-Erich Peuckert, Willy Andreas, and Aby Warburg emphasized the prominent role of astrology in pre-Reformation German culture. By contrast, many recent surveys barely mention this aspect, if indeed they touch on it at all. A number of recent specialized studies have dealt with the astrological background in relation to the great "flood panic" of 1524; see for instance Heike Talkenberger, *Sintflut: Prophetie und Zeitgeschehen in Texten und Holzschnitten astrologischer Flugschriften, 1488–1528* (Tübingen: Niemeyer, 1990), and Robin B. Barnes, "The Flood Panic, Medieval Prophetic Traditions, and the German Evangelical Movement," in Roberto Rusconi, ed., *Storia e figure dell'Apocalisse fra '500 e '600* (Rome: Viella, 1996), 145–162.

inherited medieval forms. The vernacular *Volkskalender*, for example, had appeared in various manuscript versions from the late fourteenth century. These works embodied all the major strains of traditional lay astrology, and offered a variety of other practical and devotional materials. In the later fifteenth century printed versions quickly multiplied, tending toward a more or less standardized form. The typical *Volkskalender* presented basic computational data for each month, saints' and feast days, and various astrological tables to determine for example the position of the sun and the moon in the signs of the Zodiac. It also gave basic astrological rules for health and hygiene (especially for phlebotomy), described the characteristics of each sign of the Zodiac, discussed the nature and powers of each planet, explained the workings of the four bodily humors, and listed "unlucky" days on which certain important activities, including phlebotomy, were to be avoided. Some versions even included a basic chapter on cosmology, teaching a simplified version of the Ptolemaic system.[3]

By the time the medieval *Volkskalender* was taking printed form, the traditions of folk wisdom and learning that had shaped such works were subject to a variety of new forces. Most notable in this connection were two developments. First, the late fifteenth century brought significant advances in astronomical and calendrical computation. Learned figures such as Johannes Regiomontanus and Jakob Pflaum issued technical yet relatively accessible astronomical and calendrical works that supplied powerful new tools for astrological analysis.[4] While the universities remained the center of astronomical and astrological expertise, the way was now increasingly open for local physicians and other astrological thinkers to engage in their own reckonings on the basis of uniform professional data. Second, the same era witnessed the rapidly expanding deployment of Arabic astrological concepts. In the newly published writings of such figures as Albumasar, students found major elaborations of the inherited astrological cosmology, above all a more sophisticated and comprehensive theory of planetary conjunctions. Together, these developments soon made the traditional *Volkskalender* obsolete. It would be the most inexpensive

---

[3]See Francis B. Brévart, "The German *Volkskalender* of the Fifteenth Century," *Speculum* 63, 2 (April 1988): 312–342.

[4]For editions of works by Regiomontanus and Pflaum, see Ernst Zinner, *Geschichte und Bibliographie der Astronomischen Literatur in Deutschland zur Zeit der Renaissance*, 2d ed. (Stuttgart: A. Hiersemann, 1964). The most influential vernacular work of Regiomontanus is available in a facsimile edition: Ernst Zinner, ed., *Der deutsche Kalender des Johannes Regiomontan, Nürnberg, um 1474* (Leipzig: Harrassowitz, 1937).

and most ephemeral astrological genres that also proved the most adaptable in the face of the new trends.

Most of the earliest printed "calendars" were not really calendars as we tend to think of them; often they did not even place each day in an ordered series. They were instead tables of basic astronomical and astrological data for the coming year, meant to serve the practical needs of "the common man." They were especially concerned with showing the lunar phases for mundane purposes such as astrological medicine (especially the proper times for phlebotomy), as well as planting and general husbandry. By the last decade of the fifteenth century they were often enlarged to include a full annual calendar, but they remained closely associated with astrological medicine and husbandry, commonly indicating for instance the best times to sow, reap, travel, build, bathe, cut hair and nails, wean children, and the like. They commonly indicated the expected eclipses and conjunctions for the coming year, and offered brief weather forecasts along with other general predictions. Many of the earliest printed calendars used roman numerals, but as early as 1472 arabic numerals began to appear, and soon became the rule. Until well into the sixteenth century, such annual calendars appeared most commonly in broadsheet form.[5]

From the 1470s on, the annual calendar was frequently complemented by a brief "practica" or astrological prognostication for the coming year; indeed well before 1500 many writers issued regular annual editions of both. Yearly astrological practicas in manuscript and woodblock form had circulated in Italy as early as the fourteenth century; in Germany the earliest we have date from the early fifteenth century. Like calendars, they were often reckoned for particular cities. Sometimes the annual practica was included in the broadsheet calendar, but more often the calendar directed the reader to the complementary practica; we see this already in the 1480s. Citing the authority of Greek and Arabic authorities such as Ptolemy, Aristotle, Albumasar, and Al Kindi, and drawing on the new stocks of published astronomical data, these works made predictions on the basis of conjunctions, eclipses, and comets. As pamphlets they ranged from four to around sixteen pages; they shared a basic but fairly flexible form, generally consisting of three main parts: a preface, predictions about various aspects of daily life and for various social classes and groups, and more or less detailed weather forecasts for the coming year.[6]

---

[5]A useful if hard-to-find collection of early calendars is Paul Heitz and Konrad Haebler, *Hundert Kalender-Inkunabeln* (Strassburg: Heitz, 1905). See also Adolf Dresler, *Kalender-Kunde: Eine kultur-historische Studie* (Munich: K.Thiemig, 1972).

[6]There is no collection of early "practicas" or astrological prognostications comparable to

It was not until the second half of the sixteenth century that the calendar and prognostication were regularly issued together, thus forming the handy annual work of chronological information and practical guidance that we now associate with the term "almanac." Yet it is clear that already in the 1470s, printers in many German towns regarded yearly astrological guides as a guaranteed cash cow, an almost surefire way of getting a start in the business. The famous Anton Koberger of Nuremberg, for instance, got his press established partly by issuing such works; he was later able to print the sort of humanistic writings that were his main interest.[7] Indeed the evidence strongly suggests that astrological calendars, prognostications, and related publications reached a larger audience in the German cities than anywhere else in pre-Reformation Europe. In the period before 1520, we find virtually no examples of broadsheet almanacs from Italy, France, Spain, the Netherlands, or England; nowhere outside the German-speaking lands did this form become established. The German towns also became leaders in the early production of annual prognostications. Only in Italy were more of these works published, and here, as we will see, the circumstances were significantly different.[8]

Because calendars and practicas were the most ephemeral of all printed works, they are the most likely to have been lost forever to posterity. There were surely many more published in the late fifteenth and early sixteenth centuries than survive; this is especially true of the years after 1500. A case in point is that of Johann Schöner of Nuremberg. Schöner almost certainly published broadsheet calendars for most if not all years between 1504 and 1529, but none of these works survive.[9] It is still common for fragments of previously lost or unknown calendars or prognostications to turn up as part of the binding of larger books; once the year for which it was reckoned was over, a

---

Heitz and Haebler, *Hundert Kalender-Inkunabeln*. A small sampling of such works is available in Peter Hans Pascher, *Praktiken des 15. und 16. Jahrhunderts* (Klagenfurt: Verlag Armarium, 1980). Some helpful background on early practicas is available in Gustav Hellmann, *Versuch einer Geschichte der Wettervorhersage im XVI. Jahrhundert*, in *Abhandlungen der Preussischen Akademie der Wissenschaften*, Jahrgang 1924, Nr. 1 (Berlin, 1924).

[7] Klaus Matthäus, "Zur Geschichte des Nürnberger Kalenderwesens," in *Archiv für Geschichte des Buchwesens* 9 (1969), cols. 965–1396; here 1007.

[8] See Hellmann, *Versuch einer Geschichte der Wettervorhersage.*

[9] Matthäus, "Zur Geschichte des Nürnberger Kalenderwesens," 1023. In the nineteenth century, and well into the twentieth, bibliographers were far more careful to gather and catalog ephemeral and fragmentary works from before 1501 than from the sixteenth century or later. Hence our knowledge of calendars and prognostications from the first decades of the sixteenth century remains comparatively weak.

work of this sort was as likely as not to end up in pieces at the bottom of a latrine.

We know of well over 380 annual single-leaf calendars from before 1501. If we add to this figure the number of known annual prognostications printed in Germany in this period, we reach a total of nearly six hundred works.[10] Since such ephemera are so likely to have been lost completely, a very conservative estimate of the actual number published might add a third again as many; let us offer the figure of nine hundred as a modest speculative total. If we make another conservative estimate of five hundred copies per issue, we can conclude that even before 1500 almost half a million copies of such works had circulated in German towns. For the period before 1520, the likely total would without doubt be closer to one million, if not higher. These figures do not include the many editions of calendars or prognostications for more than one year. Nor do they include *Volkskalender* editions, popular planet books, frequently reprinted works such as the astrological folk book *Lucidarius*, or other vernacular writings that included astrological references. Perhaps even more significantly, they do not include sensational best-sellers such as Johann Lichtenberger's *Pronosticatio*, probably the best known astrological work of the pre-Reformation era, which went through multiple editions before 1500.[11] These are truly astonishing numbers, especially when we consider that literacy rates were still extremely low, even in the largest towns.[12]

Striking percentages of these early astrological works were published in the vernacular. Of some 380 known calendars from before 1501, around 250 were in German, almost 75 percent. Even before 1480, in the very first decades of the commercial press, over half the known broadsheet calendars were in German. The printing of prognostications was in general a little slower to gain momentum, but we know of around 103 vernacular practicas for a single year before 1501, and some 97 Latin practicas from German-speaking lands.[13] Thus here, too, well over half of the fifteenth-century works were

---

[10]These numbers are derived from my own count of works listed in Zinner, *Geschichte und Bibliographie der Astronomischen Literatur.*

[11]On Lichtenberger see above all the important work of Dietrich Kurze, *Johannes Lichtenberger (+ 1503): Eine Studie zur Geschichte der Prophetie und Astrologie* (Lübeck: Matthiesen, 1960).

[12]For literacy rates in Germany see Rolf Engelsing, *Analphabetentum und Lektüre: Zur Sozialgeschichte des Lesens in Deutschland zwischen feudaler und industrieller Gesellschaft* (Stuttgart: Metzler, 1973), and idem, *Der Bürger als Leser: Lesergeschichte in Deutschland 1500–1800* (Stuttgart: Metzler, 1974).

[13]Again my count is based on the entries for annual works only in Zinner, *Geschichte und Bibliographie der Astronomischen Literatur.* The total here of some 580 annual works does not include several which could not be identified as either Latin or vernacular.

directly available to a non-latinate readership. Moreover, the proportion of calendars and practicas published in the vernacular continued to increase after 1500; German editions became more and more dominant. These trends take on more meaning if we realize that among all books of any kind printed in Germany before 1501, more than 80 percent were in Latin.[14] Studies of early sixteenth-century German popular "pamphlets" show that only from 1520 on did vernacular writings begin to outnumber Latin ones.[15]

Undoubtedly one reason for the early predominance of German cities in this realm was simply that printing in almost all its forms spread most rapidly here. In France, for example, the slow growth of a "popular" press naturally retarded the development of the almanac.[16] Even later, in the sixteenth century, most French almanacs were not cheap works aimed at a mass market. Closer clerical control over publication and narrower channels of distribution restricted the dissemination of astrological ideas and imagery.[17] In England there were even fewer channels by which the revival of ancient astrology could take on cultural weight. Among the earliest writers of annual printed prognostications in England was William Parron, who worked for Henry VII between c. 1490 and 1503.[18] Yet Parron had few imitators, and sixteenth-century England has with justification been called "an astrological backwater." Most of the earliest English vernacular astrological publications were in fact translations of continental works.[19]

Only in Italy can we find an interest in astrological publications comparable to that of the German cities during this early period. Here, printed prognostications proliferated quickly in the late fifteenth century, and probably outnumbered works of the same sort issued in Germany. But there is evidence

---

[14]Rudolf Hirsch, *Printing, Selling, and Reading 1450–1550*, 2d ed. (Wiesbaden: Harrassowitz, 1974), 134.

[15]Hans Joachim Köhler, "The *Flugschriften* and Their Importance in Religious Debate: A Quantitative Approach," in Paola Zambelli, ed., *'Astrologi hallucinati': Stars and the End of the World in Luther's Time* (Berlin and New York: Walter de Gruyter, 1986), 153–175; here 155.

[16]See Geneviève Bollème, *Les Almanachs Populaires aux XVIIe et XVIIIe Siècles: Essai d'histoire Sociale* (Paris: Mouton, 1969), 18. Despite the contributions of a few figures such as the famous Nostradamus, the popular almanac did not establish a secure place in the French literature of colportage until the seventeenth century, and then only after the astrological and prophetic elements had been substantially modified.

[17]Bernard Capp, *Astrology and the Popular Press: English Almanacs 1500–1800* (London and Boston: Faber and Faber, 1979), 271. See also Hellmann, *Versuch einer Geschichte der Wettervorhersage*, 20.

[18]Hilary M. Carey, *Courting Disaster: Astrology at the English Court and University in the Later Middle Ages* (London: Macmillan, 1992), 161.

[19]Capp, *Astrology and the Popular Press*, 180.

that by the first decades of the sixteenth century German printers were taking the lead in the production of such predictions.[20] More importantly, the proportion of vernacular prognostications was much lower in Italy. We do not have bibliographical data for Italy comparable to what we possess for Germany, but analysis of one large collection suggests that south of the Alps vernacular works did not outpace Latin ones until the second or third decade of the sixteenth century.[21] Thus, while more astrological practicas may have been published in Italy than in Germany before 1520, far fewer of them were intended for the popular market. Even if we leave aside the entire genre of broadsheet calendars, it seems clear that astrological notions had broader channels through which to flow in Germany than in Italy in the pre-Reformation era.

The German production of calendars and prognostications was also much more decentralized than it was in Italy and other areas. To a certain extent this was true of the German printing industry as a whole; there were numerous printing centers, each publishing at least in part for a local market. The centers of calendar production were the famous towns of the early printing industry: Augsburg, Nuremberg, Strassburg, Ulm, Leipzig, and Erfurt were among the most notable. The first leader in calendar production was Augsburg; by 1500 Nuremberg was even more active. Yet many towns that were not particularly notable centers of early printing nevertheless saw the early production of calendars, a point that underlines the great popularity of this genre in Germany.[22]

The majority of the earliest astrological calendars were issued anonymously; the authority of the calendar writers was entirely subordinated to that of the revered ancient sources. Toward the end of the century it became more common for authors to name themselves, as growing competition among publishers made it desirable to stress the fame and expertise of particular astrologers.[23] Well before 1500, writers such as Johann Virdung (Virdung von Hassfurt), a physician who served the Elector Palatine at Heidelberg, and Wenzel Faber (Faber von Budweis), a medical professor and physician at Leipzig, gained considerable fame through their popular almanacs and practicas. Such

---

[20]Gustav Hellmann's early-twentieth-century studies, while based on bibliographical data that was far from comprehensive, nevertheless validly indicate the general comparative trends in the publication of astrological prognostications; see Hellmann, *Versuch einer Geschichte der Wettervorhersage*, 4 ff.

[21]I base this claim on my own analysis of the listing presented in Klaus Wagner, "Judicia Astrologica Columbiniana: Bibliographisches Verzeichnis einer Sammlung von Practiken des 15. und 16. Jahrhunderts der Biblioteca Columbina Sevilla," in *Archiv für Geschichte des Buchwesens* 15 (1975): 1–98. The works in this collection are overwhelmingly Italian publications.

[22]Heitz and Haebler, *Hundert Kalender-Inkunabeln*, 7; Dresler, *Kalender-Kunde*, 19.

[23]Matthäus, "Zur Geschichte des Nürnberger Kalenderwesens," 1023.

renown was naturally a great boon in the eyes of printers. It appears that by the 1490s some aspiring humanists, such as Thomas Murner, saw the writing of annual practicas as a quick way of making a name for oneself while still cutting one's literary teeth.[24] Almost from the start, however, the most common figure among the calendar writers appears to have been the city physician, a fact that is hardly surprising since the main purposes of the early calendars had to do with astrological medicine.

That there was early and open competition for the market is clear from a public spat between Wenzel Faber and another figure who had begun publishing practicas for Leipzig, Paul Eck. Faber clearly regarded Eck as an unwelcome upstart and a threat. In 1489 the two writers denounced one another in a series of printed broadsides that traded accusations of greed, dishonor, and incompetence. Apparently the university faculty sided with its own, Faber, and helped him to fight off Eck's challenge to his local monopoly. This was perhaps the very first publicity battle ever carried on in print; it would not be long before such disputes were taken for granted among authors and publishers.[25] The controversy is in fact testimony to the seriousness of the business of astrological publication at a very early date.

Inventories of lay libraries from the years around 1500 confirm the assumption that such works were widely disseminated among townsmen.[26] In the early sixteenth century a typical broadsheet calendar cost about six pfennigs, around the same price as a couple of chickens.[27] The early Reformation era saw a continued rapid acceleration in the numbers of such works circulating each year: in the 1550s, one Nuremberg publisher reported printing some thirty-seven thousand copies of a single broadsheet almanac.[28] Clearly there are good reasons to believe that popular astrological works found their way into the hands of a large proportion of those German burghers who had any pretensions to literacy. Of course, these popular works could be read aloud.

There is every reason to agree, then, that the calendar and practica writers were the "purveyors of astrology to the public," and to resurrect the observation, once common among cultural historians but no longer granted its proper

---

[24]See Moriz Sondheim, *Thomas Murner als Astrolog* (Strassburg: Elsass-Lothringische wissenschaftliche Gesellschaft, 1938), 7 ff.

[25]Konrad Haebler, "Paulus Eck gegen Wenzel Faber," in *Zeitschrift für Bücherfreunde*, n.f. 6 (1914–15), 200–204.

[26]Engelsing, *Der Bürger als Leser*, 12.

[27]Ludwig Rohner, *Kalendergeschichte und Kalender* (Wiesbaden: Akademische Verlagsgesellschaft Athenaion, 1978), 27.

[28]Matthäus, "Zur Geschichte des Nürnberger Kalenderwesens," 1119; Dresler, *Kalender-Kunde*, 14.

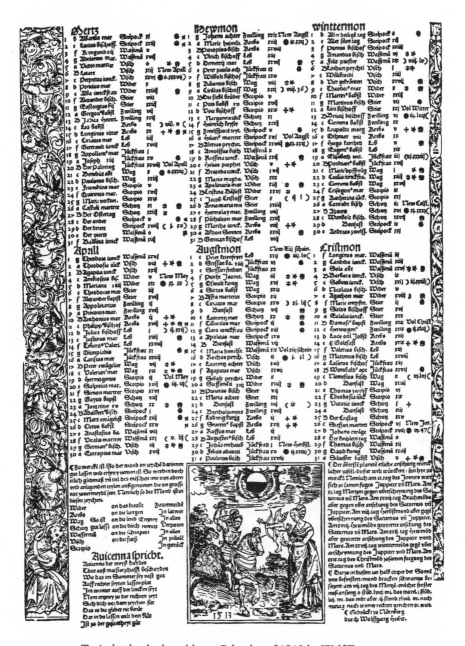

Typical calendar broadsheet. Calendar of 1513 by Wolf Traut.

weight, that the astrological notions conveyed in the calendars and practicas became a pervasive feature of German urban culture in the period around 1500.[29] Moreover, if the sorts of vernacular works I have discussed here are any reflection of broader trends, it would appear that the pre-Reformation German towns were more deeply immersed in astrological imagery than any other region of Europe. In any case, without a clear recognition of this aspect of early modern print culture in Germany, our picture of the setting in which the religious and social upheavals of the 1520s took place can hardly be complete.

[29]The reference to the almanac-makers as "purveyors" is from John North, "Celestial Influence—the major premise of astrology," in Zambelli, ed., "Astrologi hallucinati," 45–100; here 99.

SCHOLARSHIP AS PROPHECY

The Beloved City of Johann Heinrich Alsted

Robert G. Clouse

SOME INFLUENTIAL BOOKS THAT WERE WRITTEN CENTURIES AGO can still be read rather easily and with great enjoyment, while other works were "tracts for the time" and had a wide influence in their day but are difficult and dull reading for those on the threshold of the twenty-first century. This chapter deals with one of the latter type of volumes. Written by a leading scholar, *The Beloved City*, made available in English during the seventeenth century, gave people encouragement that despite the time of troubles through which they were passing, millennial glory was near. The immense prestige of its author as well as its solid scholarship gave them hope and patience to endure the hardships that they suffered. The writer of this formidable piece of scholastic Protestant exegesis was Johann Heinrich Alsted (1588–1638), a Rhineland Calvinist trained at Herborn Academy, where his father was a teacher.[1] When Alsted enrolled in the school it was just beginning to reach the height of its prestige, offering an excellent education in both Reformed theology and humanistic studies. After finishing his courses at the head of his class, Alsted went on an academic journey, visiting Marburg, Frankfurt, Heidelberg, Strassburg, and Basle. Returning

---

[1] For information about Alsted's life, see the following: Percival Richard Cole, *A Neglected Educator: Johann Heinrich Alsted* (Sydney: William Applegate Gullick, 1910); Herman Ferdinand von Creigern, *Johann Amos Comenius als Theolog* (Leipzig: C. F. Winter'sche, 1881); Heinrich Heppe, *Alsted: Allgemeine Deutsche Biographie*, vol. 1 (1875); Friedrich Adolf Max Lippert, *Johann Heinrich Alsteds Pädagogisch-Didaktische Reform-Bestrebungen und ihr Einfluss auf Johann Amos Comenius* (Meissen: Klinkicht & Sohn, 1898); Herman Pixberg, *Der Deutsche Calvinismus und die Pädagogik* (Gladbeck: Martin-Heilman, 1952); and F. W. E. Roth, "Johann Heinrich Alsted (1588-1638), Sein Leben und Seine Schriften," *Monatshefte der Comenius-Gesellschaft*, ed. Ludwig Keller (Berlin, 1895), 4:29 ff. For the most recent work on Alsted see Howard Hotson, *Johann Heinrich Alsted: Encyclopaedism, Hermeticism and the Second Reformation in Germany* (D.phil. dissertation, Oxford University, 1991), forthcoming as *Johann Heinrich Alsted: Encyclopaedism, Hermeticism, Millenarianism and the Second Reformation in Germany*, Oxford Historical Monographs (Oxford: Clarendon Press).

to his alma mater, he became a teacher in the preparatory school which was held in connection with the higher school. Later he was appointed to the faculty of philosophy at Herborn. This position did not interfere with his literary activity, and a steady stream of writing flowed from his pen, giving him an excellent reputation far beyond his native Rhineland. As this fame grew, young men came from many areas of Europe where the Reformed faith had gotten a foothold to hear Alsted's lectures. Students from Bohemia, Moravia, Poland, Transylvania, the Netherlands, Scotland, Denmark, and Latvia availed themselves of his teaching.

When dissension broke out between the Reformed and the Arminians, and the Synod of Dort was called (1618) for the purpose of settling the dispute, Alsted and John Bisterfeld were sent as the representatives of the League of Rhenish Calvinist Princes. These men participated in the victory of the Reformed at the Synod, and on his return, Alsted was promoted to professor of theology. His position at Herborn continued to improve, and when John Piscator died (1626), Alsted was made senior professor of theology.

In the meantime, however, the Thirty Years' War had begun, and large armies marching through the Rhineland brought plague and fire in their wake (1626). The fortunes of Herborn declined as a result of the reduced enrollment of the school and the seizure of the endowment by the victorious Catholic princes. Herborn continued only through the contributions of some of the leading professors. Even Alsted's reputation was not able to draw students into the war-torn area. However, he was invited by Prince Gabriel of Transylvania to come to a new institution that the prince was organizing at Stuhl-Weissenburg. Gabriel was interested in the Reformed faith and wished to secure a man who could lend prestige to his new school. The desire for an undisturbed place to do his work caused Alsted to leave Herborn in 1629 and become the first rector of the new academy. He remained at this post until his death in 1638, never returning to his homeland.

Alsted's work reflects the ideas of Protestant scholasticism or orthodoxy. He expresses the view that all study should be based on the Bible, for it contained not merely religious truth but accurate knowledge on all matters. His theological precision is coupled with a medieval scientific outlook because he lived in an age preceding that of the formulation of modern science. Alsted's Aristotelianism is tempered by an interest in the logic of Petrus Ramus,[2] known as Ramism. Ramus had discarded the logic of Aristotle and substituted invention, argument, and judgment. According to his approach, if one carefully analyzes any fact, it will yield a dichotomy and each bifurcation will again

---

[2]Latin form Pierre de La Ramée (1515–72), French philosopher and logician.

yield a dichotomy. When these dichotomies are properly arranged, knowledge is possible by accepting the true and rejecting the false. These arguments were usually arranged by Ramists in charts to facilitate the understanding of a subject.[3]

Ramism reached a climax in his most famous work, the *Encyclopedia septem tomis distincta*.[4] This book was widely used throughout the academic world of the western community in the seventeenth century. The puritan students of England and New England read it, and the Catholic students of France found it valuable. A student who had this book had all that a seventeenth-century scholar would need to know. The fame of this massive contribution to knowledge proved to be short-lived as it was overshadowed later in the century by vernacular encyclopedias with alphabetical arrangement.

Alsted was in most ways a typical product of the Reformed orthodoxy of his day. In his espousal of millennialist eschatology, however, he departed from his amillennial Calvinist legacy. In 1627 he arrived at his most radical eschatology for in that year he published the famous expression of his millenarian views, *Diatribe de mille annis Apocalypticis*.[5] This work, which has numerous Ramist diagrams, is a study of the twentieth chapter of the book of Revelation.

The English translator of this book, William Burton, was a capable scholar who studied at Queen's College, Oxford, and taught at Gloucester Hall. Burton was forced to leave the university for lack of financial support and became

[3]For further information on Ramism these books are valuable: Herschel Baker, *The Wars of Truth* (Cambridge, Mass.: Harvard University Press, 1952); Frank Graves, *Peter Ramus and the Educational Reformation of the Sixteenth Century* (New York: Macmillan, 1912); William Samuel Howell, *Logic and Rhetoric in England 1500–1700* (Princeton: Princeton University Press, 1956); Perry Miller, *The New England Mind: The Seventeenth Century* (Cambridge, Mass.: Harvard University Press, 1939); and the following works by Walter J. Ong: *Ramus, Method, and the Decay of Dialogue* (Cambridge, Mass.: Harvard University Press, 1958); *Ramus and Talon Inventory* (Cambridge, Mass.: Harvard University Press, 1958); "System, Space, and Intellect in Renaissance Symbolism," *Bibliothèque de Humanisme et Renaissance* 18 (1956): 222–39.

[4]This encyclopedia was published at Herborn in 1630 and had 2,543 pages in seven volumes. For a resume of its contents see "Encyclopaedia," in *Encyclopaedia Britannica,* 11th ed. (Cambridge, Mass.: Harvard University Press, 1910), 9, 372. As late as the 1670s Leibnitz was very interested in working out a revision of Alsted's work. LeRoy E. Loemker, "Leibnitz and the Herborn Encyclopedists," *Journal of the History of Ideas* 22/3 (July–Sept., 1961): 333.

[5]*Diatribe de mille annis apocalypticis, non illis Chiliastarum et Phantastarum, sed B. B. Danielis et Johannis,* German translation (Herborn, 1630); English translation, *The Beloved City,* trans. William Burton (London, 1643). The English and Latin versions of the book have been republished in: J. H. Alsted, *Herborns calvinistische Theologie und Wissenschaft im Spiegel der englischen Kulturreform des frühen 17. Jahrhunderts,* ed. J. Klein and J. Kramer (Frankfurt a/M: Peter Lang, 1988), 20ff.

a schoolteacher in Kent. Later he taught at Kingston-upon-Thames until shortly before his death in 1657. Burton was a noted topographer, Latinist, and philologist, and during the civil war a copy of the *Diatribe* fell into his hands. As he tells his readers: "I bethought my selfe of some meanes whereby I might mitigate my apprehension of the miseries issuing from these present distempers; When (I thinke God so directing it) this Treatise came to my hands." The regard with which Alsted was held is apparent as he continues: "The *Author* is of as generall repute among us for learning, as any late Writer we have received from beyond the Seas these many yeares...."[6] "The generall welcome and long entertainment, which the other learned workes of this same *Authour* have had in our *Schooles*, as well as in those beyond the Seas, where he professed with admirable applause, seemed to me not to deny this piece an *endenizing*, or freedome, from some hands of a better note."[7] Burton concludes his introduction by explaining that many of the leaders of the early church and certain important contemporaries agreed with Alsted's millennialism.

The Beloved City, the title that Burton gave his translation of the *Diatribe*, begins by explaining that it was written to satisfy a twofold purpose: as a sample of the writer's method of Bible study and as a proof for his millennial views. Alsted believed that there were three prerequisites to the successful study of the prophetic portions of the Bible: the help of the Holy Spirit, a diligent comparison of Scripture with Scripture, and an experience of fulfilled Bible prophecy. As the Thirty Years' War was devastating his land, he claimed that these were the signs of the end of the age, stating: "Let us set sail therefore in the Name of God, and comfort the desolation of Germany with this pious meditation."[8] The war was particularly severe in Alsted's home province of Nassau, and he was forced to move to Transylvania. Indeed, the horrors of the conflict seem to hold the key for the shift of Alsted's thought from an amillennialist to a premillenarian position. He quoted a statement by Irenaeus that every prophecy before it is fulfilled is a riddle, but when fulfilled can be understood easily. Thus the trouble in Germany helped to explain the statements of the book of Revelation and to point to the end of the age.

Alsted considered his method of Bible study to be applicable to every chapter and every verse of Scripture (see facsimile, fig. 1). When applied to Rev. 20, it showed that the author of the book is Jesus Christ working through

---

[6]William Burton, "To the Right Worshipfull, Sir John Cordwell Knight...." This is found in the first page of the dedication of *The Beloved City.*

[7]William Burton, "Introduction," in John Henry Alsted, *The Beloved City,* trans. William Burton (London: 1643), ii.

[8]Alsted, *Beloved City,* trans. Burton, 1.

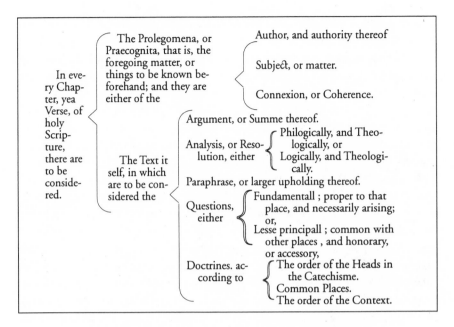

Fig. 1, facsimile p. 84 of *The Blessed City* (London, 1643)

the Apostle John and the subject is the Church, which consists of all people who have trusted in the true God. Alsted proceeds to trace the church's history on earth, beginning with Adam and the posterity of Abraham. The church continues to be limited to Abraham's descendants throughout the Old Testament and branches out to the Gentiles in the New Testament.

There are four periods of the church in the New Testament. The first is from the time of John the Baptist to the Jerusalem Council (A.D. 50), the time of the godly Jews. The second period lasts from the year 51 to the beginning of the thousand-year reign of Christ in 1694. The third period is the millennium when the martyrs for Christ will be resurrected and will reign on earth. There will be no persecution during this period and there will be a reformation in both life and doctrine. The fourth period lasts from the end of the thousand years until the last judgment and will be a time of misery because of the war of Gog and Magog. This ends in the last judgment, when the faithful share in everlasting happiness in heaven with Christ. The third part of the introduction is the connection of the passage with the rest of Scripture. This is explained by the presentation of a seven-point outline of Revelation.

Alsted then gives a summary of the chapter: God puts the dragon, Satan, into the bottomless pit for a thousand years. Because the devil is imprisoned for these years he cannot stir wicked men against the church; therefore, the

church enjoys outward peace, the dead are raised, and multitudes are converted. This happy condition is ended by the war of Gog and Magog, when
the church is again persecuted. At the close of that conflict the last judgment is
held and Satan with his followers are cast into the pit and the saints are forever
with Christ.

Alsted proceeds to analyze the passage philologically, that is, by a study of
all the important Greek words. We shall not review each of these, but a selection of key verses from the passage will be presented. Rev. 20:4 states: "And I
saw thrones, and they sat upon them, and judgment was given unto them; and
I saw the souls of them that were beheaded for the witness of Jesus, and for the
word of God, and which had not worshiped the beast, neither his image, neither had received his mark upon their foreheads, or in their hands; and they
lived and reigned with Christ a thousand years." Alsted explains that "thrones"
mean a judicial process being prepared, "judgment" is given to Christ, and his
angels and "souls" refer to men who are martyrs and are freed by the judgment. The "beast" is the second beast of Rev. 13 and 19 which had arrogated
to itself the worship of God. "And had not received his mark upon their foreheads" indicates that the martyrs did not publicly follow the opposition to
Christ. "And they lived" indicates that the martyrs lived again as a reward for
their sufferings, "'with Christ' who all this while shall reign visibly in heaven,
invisibly upon earth, his visible kingdom resigned to the martyrs."[9]   Verse 8
states that when Satan is again loosed he "shall go out to seduce the nations
which are in the four quarters of the earth, Gog and Magog, to gather them
together to battle: the number of whom is as the sand of the sea." The phrase
"the nations" means the wicked who shall remain on earth despite all the
efforts of the church to evangelize them during the thousand years. Gog and
Magog, collective names for the people that Satan shall gather, are dealt with
in verse 9: "And they went up on the breadth of the earth, and compassed the
camp of the saints about, and the beloved city: and fire came down from God
out of heaven, and devoured them." Alsted interprets "the camp of the saints"
and "the beloved city" as being the whole church scattered over the earth at
that time.

Another interpretation of interest is that for verse 12: "And I saw the
dead, small and great, stand before God; and the books were opened: and
another book was opened, which is the book of life: and the dead were judged
out of those things which were written in the books, according to their
works." The first set of books is that of every person's conscience where he has

---

[9] Alsted, *Beloved City*, trans. Burton, 17. Parenthetical references in the text refer to this
translation.

stored his thoughts, words, and deeds. The book of life is the sacred and hidden decree of God concerning the election of the saints to eternal life. The dead were judged out of these books with a sentence passed upon all, acquitting some and condemning others to hell.

Alsted's logical-theological analysis is an elaborated outline of the passage. He divides the chapter into five parts: first, the description of the angel (v. 1); second, what the angel did (vv. 2, 3); third, the happy condition of the church (vv. 2–6); fourth, the troubled state of the church (vv. 7–10); fifth, the description of the last judgment (vv. 11–15). Following the analysis, he presents his view of the passage by paraphrasing the entire chapter.

Then he answers questions that arise from his interpretation of the chapter; for example, What year will the thousand-year reign of Christ begin and who are Gog and Magog? Alsted believes that such questions can be condensed into one; namely, will there be any happiness of the church before the last day and if so, what will it be? He divides his discussion of this question into two parts by stating, "I will in the first place therefore by certain Classes, or ranks of Arguments, confirm the truth to be maintained herein: After that I will confute the Objections of the adversary part" (33). He argues in the affirmative from the context of the passage, from other passages of Scripture, from reason, and from the opinions of learned men. The contextual argument reminds his readers that Satan has never been bound, the martyrs have never been resurrected, and the war of Gog and Magog has never occurred.

Next, he takes different passages from various parts of the Bible to show that events are spoken of which require his millennial scheme. He refers to Gen. 17:4–6 where God promised Abraham that he would be the father of many nations. This meant that he would have spiritual sons as well as physical and refers to Gentiles as well as Jews. As this was a prophecy of the blessing that would come to people through Christ and since the Jewish people have never followed Christ, there must come a day when they, too, will believe and be the true sons of Abraham.

Another scriptural proof offered for the coming millennium is Isa. 2:1–4 where one reads of the supremacy of God and the peacefulness of the nations as they beat their swords into plowshares and their spears into pruning hooks. Pss. 22:27, 86:9, and 117:1 predict the conversion of all nations, but as Alsted writes: "Let us search through the Monuments of Histories, and then let us examine whether this hath been, or no. We shall finde indeed in some new found Lands, detected in ours and our fathers memory, that the works of the Conversion of the Nations hath had some beginning, and small progress: But in many parts of the East to this day, we shall find so little progresse, that not so much as a beginning thereof will any where yet appear" (42). As he gives arguments for the millennium Alsted moves beyond the scope of commentator to that of prophet when he explains Dan. 12:11, 12: "And from the time that the daily sacrifice shall be taken away and the abomination that maketh desolate set up, there shall be a thousand two hundred and ninety days. Blessed is he that waiteth, and cometh to the thousand three hundred and five and thirty days." He states that "from the time" refers to the destruction of Jerusalem by Titus and that a day in prophecy is to be understood as a year. Thus to the date of the destruction of Jerusalem in A.D. 69 one must add 1,290 years, which results in A.D. 1359. "At which we must begin the Epocha or account of 1335 dayes, or years: and so we shall be brought to the year of Christ 2694 in which the thousand years in the Revelation shall have end: and they being ended the warre of Gog and Magog shall begin, to which also the last judgment shall put an end" (50).

The next section of Alsted's work consists of an appeal to "reason." He felt that "the severall Phanomena, or Apparitions in the Heavens; namely, new Starres, and Cometes; also Earthquakes, and the like, taken notice of in these latter times, do without doubt portend and manifestly foretell some notable, and extraordinatory change" (57). He further bolsters his interpretation by appealing to the views of learned and godly men, recognizing that their opinions differ in certain respects from his, but they all believe in a future happy state of the church during a thousand-year period when evil will be restrained. Among those that he cites are Alfonsus Conradus of Mantua, Lucas Osiander, Matthew Cotterius, John Piscator, Paracelsus, Michael Sendivogius, Stephanus Pannonius, Joannes Debriciu, and Peter du Moulin. He also quotes the IV Esdras, which refers to the conversion of the Jews and the deliverance of God's people from Antichrist.

Alsted then answers thirty-six objections to his interpretation. Attention to several of these will demonstrate his approach. He quotes Matt. 24:27–39, which states that before the coming of Christ the world will be wicked as it was before the deluge in the days of Noah. If there is a great worldwide conversion during the thousand years, how will this prophecy be fulfilled? He answers that some wicked men shall continue throughout the millennium and will be strong enough to wage war at the end of the thousand years against the church. Then they shall be judged as the wicked were in the days of Noah. Others might object on the basis of Luke 18:8 ("Nevertheless when the Son of man cometh, shall he find faith on the earth?") that when Christ comes to judge the world he will find very few believers. Yet, if the millennial teaching of Alsted is correct, when Christ comes in judgment at the end of the thousand-year reign, he will find a great number of believers. The answer to this objection is that Christ did not mean that he would find few believers, but rather that they would not be as numerous as the enemies of the church, who would be as the sand of the sea in number. The familiar objection to millenarian doctrine, that Satan as mentioned in Rev. 20:2,3 was bound for a thousand years in the first century by the preaching of the gospel, is squarely rejected. Alsted writes: "Again, it is false that Satan from the year of Christ 70, was bound for a thousand years; because from that time innumerable and horrible heresies, fallings away, and scandalls, &c. have been" (66). Satan all these years was very busy deceiving the people of the world such as the Jews, Indians, and Turks.

Opponents of millennialism frequently cite verses such as Acts 14:22, where Paul and Barnabas affirm that one must enter the kingdom of God through much affliction. It seems best in this case, however, to say that they refer to their own times and do not mean to say that the church must always suffer persecution. If the church must always be under the cross, it would seem to contradict its position during the reigns of such rulers as Constantine the Great and Theodosius.

Those who spiritualize the first resurrection are also answered by Alsted. These people believe that the first resurrection refers to those who are raised from spiritual death by repentance and faith. Yet these same people, Alsted reminds us, take the second resurrection literally. He points out that these two uses of the term are contradictory, and that the first resurrection cannot be merely spiritual, especially 0since there is no mention here of the death of sin. As he states, "the first Resurrection, as it is spoken of in this place, is not opposed to the first death, of which there is here no mention; but is opposed to the second Resurrection, as appears out of these words; But the rest of the dead lived not again, untill the thousand years were finished. This is the first Resurrection" (68).

Another objection identifies Alsted's opinion with the chiliasts or millenarians who had been discredited many years before. He replies to this by stating that the astic view differs from his because the former maintains a life of physical pleasure for a thousand years, whereas he emphasizes spiritual joy. The chiliasts say that Christ reigns personally upon earth but Alsted believes that He rules through His saints. Also they claim that no ungodly people would live during the reign of Christ, but he denies this.

Alsted responds to the objection that the thousand-year reign spoken of in Rev. 20 consists of souls reigning in heaven with Christ. He believed that the term "resurrection" was used in a complete sense in Rev. 20, that is, of both soul and body (see fig. 2). The reward of the martyrs is pictured in this Scrip-

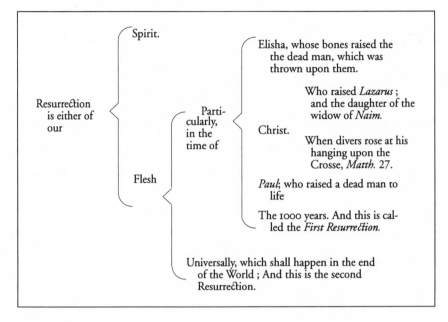

Fig. 2, facsimile of diagram on p. 18 of *The Beloved City* (London, 1643).

ture as a special blessing and yet the souls of all the saints are to reign in heaven
with Christ. Thus the martyrs must receive an additional reward, which would
be the first resurrection from the dead. This kingdom is also said to last for a
thousand years, a statement that could not be true of the rule of Christ in
heaven, which is an eternal reign.

Some accuse millenarians of being Judaizers but Alsted answers indig-
nantly: "Therefore also the Scripture doth Judaize.... we generally entertain
too mean a conceit of the conversion of the Jews, because being over-much
addicted, and carried away with Scholasticall trifles, we weigh not at all the
Mysteries, which are propounded in the Scriptures."[10] The last objection cited
by Alsted is based on Mark 13:32, "But of that day and that hour knoweth no
man, no, not the angels which are in heaven, neither the Son, but the Father,"
and Acts 1:7, "It is not for you to know the times, or seasons, which the Father
hath put in his own power." This concerns the time of the final judgment, yet
Alsted seems to have set a date for this judgment. In his answer he mentions
that the judgment and the return of Christ will come after the 2,694th year of

[10] Alsted, *Beloved City*, 76.

Christ but one cannot be certain of the exact time since the length of the war of Gog and Magog is not given. He closes his work by pointing out the doctrines that can be found in this passage concerning such matters as God's providence, the angels, predestination, the church, martyrdom, the resurrection of the flesh, the last judgment, eternal life, and eternal death.

From this book we see Alsted's millennial teaching to be a mixture of radical and conservative elements. He does not describe in great detail all the aspects of Scripture that pertain to life during the millennium, yet he believes in a literal first resurrection of the martyrs and a thousand-year reign of the righteous upon the earth. He does not hesitate to set the date for the beginning of this glorious kingdom: it would come in 1694. When he predicted the time of the arrival of the millennium Alsted went beyond the role of scholar and became a prophet. His work as a renowned polyhistor, theologian, and biblical scholar gave a firm basis to this date setting. His work reached a broad audience in England because of Burton's translation. The extent of literacy during this era is a matter of considerable debate because of the problem of defining literacy and the scarcity of records about those who did not read Latin.[11] Obviously there was an increase in the English-reading public as evidenced by the numerous pamphlets published during the Civil War and the Interregnum. This was especially true of material dealing with the Bible. As Patrick Collinson has stated, even humble artisans had minds that were "so steeped in the cross-references and resonant concordances of Scripture as to be incapable of exercising themselves in any other way."[12] With such people, and even their social superiors, the work of Alsted, when translated and published in English, had a tremendous prophetic impact. *The Beloved City* is often referred to by Fifth Monarchists and other millenarian sects that appealed to the common people.[13]

[11]Capable guides to the labyrinth of debates about seventeenth-century literacy can be found in Peter Clark, "Ownership of Books in England 1560–1649" *Schooling and Society*, ed. Lawrence Stone (Princeton: Princeton University Press, 1976), 95–111; Wyn Ford, "The Problem of Literacy in Early Modern England" *History*, 78 (Feb. 1993): 22–37; Harvey J. Graff, *The Labyrinths of Literacy, Reflections on Literacy Past and Present* (Pittsburgh: University of Pittsburgh Press, 1995); David Cressy, *Literacy and the Social Order, Reading and Writing in Tudor and Stuart England* (Cambridge: Cambridge University Press, 1980).

[12]Patrick Collinson, *The Birthpangs of Modern England, Religious and Cultural Change in the Sixteenth and Seventeenth Centuries* (New York: St. Martin's, 1988), 124.

[13]For further information on seventeenth-century English millennialism see Bryan W. Ball, *A Great Expectation: Eschatological Thought in English Protestantism to 1660* (Leiden: Brill, 1975); Bernard S. Capp, *The Fifth Monarchy Men: A Study in Seventeenth-Century English Millenarianism* (Totawa; N.J.: Rowman and Littlefield, 1972); Paul Christianson, *Reformers and Babylon: English Apocalyptic Visions from the Eve of the Reformation to the Eve of the Civil War* (Toronto: University of

Perhaps as one approaches the year 2000 these seventeenth-century readers can be understood a little better than they were by previous generations of
scholars. Contemporary paranoia about the millennial year is very great with
even secular writers worrying about the Y2K phenomenon, that is, that most
mainframes will crash on New Year's Eve 1999, leaving the world without
phone records, medical data, equity holdings, bank accounts, and other vital
files. More religious people believe that in the year 2000 the Antichrist will be
revealed and God's people will be "raptured" or taken from the world in
UFOs. Some New Age writers claim that Princess Diana was an ambassador
sent from a distant fairy realm to guide us into the new millennium. In a con-
temporry admosphere seething with such currents of thought, one may
excuse the eagerness of seventeenth-century English people to accept the pre-
dictins of the sage of herborn

Toronto Press, 1978); James A. De Jong, *As the Waters Cover the Sea: Millennial Expectations in the
Rise of Anglo-American Missions 1640–1810* (Kampen: Kok, 1970); Katherine R. Firth, *The Apoc-
alyptic Tradition in Reformation Britain 1530–1645* (Oxford: Oxford University Press, 1979);
Christopher Hill, *Antichrist in Seventeenth Century England* (London: Oxford University Press,
1971); Ian Murray, *The Puritan Hope: A Study in Revival and the Interpretation of Prophecy* (London:
Banner of Truth Trust, 1971); and James West Davidson, *The Logic of Millennial Thought* (New
Haven: Yale University Press, 1977). For a perceptive analysis of the main millennial views in
Tudor-Stuart times see George Kroeze, "The Variety of Millennial Hopes in the English Refor-
mation 1550–1660" (Ph.D. dissertation, Fuller Theological Seminary, 1984).

Interpreting an Early Reformation Pamphlet by Urbanus Rhegius

Richard Cole

The printed sermon of sixteenth-century Germany is an underutilized genre of the many printed documents relating to that early Reformation period. Some of those sermons are fairly straightforward, but others are wrapped in several layers of meanings, some of which are not immediately understandable. These sermons often reflected the chaos and seemingly unrelated currents of the moment in which they were delivered. It is useful to explore in depth the contents and setting of one such document.

The time and place is December 14, 1521, in the South German city of Augsburg. The event is the delivery of a printed sermon, *Ain Predig der hailigenjunckfrauwen Catharina* (A Sermon about the Holy Virgin Catherine) by the printer Sylvan Otmar.[1] The sermon had been preached only three weeks earlier, on November 25, 1521, St. Catherine's Day, in Augsburg's St. Ann's Church by a guest preacher, one Urbanus Rhegius, one of the first Lutheran reformers in that city.[2] Rhegius' sermon in many ways reflects the crosscurrents of the early Reformation period. This is the sermon genre one would expect to hear preached on November 25, a day in medieval hagiography that honors St. Catherine of Alexandria. Robert Kolb suggests that it was not

---

[1]Urbanus Rhegius, *Ain Predig der hailigenjunckfrawen Catharina* (Augsburg: Sylvan Otmar, 1521). The pamphlet is partially paginated. I use the existing A and B signatures and number consecutively each section. This pamphlet is located in the Flugschriften-sammlung Gustav Freytag in the Stadt- und Universitätsbibliothek in Frankfurt a/M. For catalog reference, see Paul Hohenemser, *Flugschriften-sammlung Gustav Freytag* (Hildesheim: Olms, rept. 1966), no. 2884.

[2]Recent discussion of Rhegius can be found in Hellmut Zschoch, *Reformatorische Existenz und konfessionelle Identität: Urbanus Rhegius als evangelischer Theologe in den Jahren 1520 bis 1530* (Tubingen: Mohr, 1995), and in Scott H. Hendrix, "Validating the Reformation: The Use of the church Fathers by Urbanus Rhegius," in *Ecclesia Militans: Studien zur Konzilien- und Reformationsgeschichte*, ed. Walter Brandmüller, Herbert Immenkötter, and Erwin Iserloh (Paderborn: Schöningh, 1988), 2:281–305; and idem, "The Use of Scripture in Establishing Protestantism: The Case of Urbanus Rhegius," in David C. Steinmetz, *The Bible in the Sixteenth Century* (Durham, N.C.: Duke University Press, 1990), 37–49. Older but still useful is Gerhard Uhlhorn, *Urbanus Rhegius: Leben und ausgewählte Schriften* (Elberfeld: R. L. Friedrichs, 1861).

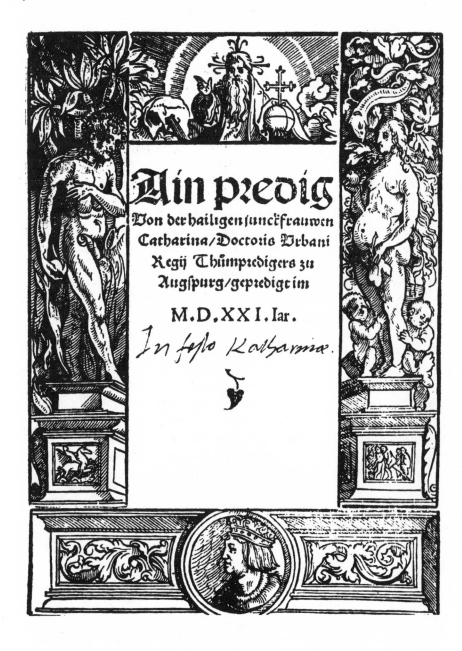

Title page of *Ain Predig der hailigenjunckfrawen Catarina,* by Urbanus Rhegius, printed in Augsburg by Sylvan Otmar, 1521 (shown at 65 percent).

uncommon for Lutheran pastors to preach about the various saints beloved by the medieval church.[3] Even though the year 1521 is very early in the reforming career of Rhegius, there is something new and out of the ordinary in this sermon. To probe the text one needs to ask a number of questions: Does the text reflect the authority of the traditional Christian church or the spirit of the early Reformation? Will an examination of an ignored text shed some light on the triangular relationships arising among the text conceived by the author, printed by the publisher, and read or heard by its audience? Kolb's evaluation is insightful and well documented, yet it appears that in his sermon of November 25, 1521, Rhegius not only commemorates a popular saint in the Catholic church but also uses the day of commemoration for something else: he reflects on Renaissance humanism, elements of Reformation biblicism, and the perils of contemporary politics (especially relating to the dreaded threat from the Moslem Turks), and perhaps he assesses the potential for influence by and profit from the new printed genre, the polemical pamphlet (*Flugschriften*).

Rhegius, who had watched closely the indulgence controversy of Martin Luther and subsequent events in Wittenberg, moved in this sermon from his academic humanist environment to the realms of both the marketplace and the Reformation.[4] At the universities of Freiburg im Breisgau and Ingolstadt, Rhegius had studied the humanist way toward the life of the mind, a way predicated on increased focus on grammar and rhetoric.[5] After completing his formal study, Rhegius was hired by the University of Ingolstadt to lecture on poetry and rhetoric; he wanted the *belles lettres,* "which had been so long neglected," to bloom again and return to the brilliancy of former times.[6] Rhegius became a poet immersed in Greek and Roman mythology and was rewarded for his efforts by being named Poet Laureate of the Holy Roman Empire by Emperor Maximilian in 1517.[7]

Shortly thereafter Rhegius left Ingolstadt, and after a brief stay in the diocese of Constance he accepted a call in July 1520 to become the cathedral preacher in Augsburg. Now, as preacher instead of classroom lecturer, Rhegius

---

[3]Robert Kolb, *For All the Saints: Changing Perceptions of Martyrdom and Sainthood in the Lutheran Reformation* (Macon, GA: Mercer University Press, 1987), 141. See also Roger Chartier, "Texts, Printing, Readings," in *The New Cultural History,* ed. Lynn Hunt (Berkeley: University of California Press, 1989), 154–175.

[4]Manfred Hannemann, *The Diffusion of the Reformation in Southwestern Germany, 1518–1534* (Chicago: University of Chicago Reserve Paper, 1975), 16.

[5]Douglas Hampton, "Urbanus Rhegius and the Spread of the German Reformation" (Ph.D. diss., Ohio State University, 1973), 7.

[6]Uhlhorn, *Urbanus Rhegius,* 9–10.

[7]Rhegius, *Ain Predig,* Aii.

switched from being a poet of classical themes to become a preacher who astutely observed his times and who became a spokesman for the Reformation.

On November 25, 1521, Rhegius had the opportunity to express publicly the gist of his newly acquired Reformation thinking. In "A Sermon about the Holy Virgin Catherine," Rhegius reminded his listeners that the church obliges its members to praise the saintly Catherine. He tells the story related in Matt. 13:44–46, that sometimes treasures are found like a pearl hidden in a farmer's field, a treasure the finder may keep without repayment just like the treasure of one knowing Christ through the Scriptures; yet sometimes one must give up the treasures of the world. In the humanist mind of Rhegius, Catherine had all the virtues to be most admired:

> Now we will see how the holy maiden Catherine handled these treasures. The wise maiden Catherine had the best that was observed in the world, that is, a deep knowledge of all philosophical or worldly wisdom; that is, the seven liberal arts [*siben freyen kuensten*]: grammar, logic, rhetoric, all power, cleverness of the tongue, sharp argument, diverse calculation in numbers, Geometric descriptions of earth, and the marking of musical chords in music....[8]

Up to this point Urbanus Rhegius' sermon is what one would expect; but he was already in trouble with the Catholic hierarchy for his strong Reformation views attacking indulgences. Eulogizing a saint who had been martyred in 307 A.D. was perhaps a laudatory action in the eyes of the Catholic bishops, but the whole realm of sainthood obscured Martin Luther's views on the christological foundation of soteriology. Even though many saint's days were retained in later Protestant church orders and many pastors continued to use and reinterpret saints for Lutheran usage, preaching on them was rare for Rhegius.[9] Douglas Hampton, a biographer of Rhegius, concluded, perhaps erroneously, that the voice of Rhegius is that of a conservative reformer not venturing so far from the old faith as many of the other reformers who were

---

[8]Rhegius, *Ain Predig*, Aiiii. "Was ist mir nütz zü zu dem ewigen leben / wen ich gleich waiss in der Grammatica / Logica / Rhetorica / alle kraft / scharpffe argument / klugheit in det rede / die tieff und vilfeltig aussrechnung aller zal in der Arithmetica. Die kunstreich abmessung aller grosse / beschreibung aller formen / abmessung des umkraiss und tieffe der erden / in der Geometria / Item underschaid der don / ausstaillung der interuallen allerlay gesangs auff dem Monochordo in Musica...."

[9]Cf. Kolb, *For All the Saints,* 87.

caught up in the flow of the Reformation.[10] But Rhegius' actions cannot be explained easily by his conservatism; rather, the conditions of the moment caused some confusion and uncertainty for reformers during the early years of the Reformation.

What did the life of Catherine signify to Rhegius' two audiences—those who heard him preach and those who read the printed sermon—and to the church? Catherine was the daughter of King Costos of Cyprus, whom the Roman emperor Diocletian appointed to head the government of Egypt. At the death of her father, Catherine left Alexandria in Egypt and returned to Cyprus, where she was thrown into prison for being a Christian and was martyred on November 25, 307. The story of Catherine passed into the oral tradition of medieval Europe and was finally recorded in the thirteenth century by the bishop of Genoa, Jacobus de Voragine, in his widely popular book *The Golden Legend*, which recorded the lives of two hundred saints (of which forty-one were women). Voragine tells us that when Emperor Maxentius summoned all to offer sacrifices to idols, the well-educated eighteen-year-old Catherine argued with Maxentius using syllogistic reasoning, allegories, metaphors, and logical and mystical inferences to reject false gods. Intimidated, Maxentius ordered fifty scholars, orators, and rhetoricians to debate Catherine.[11] Rhegius mentions this colloquy, as it was passed on to him by Voragine, in his sermon: "The knowledge of Jesus Christ ... is the power with which the noble maiden Catherine overturned the ideas of the *fuenfftzig haidnischer maister.*" Here the reader or hearer of the sermon may relate to the transforming idea of the centrality of Christ in Reformation doctrine. Rhegius continues, "The few words of the wise Catherine which stemmed from the belief in and love of God ... were worth more than the clever speech and sharp arguments of the heathens."[12] Catherine easily put down the arguments of the fifty

---

[10]Hampton, "Urbanus Rhegius and the Spread of the German Reformation," 58. *The Oxford Encyclopedia of the Reformation* (1996), 429, tells us that Rhegius served in Augsburg until he was replaced as cathedral preacher in 1522; he was recalled in 1523 by the council at Augsburg and remained a Lutheran preacher in the city until 1530. It is well known that in 1524 he and his coworker Johannes Frosh (1483–1533) were the first to give the cup to the laity during the Eucharist, thereby formally instigating the Reformation in Augsburg, and that, following Luther's lead, both of the reformers married in 1525.

[11]See Jacobus de Voragine, *The Golden Legend,* trans. William Granger (Princeton, NJ: Princeton University Press, 1993), 334–335.

[12]Rhegius, *Ain Predig,* A5: "Ich hat mich unnder euch nichtz beriembt zuwissen / dann Jesum Christii unsenselben gecreuetzget. Das is die recht war kunst edel Junckfrolin Catherina fuenfftzig haidnischer maister ritterlichuberwunden / und all ir haidnische weisshait und kunst zu ainer Lautern torheit gemacht hat."

men, who were subsequently executed for losing the debate with her. Apparently, as legend tells it, Catherine had a broad knowledge of all levels of philosophy in its practical, theoretical, and logical components. She had eloquence and dignity, and she was chaste.[13] Was Rhegius in his praise of Catherine exhibiting conservative theology or was he merely softening his audience by appealing to stories already familiar to them? He showed some significant constraint vis-à-vis miracles by omitting parts of the Catherine legend, at least as the bishop of Genoa tells it; Rhegius failed to report that when Catherine was beheaded milk not blood flowed from her body.[14]

Part of the contemporary context of Rhegius' 1521 sermon is "the Turkish problem," that is, Turkey's successful intrusion into the relatively weak and disorganized Balkans and its subsequent rush into a vacuum created in part by an increased western interest in Atlantic exploration.[15] By late August 1521 Suleiman had captured the Slavic city of Belgrade, opening the gates for further Islamic conquest in Hungary and Austria. The large number of extant sixteenth-century anti-Turkish pamphlets confirm the panic and fear of Islamic domination indicated by Rhegius. He told his audience that Turks were in no uncertain terms "the enemy of our present holy beliefs."[16] He continues: "The weapons Catherine used, the evangelical power generated by the writings of the apostles will be more important than spears, muskets, and steel halberds [spiessen/buechsen und helmparten]; we will yet make Christians out of the Turks."[17] At this point the sermon reflects the conjoined power of religion and the interests of the small independent German cities and fiefdoms. Certainly the impending threat of invasion by infidels was an important part of the political context of the moment.

One notes quickly in this sermon about St. Catherine the omnipresence of the central ingredients of the evangelical Christian religion. Rhegius' use of citations of key biblical verses, for the most part his own German translations of the Vulgate, to make his arguments scripturally based, are a cardinal feature of the pamphlet.[18] He cited biblical verses and the church fathers such as

---

[13]Voragine, *Golden Legend*, 339.   [14]Voragine, *Golden Legend*, 339.

[15]Fernand Braudel, *The Mediterranean and the Mediterranean World in the Age of Philip II*, 2 vols., trans. Sion Reynolds (New York: Harper & Row, 1966): 2:667–668.

[16]Rhegius, *Ain Predig*, B1. "auf den heutigen tag die feind unsers haligen glaube / ...."

[17]Rhegius, *Ain Predig*, B1.

[18]Rhegius, *Ain Predig*, A3. Rhegius made his own vernacular translation from the Vulgate of the biblical verses he cites. An example which indicates the clarity of biblical translation is John 3:16: "Aber der guting got / ... / hat die welt so leib gehaptt/ das er sein aingeprornen sun geben hat / damit das alle / die in glauben/ nit verloren und verdampt werden / sonnder das ewig Leben haben."

Jerome and Cyprian at great length to underscore the blessedness of the maid-enhood of Catherine, the noble lady of Cyprus. Rhegius wrote that since the fall of humanity in the Garden of Eden, virginity and hence purity was a trea-sure. He cited Matt. 5:8: "Blessed are the pure in heart, for they shall see God." He continued by citing Cyprian, who called virginity, maidenhood, the most treasured part of the flock of Christ ("den schoener herzlichen tail der scar Christi"). He concluded his sentence with a citation from Rev. 14:4: "These are those who follow the spotless lamb whithersoever he goes" ("sy volgen demm vnuermassgeten lemblin nach wo es hin gat").[19] These ideas do not only pertain to women. Rhegius declared that indeed Christ is a virgin ("Christus ist ain junckfraw").[20] He pursued his idea of purity of heart with great enthusiasm, and he concluded his work with yet further adulation for Catherine: "Die kirch singt in person der hailigen Catherine."[21]

Rhegius' St. Catherine's Day sermon was printed with unusual speed—three weeks after its oral delivery. The city of Augsburg was already by 1521 the locus of much Reformation printing activity. There were at least fourteen printers in Augsburg in the 1520s and the majority of them printed works by Martin Luther or Reformation tracts of the genre of Rhegius' works. Sylvan Otmar, the printer/publisher of the sermon tract, may easily be considered one of the most prolific printers not only in Augsburg but in all the German lands during the early German Reformation.[22] The potential for the sale and dissemination of Rhegius' work was clearly favorable.

There are few records indicating the motives of Reformation printers but we do know that Otmar rushed the Rhegius sermon under review into print. Otmar knew well the commercial potential of books and pamphlets that con-cerned issues of reform. He knew that sainthood would be revered, and he knew that his readers could be reassured that the Turkish menace could be overcome. The quick publication was a good measure of Otmar's reading of the readiness of his market for the information he could print.

For Rhegius, the sermon reflects the culmination of a number of variables that affected his life. He was rapidly coming to terms with the idea of Refor-mation, to which he had become totally committed by 1525. He believed in the power of the sermon in the best evangelistic tradition. Even though the St. Catherine's Day sermon pamphlet points backwards to the church fathers and

---

[19]Rhegius, *Ain Predig*, B3a. Rhegius adds "spotless lamb" to the Vulgate text.

[20]Rhegius, *Ain Predig*, B3a.

[21]Rhegius, *Ain Predig*, B6.

[22]Richard Cole, "Reformation Printers: Unsung Heroes," *Sixteenth Century Journal* 15 (Fall 1984): 332, 336.

old, established ideas of the sanctity of a virginal state and traditional ideas of sainthood, the pamphlet itself has a very modern appearance. It was printed in the vernacular with a title page enhanced by a woodcut illustration that details the humanistic proportions of Adam and Eve.

Further, Rhegius' pamphlet reflects his own connections with the humanist milieu. He cites, for example, the father of Italian humanism, Petrarch, who envisioned a synthesis of wisdom and eloquence in oral expression.[23] In the section extolling plainness over the sensual sin in human life, Rhegius quotes Petrarch: "The brightest and clearest part of the body, which is the eyes, reveal to us the darkness of humanity."[24]

Clearly there are many crosscurrents in the sermon by Rhegius. The year 1521 was a period of significant Reformation change and turmoil, much of which is revealed in the pamphlet under study. The rhetoric and content of this sermon text point in a new direction, the new order of Reformation Europe. Perhaps Urbanus Rhegius did not realize in 1521 the ultimate dimensions of the Reformation in the making, but the tone of his sermon and the quick rush to print were important aspects of the unfurling Reformation.

---

[23]George A. Kenney, *Classical Rhetoric and Its Christian and Secular Tradition from Ancient to Modern Times* (Chapel Hill: University of North Carolina Press, 1980), 197.

[24]Rhegius, *Ain Predig,* B: "Der allerhellest klarest tail des leibs / das seind die augen ★★★/ zeucht offt den ganntzen mensch in the finsternuss.".

Publishing the Reformation in Habsburg Hungary

David P. Daniel

REFORMATION IDEAS BEGAN TO PENETRATE HUNGARY during the early 1520s. The first reports about Luther, as well as copies of his early publications, were brought to Hungary by merchants and others who regularly traveled to Bohemia, Poland, and the Empire, or were sent to individuals in the kingdom by correspondents in these lands.[1] Unsubstantiated reports from the early seventeenth century maintain that booksellers first brought works of the Wittenberg Reformer to Hungary in 1519 and that in 1520 Thomas Preisner read the Ninety-Five Theses of Luther from his pulpit in L'ubica in Spiš county.[2] Better documented are the first manifestations of sympathy for Luther and the Reformation in the mining cities of central upper Hungary.

On August 28, 1521, John Korb, prior of the cloister in Königstein near Dresden, sent a letter and several publications of Luther's to Gregor Soravius, pastor in Banská Štiavnica (Selmecbánya, Schemnitz).[3] During the same year, in nearby Banská Bystrica (Besztercebánya, Neusohl), the mayor, Valentine Schneider, and his brother-in-law, Henrich Kindlinger, the church warden, sought to have Simon Bernhardt from Opava in Silesia serve as a preacher of the evangelical faith. This initiated a struggle over patronage rights with the Roman Catholic city pastor, Nicolaus of Sabinov, which lasted until the end

---

[1]For the course of the early Reformation in Hungary see especially Mihaly Bucsay, *Der Protestantismus in Ungarn 1521–1978, Ungarns Reformationskirchen im Geschichte und Gegenwart: 1. Im Zeitalter der Reformation, Gegen-reformation und katholischen Reform* (Vienna: Böhlau, 1977), and David P. Daniel, "Hungary," in *The Early Reformation in Europe*, ed. Andrew Pettegree (Cambridge: Cambridge University Press, 1992), 49–69.

[2]Győző Bruckner, *A reformáció és ellenreformácio története a Szepességen*, vol. 1 (Budapest, 1922), 54; Mathias Szlavík, *Die Reformation in Ungarn* (Halle:Buchdruckerei des Weisenhauses, 1884), 2.

[3]Letter dated August 28, 1521;V. Bunyitay, R. Rapiacs, J. Karácsonyi, eds., *Egyháztörténelmi emlékek a magyarországi hitujítás korából*, vol. 1 (Budapest: Societatis S. Stephani, 1902), 41. Soravius was from Sorau in Lower Lusatia.

of the decade.[4] In 1522 George Baumheckel of Banská Bystrica became the first student from Hungary to enroll at the University of Wittenberg. He was joined there, in 1523, by Matthias Thome, also from Banská Bystrica.[5] In a letter of May 19, 1522, to the notary of Kremnica (Körmöcbánya, Kremnitz), Bartolomeus Frankfordinus of Banská Štiavnica referred to "our Luther" and "our Conrad."[6] The latter may have been a reference to Conrad Cordatus, who served as preacher in Buda and was briefly the court chaplain of Queen Mary of Habsburg until his Lutheran views led to his dismissal and departure for Kremnica[7] and then for Wittenberg.[8] He was replaced by Johann Henckel, formerly pastor in Levoča (Löcsei, Leutschau) in Spiš (Szepes, Zips), who, like the queen, sympathized more with the views of Erasmus than with those of Luther.[9]

Support for Luther was, therefore, not only manifested in the upper Hungarian mining cities during the early 1520s, but also by a small circle of individuals with contacts to the court of Queen Mary in Buda and who likewise supported the Habsburg in Hungary. Among these were the humanists Simon Grynaeus, Viet Winsheim, John Kressling, and Conrad Cordatus.[10] But it was Margrave George of Brandenburg-Ansbach, the military tutor of Louis II (still in his teens and confidant of Mary) who was the most prominent advocate of the Wittenberg reformers. In 1523 George wrote to Luther noting that he had defended the Reformer before his wards, indicating the substance of his defense and asking several questions concerning the reception of the sacrament, which actually may have been posed by the queen.[11] But the influence of these supporters of Luther declined with the appointment of Henckel as

---

[4]Alžběta Göllnerová, "Počátky reformace v Banské Bystrici," *Bratislava* 4 (1930): 589.

[5]Göllnerová, "Počátky reformace v Banské Bystrici," 587.

[6]Bunyitay, et al., *Egyháztörténelmi emlékek a magyarországi hitujítás korából*, 1:57.

[7]Ján Kvačala, "Kralovna Maria a jej účast v dejoch reformácie," *Viera a veda* 1 (1930): 16.

[8]Vilmos Frankl (Fraknói), *A hazai és külföldi iskolázás a XVI században* (Budapest: Athenaeum, 1873), 296.

[9]Adalbert Hudak, "Der Hofprediger Johannes Henckel und seine Beziehungen zu Erasmus von Rotterdam," *Kirche im Osten* 2 (1959): 106–113; Gustav Bauch, "Dr. Johann Henckel der Hofprediger der Königen Maria von Ungarn," *Ungarische Revue* 4 (1889): 599–627. After the death of Louis II at Mohacs in 1526, Luther prepared for Mary his *Vier tröstliche Psalmen an die Königen zu Ungarn* (Wittenberg, 1526) while Erasmus, after repeated requests from Henckel, sent Mary a copy of his *De Vidua Christiana*.

[10]Gustav Hammann, "Conrad Cordatus Leombachensis: Sein Leben in Österreich," *Jahrbuch des oberösterreichischen Musealvereins* 109 (1964): 250–278; idem, "Bartolomeus Fancfordinus Pannonius, Simon Grynäus in Ungarn," *Zeitschrift für Ostforschung* 14 (1965): 228–242.

[11]WA, Br III, no. 568, pp. 8–10. See also Louis Neustadt, *Markgraf Georg von Brandenburg als Erzieher am ungarischen Hofe* (Breslau: T. Schatzky, 1883).

court preacher, the increase in antiforeigner sentiments, and the uprising of the mine workers in upper Hungary during 1525 and 1526.

Relatively swift response was made to the "German heresy" by the archbishop of Esztergom (Ostrihom, Gran), the Roman Catholic hierarchy, and the lesser Magyar nobility led by Stephen Werböczy, leader of the group of Magyar nobles who resented foreign influences in the country and especially in the court. The archbishop ordered the promulgation of the papal bull *Decet Romanum* throughout Hungary. In April 1523, the Hungarian Diet decreed that "all Lutherans and those favoring them...should have their property confiscated and themselves punished with death."[12] In April 1524, the archbishop of Esztergom, Ladislav Szalkai, sent a commission to the mining city to search for and destroy publications by Luther.[13] In August of the same year, the papal nuncio, Anton Burgio, wrote that a noble on the western borders of Hungary had captured and burned on the spot several Germans who were sellers of books by Luther[14]i; John Horvath de Lomnitz, provost of Spiš county, issued an injunction against Lutherans.[15] During the course of the uprising of the miners of the mining cites (1525–26), Cordatus and Kressling were briefly imprisoned by the archbishop of Esztergom. They were released only after appeals from the cities of Kremnica and Banská Bystrica.[16] In May 1525, the Hungarian Diet meeting at Campo Rákos approved an article that those selling or reading heretical publications should be purged from the land and both the secular and clerical authorities should pursue, imprison, and burn all Lutherans and other heretics.[17]

These attempts to halt the spread of reform ideas by destroying publications and those who promulgated them were brought to a standstill by the catastrophic defeat of the Hungarian army by Suleiman II on the right bank of the Danube at Mohács in southern Hungary on August 29, 1526. Louis, two archbishops, five bishops, twenty-eight magnates, five hundred nobles, and more than sixteen thousand soldiers died in the battle and its aftermath. The country was thrown into turmoil. Ferdinand and John Zápolya struggled with

---

[12]Article 54, 1523 *Corpus Juris Hungarici,* 1 (Budae: Reg. Universitatis Hungaricae, 1844).

[13]Gustav Hammann, "Magister Nicolaus von Sabinov, ein Beitrag über den Humanismus und die frühe Reformation in der Slowakei," *Zeitschrift für Ostforschung* 16 (1967): 25–44.

[14]Branislav Varsik, *Husiti a Reformácia na Slovensku do Žilinskej synody, Sborník filozofickej fakulty unverzity Komenského* (Bratislava: Univerzity Komenského, 1932).

[15]Johannes Ribini, *Memorabilia Augustanae Confessionis in regno Hungariae II* (Posonii: G. Lippert, 1789), 636.

[16]Bunyitay, et al., *Egyháztörténelmi emlékek a magyarországi hitujítás korából,* 1:203, 227, City Archive Kremnica Fons 19, fasc. 1, no. 28.

[17]Article 4, 1525, *Corpus Juris Hungarici.*

each other for the right to wear the "Holy Crown" while ineffectively and sporadically fighting the Turks. By 1541 Hungary had effectively been divided into three parts, a division which would last for more than one and a half centuries. Western and northern Hungary remained Habsburg or royal Hungary. Transylvania (Erdelyi, Siebenbürgen) and the Partium (lands between the left bank of the Tisza (Theiss) River and Transylvania was governed by Zápolya and his successors. The Turks occupied central Hungary from above the bend of the Danube at Esztergom to its southern borders. Not until midcentury, after defeat of the German Protestants at Schmalkald and the convocation of the Council of Trent, was the Catholic hierarchy in a position to attempt to mount a counterreformation. But by then the major cities and many of the magnates had adopted Reformation practices and teachings. They confiscated or secularized the administration of church property and called evangelical pastors and teachers to serve vacant parishes and reformed or newly established schools. Even the king, Maximilian II, was suspected of sympathizing with the Reformation.[18]

As elsewhere in Europe, the introduction, spread, and consolidation of the Reformation in Hungary can be ascribed not only to political, economic, and social circumstances but also to the power of the spoken and written word. It is clear that prior to the battle at Mohács, Reformation ideas and practices were accepted by a small but influential group of individuals: members of city councils and clerics who had obtained publications from Germany or maintained contact with individuals and centers of humanist learning within the empire and Poland, most notably Cracow. After 1526, the spread and consolidation of the Reformation was the work of those Germans, Magyars, and Slavs who attended Wittenberg or other centers of humanist evangelical learning supported by city councils and the nobles who were their patrons.

During the sixteenth century more than a thousand individuals from Hungary enrolled at Wittenberg. Of these, 43 percent (442 of 1,018) entered the university before the death of Melanchthon in 1560.[19] An additional 311 individuals from Hungary, primarily from upper Hungary (roughly congruent with modern-day Slovakia), traveled to Wittenberg to obtain ordination as pastors. Some of those who attended Wittenberg also were among the 304 students from Hungary who studied at the University of Heidelberg before

---

[18]Viktor Bibl, *Zur Frage der religiösen Haltung Kaiser Maximilians I, Archiv für österreichische Geschichte* 106/2 (Wien: Österreichische Akademie der Wissenschaft, 1848).

[19]Ioannis Ladislai Bartholomaeides, *Memoriae Ungarorum qui in Alma concam Universitate Vitebergensi a tribus proxime concludendis seculis studiea in Ludis Patriis Coepta Confirmarunt* (Pest: Joannis Thomae Trattner, 1817).

1620. Slovaks and other western Slavs generally preferred, especially during the second half of the century, to study in Prague or other academies in Bohemia and Moravia where the views of the neo-Utraquist Hussites and Lutherans had converged. Most returned to Hungary and became influential figures in the intellectual and religious life of the nation.

The foreign experience of these students and the contacts they established were essential for the spread and consolidation of the Reformation. During their foreign sojourn they acquired publications for themselves and for their noble or urban patrons. Upon returning home to serve as pastors and schoolmasters and participate in public life, they remained in touch with their former teachers and colleagues, exchanging information and publications and arranging for the publication of their own works abroad.

While the penetration of Hungary by the Reformation depended upon the spoken and written word—unlike the situation in Bohemia where there is evidence that Luther's works imported from Germany or in Czech translation were available during the 1520s[20]—the paucity of documentary evidence from early-sixteenth-century Hungary makes it difficult to determine precisely which published works of the Reformers were circulating in Hungary during the early Reformation or who imported them. Nevertheless, it seems evident that humanists and publications imported from abroad were significant instruments employed to introduce and consolidate the Reformation in Hungary. The creation of a domestic publishing industry in Hungary, primarily during the second half of the sixteenth century, emerged as the broad evangelical humanist reform movement fragmented into distinct confessional communities and subsequently, sought to establish doctrinal conformity within each of the respective communities.[21] The domestic publishing industry in Hungary focused on meeting the instructional needs of the Protestant schools and the liturgical and devotional needs of the various confessional groups. Moreover, while the authors in Hungary and especially in Transylvania adopted the views and used the publications of the broader European Reformation, they interpreted, adapted, and applied them in accordance with their own linguistic, sociocultural, and even political situations.

[20]Rudolf Říčan, "Tschechische Übersetzungen von Luthers Schriften bis zum Schmalkaldischen Krieg" *Vierhundertfünfzig Jahre lutherische Reformation 1517–1967: Festschrift für Franz Lau zur 60. Geburtstag* (Göttingen: Vandenhoeck & Ruprecht, 1967), 282–301. Mirjam Bohatcova, "Erasmus, Luther, Melanchthon und Calvin in Gedruckten Tschechischen Übersetzungen aus dem 16. und 17. Jahrhundert," *Gutenberg Jahrbuch* 49 (1974): 158–65.

[21]David P. Daniel, "Calvinism in Hungary: The Theological and Ecclesiastical Transition to the Reformed Faith, " in *Calvinism in Europe, 1540–1620,* ed. Andrew Pettegree, Alastair Duke, and Gillian Lewis (Cambridge: Cambridge University Press, 1994), 205–230.

The attempts by a revived Roman Catholic hierarchy and the Habsburgs to implement the canons and decrees of Trent and counter the spread of Reformation views proved ineffective for most of the sixteenth century. By the end of the sixteenth century, Lutheranism had become the faith of most of those in Habsburg Hungary while Helvetic views were dominant in the regions of Hungary occupied by the Turks and in part of trans-Danubia that bordered the Habsburg patrimonial lands. In Transylvania, the diet at Torda in 1568 extended to the Antitrinitarians the religious toleration earlier granted to the Lutherans and the Helvetic Reformed. It thus became a land of three nations and four recognized religions. In royal Hungary, the Protestant communities remained legally under the control of the Roman Catholic hierarchy until the revolt of the estates, led by the Reformed magnate Stefan Bocskay, forced the Habsburgs to grant to the Lutherans and the Helvetic Reformed legal recognition and the right to establish separate ecclesiastical institutions according to the provisions of the Peace of Vienna (1606) and the articles approved by the diet of 1608. These religious and political divisions were reflected in the development of printing and book culture in Hungary.[22]

Although the first books printed in Hungary appeared during the 1470s and were probably the products of traveling printers who used portable presses, the two presses in Buda printed only a handful of items and ceased to function after 1480.[23] From 1477 to 1480 a small press might also have operated in Bratislava (Pressburg, Pozsony) in connection with activity of the Academia Istropolitana, which the monarch, Matthias Corvinus, had established.[24] Two volumes ascribed to the publisher Lukas Trapoldner of Sibiu (Nagyszeben, Hermannstadt), a Latin grammar that appeared in 1529 and a 1530 German tract on how to act during a plague are the only known publications of this press and actually may have been printed outside of Hungary.[25]

During the late fifteenth and the early sixteenth centuries, authors who prepared works intended for distribution in Hungary had to have them printed abroad, primarily in Cracow and Vienna. After the Reformation was

---

[22]Geza Lencz, *Der Aufstand Bocskays und der Wiener Friede: Eine Kirchenhistorische Studie* (Debreczen: Hegedüs & Sandor, 1917). David P. Daniel, "The Fifteen Years' War and the Protestant Response to Habsburg Absolutism in Hungary," *East Central Europe/L'Europe du Centre-est* (1981): 38–51.

[23]Gedeon Borsa, "Die volkssprachigen Drucke im 15. und 16. Jahrhundert in Ungarn," *Gutenberg Jahrbuch* 62 (1987): 104. Gedeon Borsa et al., eds., *Régi Magyarországi Nyomtatványok 1473–1600* (Budapest: Akadémiai Kiadó, 1971), 65–71 (hereafter cited as RMN).

[24]Ján Čaplovič, *Bibliografia tlačí vydaných na Slovensku do roku 1700*, 2 vols. (Martin: Matica slovenská, 1972, 1984), 1:134 (hereafter cited as BTS).

[25]RMN, 9–10.

established in Hungary, some individuals, especially those active in upper Hungary, continued to have their works published abroad, in Wittenberg or other cities in the empire. During the sixteenth century at least thirty books for Hungary were issued in Vienna by ten different printers between 1536 and 1581, and thirty-three books appeared in Cracow between 1527 and 1580, including the first book published completely in Hungarian—a translation of the epistles of Saint Paul by the Erasmian Benedek Komjáti and issued by Vietor in 1533.[26] Vietor also printed works by two of the early Magyar reformers, *De Christo et eius ecclesia* by Imre Ozorai in 1535 and in 1538 the first work in Hungarian on the Hungarian language, the *Orthographia Ungarica* by Matthias Bíró Dévai.[27] In Vienna, translations by the humanist Gábor Pesti of Aesop's fables and of the four Gospels into Hungarian were printed in 1536 by Johann Singriener, who also published in 1539 a multilingual dictionary which had recently appeared in Nüremberg to which Pesti added Hungarian.[28] Vienna and Cracow not only attracted many students from Hungary to their universities during the late fifteenth and early sixteenth centuries but they also were important trading centers. It seems, moreover, that for most of the sixteenth century the book needs of Bratislava, the functional capital of Hungary after the occupation of Buda by the Turks, were met by printers in Vienna.

The first major publishing operation in Hungary was established in Siebenbürgen by the reformer Johann Honter in Braşov (Brassó, Cronstadt) in 1539 in the southeastern corner of the kingdom. By the end of the sixteenth century, at least 814 books had been printed by twenty publishers in at least thirty locations throughout the kingdom.[29] The vast majority of the works, more than 87 percent, were published in either Latin or Hungarian. The proportion of Hungarian titles surpassed those produced in Latin during the 1570s so that the ratio of Hungarian titles to Latin titles for the entire second half of the sixteenth century was 3:2.[30] The presses of both John Honter and Valentin Wagner in Braşov published eleven items in Greek. German titles were also relatively rare. Of the forty titles printed in German, thirty were produced in eastern Hungary and only ten in southwestern Hungary. The largest number appeared in Bardejov (eleven) and in Braşov (eight). While editions of Lutheran liturgical, devotional, and didactic works, including the Small Catechism of Luther and hymnbooks, were printed in Braşov, in Bardejov the works in German were primarily polemical, historical, or devotional.

---

[26]RMN, 12.   [27]RMN, 15, 22.
[28]RMN, 17, 16, and 21; Borsa, "Die volksprachigen Drucke," 105–106.
[29]Borsa, "Die volksprachigen Drucke," 107.   [30]Ibid., 108.

If Hungary were divided into an eastern and a western half by a line following the north-to-south flow of the Danube, presses operated in eighteen locations to the west of this line while only twelve operated to the east. However, in the western half only 145 items were known to have been issued by the eleven publishers. Forty-two of these works were issued by the press in Trnava (Nagyszombat), which was founded by the bishop of Péc and the administrator of the archbishopric of Esztergom, Miklos Telegdi, in 1578. After 1588 this press was managed by the chapter of Esztergom and continued operations into the seventeenth century, when it came under the control of the Jesuit university established by Peter Pazmany.[31] Forty-one works were published by Joannes Manlius in five locations (Güssing, Németújvar; Eberau, Monyorókerék; Deutsch-Schützen, Sicz; Deutschkreutz, Keresztúr; and Sárvár) and twenty-one were produced in three locations by Peter Bornemisza (Šintava, Sempte; Plavecký Hrad, Detrekő; and Rohožník, Rárbók, Rohrbach) in the latter two locations in cooperation with Valentin Mantskovit (Farinola), who later produced five works in Hlohovec (Galgóc, Freistadt) and then seven in Vízsolyi in eastern Hungary. Thus, two thirds of the total production resulted from the work of three presses. Except for the press in Trnava and in the Franciscan monastery in Winpassing an der Leithe (Vimpác), which produced three volumes in 1593 and one in 1599, all of the presses in western Hungary were operated by reformers. None of them, however, operated for more than a few years, nor did any survive into the seventeenth century. Nevertheless, the first book entirely in Hungarian and printed in Hungary was produced in 1541 and was one of the five volumes that issued from the press of Jan Sylvester on the estates of Thomas Nádasdy in Sárvár. Gál Huszar published three volumes in Mosonmagyaróvár during his short stay in western Hungary (1558–59) and his son, David Huszár, produced three works in Pápa during 1577. Rudolf Hoffhalter, who worked primarily in Debrecen and briefly in Varad in eastern Hungary, produced four publications in Dolnja Lendava (Alsólindva) and three in Nedelisce (Drávavásárhely) during 1573 and 1574. In the mining cities of upper Hungary the press of Christopher Sculteti (Scholtz) produced only two works, a confession of faith by Gregor Meltzer (which also included the Confessio Montana of 1559) and a tract concerning the comet of 1577, both printed in 1578.[32]

The presses operating in twelve locations in eastern Hungary produced 669 publications, but 582 of these were produced in just four cities: Cluj (Kolozsvár, Klausenburg), 208 items; Debrecen, 157 works; Braşov (Brassó,

[31]Július Valach, *Staré tlačiarne a tlačiari na Slovensku* (Martin: Matica slovenská, 1987), 53–65.
[32]*BTS*,1:47.

Kronstadt), 119 items; and Bardejov (Bartfa, Bartfeld), 98 publications. In each of four locations only one work was published during the entire sixteenth century: Košice (Kassa, Kaschau), Oraştie (Szászváros), Sebeş (Szászsebes), and Abrud (Abrudbánya). Thirteen volumes were produced in Viszoly, including the first complete translation of the Bible into Hungarian by Caspar Károlyi; ten were issued in Oradea (Nagyvárad); twenty-five in Alba Iulia (Gyulafehér-var); and thirty-seven in Sibiu (Szeben, Hermannstadt). All of the presses in eastern Hungary were operated by supporters of the Reformation, although several also sought to serve the needs of the orthodox community by produc-ing works in Romanian (eleven) and Old Church Slavonic (twenty-three).

To obtain a clearer picture of publishing in Hungary during the Refor-mation the division between east and west—separated by the territory occu-pied by the Turks where no presses were established during the sixteenth century—should be overlaid with the political division of the kingdom. In the east, presses functioned in ten locations in the practically autonomous Transyl-vania and in the Partium. Two cities, Bardejov and Košice, were in northern or upper Hungary (Felvidek), roughly congruous with modern Slovakia. While only one book, a hymnbook and Psalter by Gál Huszár, was printed in Košice in 1560, Bardejov was the most significant center of publishing in upper Hungary, home to one of its most noted schools and known for its orthodox Lutheranism.[33] In the west, the presses in Bratislava, Plavecký Hrad, Hlohovec, Rohožnik, Šintava, Trnava, Komjatice, and Banská Bystrica were also located in upper Hungary. Thus ten press locations existed in Transylvania, ten in trans-Danubia on the border with Austria, and ten in upper Hungary.

In is noteworthy that in upper Hungary Lutheranism became widespread during the sixteenth century, not only among the largely German population of the cities but also among the Slovaks. Yet only two publications in Slovak appeared during the sixteenth century: a translation of Luther's *Small Cate-chism,* published in Bardejov in 1581[34] and another Latin-Slovak edition pre-pared by John Pruno and published by Valentin Mantkovits in 1585.[35] The overwhelming proportion of the 177 works published in upper Hungary (21.5 percent of the total book production in Hungary of 816 items) were issued in either Latin (seventy-five) or Hungarian (eighty). Only fifteen were issued in German and two in Slovakized Czech. Between 1577 and 1599 the press of David Guttgesel published ninety works, forty-three in Latin, twenty-two in

---

[33]David P. Daniel, "Bartfeld/Bardejov zur Zeit der Reformation," ed. Karl Schwarz and Peter Švorc, *Die Reformation und ihre Wirkungsgeschichte in der Slowakei. Kirchen- und konfessionsge-schichtliche Beiträge* (Wien: Evangelischer Presseverband, 1996), 37–49.

[34]*BTS,* 1:195.   [35]*BTS,* 1:55.

Hungarian, fourteen in German, and one in Slovakized Czech while between 1597 and 1600 Jacob Klös published thirteen works in Latin and five in Hungarian. In the Catholic press in Trnava, only twelve publications were in Latin and thirty were in Hungarian while one was in both languages. All eight works printed by Peter Bornemisza in Šintava were in Hungarian as were eleven of the twelve items published at Plavecký Hrad and the one in Rohožnik. The exception was the *Acta Concordiae* of Paul Kyrmezer.[36] The only item possibly published in Bratislava (Pozsony, Pressburg) was a German report about a victory over the Turks published by Johann Walo in 1594,[37] and the two works printed in Banská Bystrica by Christopher Scultetus were in Latin.

Except for those printed in Trnava, the majority of the books on religious topics published in upper Hungary were Lutheran in orientation, as were those published in Braşov and Sibiu, while most of those issued in trans-Danubian Hungary bordering Austria and in Cluj and Debrecen exhibited support for Helvetic Reformed views. Several religious works by Reformers in Germany (Luther, Melanchthon, Brenz, Bugenhagen, and Chemnitz) and Switzerland (two tracts addressed to the Hungarians by Bullinger) were printed in Hungary, either in Latin or in translation. However, the major theological works by the best-known European Reformers were neither translated nor reprinted in Hungary. The majority of the religious literature produced in Hungary was in Hungarian and included translations of portions of the Bible, the whole Bible, hymnbooks, catechisms, and sermons; the greater part of this Hungarian religious literature was Helvetic Reformed in orientation. The few items in German and Hungarian produced in Siebenbürgen and by Peter Bornemisza in upper Hungary were designed to meet the liturgical and didactic needs of the German and Magyar Lutherans.

The divergence of theological views among the Reformation communities during the second half of the sixteenth century reflected, on the one hand, the influence of foreign theological developments upon the evangelicals in Hungary and, on the other hand, stimulated the domestic production of publications. After 1547 the Catholic hierarchy sought to halt the spread of religious innovations—that is, Reformation theology and practices—through conducting visitations and issuing prohibitions on the publication of heretical books and the operation of unlicensed presses. In 1584 Rudolf II issued an edict prohibiting anyone from engaging in the printing trade without a royal license. Only the press in Trnava was freed from the provisions of the edict.[38]

---

[36]*BTS,*, 2:569.   [37]*BTS,* 1:136.
[38]Valach, *Staré tlačiarne a tlačiari na Slovensku,* 13.

While these actions had little real direct impact upon Transylvania, in Habsburg Hungary the Lutherans prepared and presented to ecclesiastical and political authorities three confessions of faith which sought to express both their catholicity and their rejection of Anabaptism and Sacramentarianism. The Evangelical humanists in Transylvania and the Partium followed suit, and the differences between the Helvetic Reformed Magyars and the German and Magyar Lutherans were more clearly defined. Moreover, as Antitrinitarianism, imported from Italy and Poland, gained an increasing number of supporters among the Szeklers and Magyars in Transylvania, the Helvetic Reformed felt compelled to disavow and condemn these radical views, especially since one of the leaders of the Antitrinitarian movement, Francis David, had been one of their own. Shortly thereafter, in northeastern Hungary, as several leading Lutheran clerics and patrons sought to have the Formula and Book of Concord adopted as a doctrinal norm, a struggle between the Concordists and the Crypto-Calvinists erupted, and lasted nearly two decades. This confessionalization of the Reformation communities in Hungary and the subsequent attempt by each community to define their theological norms led to the most creative and productive domestic production of theological publications. The score of confessions and another two score of polemical treatises in Latin and Hungarian led to a substantial increase in both the number of printers active in eastern Hungary and the number of works issued primarily by domestic presses.[39] Moreover, it is interesting that as the confessionalization of the communities became complete, the number of publications issued declined. As the century ended, and during the first years of the seventeenth century, only six presses continued to function. Three of them were in Transylvania: Johann Fabricius in Sibiu, the Heltai press in Cluj, and the press of Paul Rheda (Lipsensis) in Debrecen. Two were in upper Hungary, the Klös press in Bardejov and the Catholic Esztergom Chapter press in Trnava. In trans-Danubian western Hungary only one press, that of John Melius, continued operations in Sárvár. However, with the attempts of the Catholic hierarchy and Archduke Matthias finally to implement counterreformation measures during the first decade of the seventeenth century, the domestic publishing industry was again revitalized by the resulting religious and political strife.

Despite the emergence of a domestic printing industry in Hungary during the second half of the sixteenth century, according to the evidence available, foreign publications continued to comprise a significant proportion of materials in institutional and private libraries. Although most of the more than two

---

[39]David P. Daniel, "Calvinism in Hungary," 216–226; and idem, "The Acceptance of the Formula of Concord in Slovakia," *Archiv für Reformationsgeschichte* 70 (1979): 260–277.

thousand volumes of the unique *Bibliotheca Corvina* of King Matthias Corvinus Hunyadi were dispersed and then destroyed during the occupation of Buda by the Turks, there were several very large personal and institutional libraries in Hungary. John Dernschwam from Bohemia, the administrator of Fugger property and operations in upper Hungary, had assembled a library of 1,162 printed volumes by the time of his death in 1568 in Banská Bystrica. While one third of the volumes included titles from classical antiquity and the Middle Ages, two thirds of the works were by Renaissance and Reformation authors, both Lutheran and Reformed.[40] Even larger was the library of John Sambucus (Zsámboky) from Trnava, who studied in Paris, Padua, and Vienna, where he ultimately settled, working as the physician and historian of Maximilian II. Among its nearly six thousand volumes and 730 codices, there were relatively few German or Hungarian volumes. Works on language and literature were proportionately the most numerous, followed by religious and theological publications, including those by Reformation authors. As could be expected, historical, geographical, and medical and natural science works were also well represented. Both of these collections were acquired by the court library in Vienna.[41]

These libraries were exceptional in their size and scope but not in the fact that they were cosmopolitan and incorporated works from throughout Europe and included works by the Reformers of the early sixteenth century. Studies of the book culture in the mining cities of central upper Hungary which utilize last wills and testaments provide an insight into the size and scope of private libraries among the urban population of Hungary during the sixteenth century. In Banská Štiavnica, twenty-four private libraries contained a total of 1,069 books. The 334 titles in the library of John Haunold, a teacher and later city captain, was the largest single collection. Martin Endter owned 206 volumes; the city scribe, Martin Barbaritsch, owned 110 volumes; and private mine owner, Matej Moldner, owned 106 works. Thus, 80 percent of the recorded private book stock was owned by 16 percent of those whose libraries were recorded. Fifty percent possessed small libraries of less than twenty volumes. In 1580 the will of preacher John Schedl listed twelve volumes while that of Mikuláš Horn in 1600 listed forty-eight books.[42]

---

[40]Jenő Berlász, "Dernschwam János könyvtára," *Magyar Könyvszemle* 79 (1963): 301–316; ibid., 80 (1962), 1–32.

[41]Csaba Csapodi, "Ungarische Bibliotheksgeschichte: Vom Mittelalter bis zum Fireden von Szathmár (1711)," *Gutenberg Jahrbuch* 59 (1984): 350.

[42]Viliam Čičaj, *Knižná kultúra na strednom Slovensku v 16–18 storočí: Historické štúdie* 28/2 (Bratislava: Slovenská Akadémia Vied, 1985), 21–23.

In Banská Bystrica the three private libraries listed in testaments held 113 books altogether. The largest, holding fifty-one items, was the library of the pastor Rafael Steger, who had studied abroad. In Kremnica the largest of nine libraries was that of Wolfgang Roll with 129 volumes, while four individuals had libraries ranging from twenty-six to thirty-five volumes.[43] However, other inventories indicate that in 1552 the library of the parish church of Banská Bystica owned 153 books.[44] An earlier survey of the parish church property in 1532 noted that it owned 158 volumes "old and new"[45] while an inventory from 1533 of the library of the deceased rector of the Hospital of Saint Elizabeth in Banská Bystrica lists the titles of seventy works.[46]

Registers and lists of property connected with testaments also provide information on libraries elsewhere in upper Hungary. In 1525, an evangelical preacher in Prešov (Eperies) owned seventy-seven books, the preacher Jacob Benedict in Kežmarok owned seventy-six volumes in 1601, while in 1589 the library of Baltazár Alitisa, a teacher in Zvolen, contained ninety titles.[47]

Inventories of the book collections of nobles are also instructive and diverse. While Stanislaus Thurzo, the noble administrator of Spiš county, owned 111 volumes, scarcely any were religious works.[48] Quite the opposite was the collection of Imrich Forgach, who in 1589 donated to the city school in Trenčín a collection of 177 volumes.[49]

From this rather randomly selected evidence it can be concluded that large libraries of more than one hundred volumes were exceptional during the sixteenth century. Pastors and teachers in relatively prosperous cities may have owned middle-sized collections of forty to a hundred books, but assistant preachers and teachers might possess just a few books. In smaller towns they probably possessed just a few fundamental publications. The destruction of libraries and archives during the sixteenth and especially the seventeenth century makes it difficult to ascertain the number and subject matter of books owned by representative samples of various segments of the population.

However, on the basis of the fragmentary information available it can be assumed that the libraries of schools must have included the standard humanist

---

[43]Čičaj, *Knižná kultúra na strednom Slovensku v 16–18 storočí*, 37.

[44]Jozef Kuzmík, *Knisná kultúra na Slovensku v strodoveku a renesancii* (Martin: Matica slovensaá, 1987), 211.211.

[45]Štatný okresný archív, Banská Bystrica, fasc. 168/3.

[46]Ibid., Fond Mesto 1255–1922, varia V/63, fols. 23–24.

[47]Kuzmík, *Knisná kultúra na Slovensku*, 211–214.

[48]Csapodi, "Ungarische Bibliotheksgeschichte," 351.

[49]Štatný okresný archív, Trenčín, Fond Magistrat mesta Trenčína, Mestský protokol, 1564–1700, fols. 34–42.

linguistic and didactic materials referred to in their curricula as well as reformation catechisms and the *Loci Communes* of Melanchthon or the *Corpus Doctrinae Misnicum* (a collection of his doctrinal writings) as well as Bibles and possibly Greek New Testaments and a few works in German.[50] In private libraries general works on religion were more numerous than on other topics, and in upper Hungary Latin works outnumbered works in German except in small libraries in the towns. Volumes of Protestant homiletical, polemical literature and general theological works including Bibles were more numerous than collected writings of theologians, catechisms, and liturgical works.[51]

It is striking that in many of the inventories of sixteenth-century libraries in upper Hungary (today's Slovakia), works published by domestic presses are not extensively represented. The religious literature needs of the Lutherans of royal Hungary were largely met by publications imported from abroad. However, in Hungarian-speaking areas, domestic publications were being distributed by the growing number of booksellers in the country. This is shown by the 1583 inventory of the stock of John Gallen, a book merchant from Košice.[52] It lists the titles of more than six hundred items, their prices, and the number of copies in stock. The total number of volumes exceeded one thousand copies; a substantial capital investment would have been required to acquire this extensive book stock. But what makes the stock most fascinating is that it includes both imported works and those of the domestic publishing industry—works in Latin, German, Hungarian, Czech, Greek, and even French. Multiple works by the leading figures of the European Reformation and of Hungary are included. It is clear that this collection had been prepared by one who was confident that he knew his market and that the market in eastern Hungary was theologically and culturally diverse. This list is an indication that the size and the scope of the market for Reformation publications was larger than might be deduced from extant inventories and other fragmentary documentation.

Publications from abroad introduced the Reformation to Hungary. They promoted reform but also accentuated divisions both within the country and among the reformers, making necessary the creation of a domestic publishing industry. During the sixteenth century, publishing disseminated, defined, divided, and defended the Reformation in Hungary.

---

[50]Peter Vajcik, *Školstvo, Študijné a Školské poriadky na Slovensku v XVI. storoci* (Bratislava: Slovenskej adadéme vied, 1955), 120–22.

[51]Čičaj, *Knižná kultúra na strednom Slovensku v 16–18 storočí*, 74–86.

[52]Lajos Kemény, "Egy XVI. szάzadbeli könyvkereskedő raktára," *Magyar Könyvszemle* 3 (1895): 310–320.

THE BOOK TRADE AS CHRISTIAN CALLING

Johann Friedrich Coelestin's Admonition
to Printers and Bookdealers

Robert A. Kolb

A. G. DICKENS' OBSERVATION that for the Lutheran Reformation "it seems difficult to exaggerate the significance of the Press, without which a revolution of this magnitude could scarcely have been consummated"[1] repeats a commonplace among modern Reformation scholars, one which arose in the period itself. Luther's followers saw the printing press as a gift of God, part of a certain "fullness of time" that portended the end of the world. Matthaeus Judex, a student in Wittenberg toward the end of Luther's lifetime, attributed the invention of the printing press "to the singular goodwill of God, for the sake of the cleansing of the church and the propagation of the gospel against the idolatries of the Antichrist."[2] Judex's comrade in the camp of the Gnesio-Lutherans, the more radical party among Luther's students and followers,[3] Johann Friedrich Coelestin, agreed. In writing on the calling of "bookdealers[4] and printers" he acknowledges the art of printing as "a magnificent great gift and benefit which God has bestowed and revealed in these last times. It had remained unknown and hidden from all humankind for so many thousand

---

[1]Arthur Geoffrey Dickens, *Reformation and Society in Sixteenth Century Europe* (New York: Harcourt, Brace & World, 1968), 51.

[2]Matthaeus Judex, *De typographiae inventione, et de praelorvm legitima inspectione, libellvs brevis et vtilis* (Copenhagen: Johannes Zimmermann, 1566), 25. See Robert Kolb, "Matthaeus Judex's Condemnation of Princely Censorship of Theologians' Publications," *Church History* 50 (1981): 401–414; reprinted in idem, *Luther's Heirs Define His Legacy: Studies on Lutheran Confessionalization* (Aldershot, Hampshire:Variorum, 1996), no. 14.

[3]Robert Kolb, "Dynamics of Party Conflict in the Saxon Late Reformation, Gnesio-Lutherans vs. Philippists," *Journal of Modern History* 49 (1977): 1289–1305, reprinted in Kolb, *Luther's Heirs*, no. 1.

[4]The German words *Buchhändler* and *Buchführer* refer to people involved in the sale of books—the former to the retailer, the latter to the wholesaler. Here the words are translated with the single term "bookdealer" when Coelestin uses them together.

years, but God has revealed and bestowed this gift initially in a special way to the German nation and to no other." The reason was clear, Coelestin believed: "so that, along with other good and useful illustrations, writings, and books," printers might publish particularly those works that convey the truth of the Gospel, "which had long been hidden." The printing press was making it easier to teach, learn, and spread this Gospel "just before the Last Day, as a farewell for all the world, according to the prophecy of Christ, as a witness to all peoples (Matt. 24:14), to defend this truth against the accursed papacy, all heretics, sects, and schisms, and as a comfort and warning for the chosen people of God, so that they might be preserved to the end of the world."[5]

Yet at the same time Coelestin also believed that Satan had been able to pervert this gift of God into an instrument that could also be used to undermine the true faith. That moved him to write a word of warning and admonition to those involved in the book trade. In so doing he demonstrated how his Lutheran theology conceived of and addressed the daily activities of those involved in this new aspect of Western economic and cultural life.

Johann Friedrich Coelestin's date of birth is unknown; he probably studied at the University of Wittenberg in the second half of the 1550s. Like most others among the more radical followers of Luther, Coelestin had absorbed the literary skills cultivated above all by Philip Melanchthon in the circle of the Wittenberg scholars, and his interests, written style, and publications reflected this humanistic orientation.[6] After teaching at the secondary level, he became professor of Greek at the University of Jena in 1560, at the time when Matthias Flacius, Johannes Wigand, Matthaeus Judex, and other theologians at court and on the faculty were engaged in a struggle over the integrity of the church against their prince, Johann Friedrich the Middler, who as a typical early modern ruler, was trying to bring the church more tightly under his

---

[5] *Von Buchhendlern/ Buchdruckern vnd Buchfu[e]rern: Ob auch one su[e]nde/ vnd gefahr jrer Seligkeit/ Vnchristliche/ Ketzerische/ Bepstische/ Vnzu[e]chtige/ oder sonst bo[e]se Bu[e]cher drucken/ vnd offentlich feil haben/ oder von andern kauffen/ vnnd widerumb/ one vnterscheidt/ menniglich verkauffen mo[e]gen. Auch Allen andern Christen/ sonderlich Kremern/ Kauff/ Handels vnd Handwerckleuten/ zu diesen gefehrlichen zeitten nu[e]tzlich zulesen* (s.l., 1569).

[6] See Wilhelm Preger, "Coelestin, Johann Friedrich," in *Allgemeine Deutsche Biographie* 4 (1876; Berlin: Duncker & Humblot, 1968): 389–391. Preger does not identify the place of Coelestin's university studies, but he is probably the "Johannes Caelestinus Plauensis" who matriculated in Wittenberg in 1556 (his brother Georg was born in Plauen); see *Album Academiae Vitebergensis ab A. Ch. MDII usque ad A. MDLX* (Leipzig: Tauchnitz, 1841), 1:320b. On his and others' use of the Melanchthonian rhetoric and dialectic, see Robert Kolb, "Philip's Foes, but Followers Nonetheless: Late Humanism among the Gnesio-Lutherans," in *The Harvest of Humanism in Central Europe: Essays in Honor of Lewis Spitz*, ed. Manfred P. Fleischer (Saint Louis: Concordia, 1992), 159–177; *Luther's Heirs*, no. 15.

control. At the same time these theologians were defending their understanding of Luther's message against others inside and outside ducal Saxony, and thus they ran afoul of their prince, for their polemic was so sharp that it endangered his diplomatic relationships with Roman Catholic princes, especially the emperor. Karl Heussi reports that the jurist on the Jena faculty, Basilius Monner, "infected" Coelestin with Flacian ideas and that Coelestin left Jena under ducal threat of house arrest, following Flacius and the others into exile in January 1562.[7] He traveled to Frankfurt an der Oder and there attained his doctorate and was ordained. He then moved to Bavaria, where he helped with the local introduction of the Reformation. After the troops of Duke Albrecht V of Bavaria had occupied the county of Ortenburg where he was working and driven him into exile, Coelestin was called as a professor of theology at the academy that Count Palatinate Wolfgang of Neuburg had founded in Lauingen. From there he fired his return salvo at the occupiers of Ortenburg, his *Pantheum, or Anatomy and Symphony of the Papacy … that is, a Thorough and Incontrovertible Demonstration that the Pope is the Real, Unmasked Antichrist*,[8] a work praised for its "sprightly, clever insight and breadth of literary references."[9] In the same year he wrote a treatise on schools;[10] the following year he further demonstrated his interest in learning and scholarship with his *On Bookdealers*.

In its preface he conceded to Wolfgang Moser, a bookdealer in Regensburg,[11] that he had a reputation as a contentious, sharp-tongued person "who cannot leave anything or anyone in peace but must himself remain above reproach and secure." Such a judgment hurts the pious heart more than any physical persecution or even death itself, Coelestin claimed.[12] That may have

---

[7]Karl Heussi, *Geschichte der theologischen Fakultät zu Jena* (Weimar: Böhlau, 1954), 79–80. See also Martin Kruse, *Speners Kritik am landesherrlichen Kirchenregiment und ihre Vorgeschichte* (Witten: Luther-Verlag, 1971), 57–63. On the roots of Gnesio-Lutheran resistance theory, see Oliver K. Olson, "Theology of Revolution: Magdeburg, 1550–1551," *Sixteenth Century Journal* 3 (1972): 56–79.

[8]*Panthevm sive Anatomia et Symphonia Papatvs, et praecipuarum Haeresum veterum & praesentium: Das ist / Gru[e]ndliche vnd vnwidersprechliche beweysung/ aus Gottes Wort/ Kirchen Historien / vnd der Papisten / Ketzer vnd Secten selbsteignen gewirdigten Bu[e]chern: Das der Babst der Warhafftige offenbahrte Antichrist sey…* (Regensburg: Heinrich Geißler, 1568).

[9]Preger, *Allgemeine Deutsche Biographie*, 4:390.

[10]*Von Schulen* (Strassburg: Samuel Emmel, 1568). See Remigius Stölze, "Johann Friedrich Coelestin als Erziehungstheoretiker," *Archiv für Reformationsgeschichte* 15 (1918): 204–225.

[11]On Moser, see Karl Schottenloher, *Das Regensburger Buchgewerbe im 15. und 16. Jahrhundert*, Veröffentlichungen der Gutenberg-Gesellschaft XIV–XIX (Mainz: Gutenberg-Gesellschaft, 1920), 68; cf. 35, 131, 133, 211.

[12]*Von Buchhendlern*, A2a.

been, but he remained deeply involved in controversy over the proper interpretation of Luther's teaching for the rest of his life. He returned to the theological faculty in Jena (1568–72) and joined his new colleagues, Wigand,
Tileman Hesshus, and Timotheus Kirchner, in representing the concerns of
their theological position against Philippists from electoral Saxony, the group
whose teachings Coelestin had criticized in public exchanges for a decade and
in his treatise on bookdealers. He spent most of the last six years of his life
leading the party in Austria that supported Flacius' doctrine of original sin.[13]

Coelestin wrote on the calling of bookdealers and printers in the context
of his times, times he saw from an eschatological perspective. Like most of his
Lutheran contemporaries, he remained unshaken in Luther's conviction that
the end of the world was at hand and that in its last days Satan was trying to
lead people astray, both by false teaching and by the corruption of morals, private and public, as Christ (Matt. 18:7) and Paul (1 Cor. 11:18–19) had
warned.[14] Coelestin's preface noted that the devil and false teachers were con-
fusing particularly the church in Austria[15] through unnecessary disputations
and quarrels, and that heretics, false brethren, and Epicureans were depriving
the church of peace. Hypocritical preachers were keeping quiet or using flat-
tery instead of reminding parishioners of their sins, and thus they were letting
the world go its own way. The result was a torrent of sins flowing from the
lusts of the flesh, in the form of idolatry, heresy, impurity, brazenness, greed,
usury, financial tricks, and similar sins. Temporal and eternal harm was being
visited upon both world and church.[16]

Coelestin focused especially on the sin of greed: it was the cause of the
failure of those in the book trade to fulfill the responsibilities of their calling.
Greed is a weed, Coelestin claimed, and he used 1 Tim. 6:6–10 as a "mirror
for tradespeople"—including bookdealers and printers—in which they could
see the proper reflection of God's design for their calling.[17] The concluding
sentence of the treatise's title suggested that other tradespeople and artisans

---

[13]Flacius taught that original sin is the formal essence of the fallen human creature. On
Coelestin's activities in defense of his teaching in Austria, as well as his earlier defense of Gnesio-
Lutheran positions, see Irene Dingel, *Concordia controversa: Die öffentliche Diskussion um das Kon-
kordienwerk am Ende des 16. Jahrhunderts* (Gütersloh: Gütersloher Verlagshaus, 1996), 475–476,
481, 484, 504.

[14]*Von Buchhendlern*, A4a. On Lutheran eschatological expectations after Luther's death, see
Robin B. Barnes, *Prophecy and Gnosis: Apocalypticism in the Wake of the Lutheran Reformation* (Stanford: Stanford University Press, 1988), 60–99.

[15]Coelestin's mention of the church in Austria in his preface to Moser may rest upon the
bookdealer's activities there.

[16]*Von Buchhendlern*, A4a, A7a–b.   [17]Ibid., Cb–C6a.

would also find its admonitions useful. The genre of the "mirror literature" of the Reformation period usually presented a positive standard, for instance the ideal for the life of the ruler (though other forms of "mirrors" also appeared from the pens of humanist scholars in the sixteenth century on the basis of medieval models).[18] Coelestin used this particular apostolic "mirror" less to reflect the ideal of commercial life than to call those who abused it to repentance. Such a call for abandoning specific sins frequently found expression from his contemporary Gnesio-Lutheran theologians in the genre of *Teufelbuch*, which focused on what was wrong with a particular way of life or practice and which aimed at inducing repentance.[19] Allusions to the devilish nature of the struggle against sin reinforce the impression that Coelestin used God's law chiefly as a means to evaluate the failure to serve God and neighbor rather than give specific instruction on how Christians should carry out their responsibilities. He presumed that Christian wisdom and natural human intelligence would know how to carry out a calling properly, but he also believed that sin distracts and deceives such wisdom and intelligence. Therefore, he warned his readers against the paper-greed devil and against "devilish, murderous greed" that brings God's wrath down upon those who produce and merchandise books in a way that harms their customers and society in general.[20] With the eschatological language common to his circle, Coelestin emphasized that God's wrath had swept away many whose fleshly lusts had led them into collecting earthly rather than heavenly treasures, and into doing so at the expense of the poor and oppressed.

To confirm his point, Coelestin used rhetorical tools that he had learned as a student of Melanchthon's approach to communicating the biblical message. He marshaled both citations and examples from biblical, ancient, and

---

[18]Followers of Luther also produced handbooks for pious living according to this model; for example, see Sigismund Schwabe, *Sigismund Suevus Erbauungsschriften, Spiegel des menschlichen Lebens, Eine Auswahl*, ed. M. A. van den Broek (Amsterdam: Rodopi, 1984). From lay circles around the Gnesio-Lutheran movement came a *Fürstenspiegel* by the Mansfeld chancellor Georg Lauterbeck; see Michael Philips, "Regierungskunst im Zeitalter der konfessionellen Spaltung: Politische Lehren des mansfeldischen Kanzlers Georg Lauterbeck," in *Politische Tugendlehre und Regierungskunst: Studien zum Fürstenspiegel der frühen Neuzeit*, ed. Hans-Otto Mühleisen and Theo Stammen (Tübingen: Max Niemeyer, 1990), 71–115.

[19]See Heinrich Grimm, "Die deutschen 'Teufelbücher' des 16. Jahrhunderts: Ihre Rolle im Buchwesen und ihre Bedeutung," *Archiv für Geschichte des Buchwesens* 16 (1959): 13–70; Wolfgang Brückner, "Das Wirken des Teufels: Theologie und Sage im 16. Jahrhundert," in *Volserzählung und Reformation: Ein Handbuch zu Tradierung und Funktion von Erzählstoff und Erzählliteratur im Protestantismus*, ed. Wolfgang Brückner (Berlin: Erich Schmidt, 1974), 393–416; and Rainer Alsheimer, "Katalog protestantischer Teufelerzählungen des 16. Jahrhunderts," ibid., 417–519.

[20]*Von Buchhendlern*, A5a.

more recent history, and he could employ a good story as well. The Roman poet Horace had written, "A merchant runs, chases, and travels indefatigably from one end of the world to another, over hurdle and rock, water and fire, so that he can stave off [*erwehren*] poverty and stack up [*erwerben*] money and goods." Augustine had taught, "All unjust gain brings with it a certain just punishment and harm upon itself. Whoever steals stuff loses trust. Unjust gain in the strongbox means condemnation in the conscience." A monk once asked the devil what the greatest, most tenacious sin might be, of which a person could never have enough. The devil replied, "Greed, for other sins give satisfaction, but greed never does."[21] God's refusal to let greed go unpunished could be seen in the examples of Pharaoh (Exod. 14:15–31), Saul (1 Sam. 31:1–7), Sennacherib (2 Kings 19:35–37), Nebuchhadnezzar (Dan. 4:28–33), Balthasar (Dan. 5:13), Absalom (2 Sam. 18:9–15), Ahitophel (2 Sam. 17), Haman (Esth. 9:24–25), Jezebel (1 Kings 21:23; 2 Kings 9:30–37), the Syrian oppressor of the Jews at the time of the Maccabees Antiochus Epiphanes, Herod Antipas (Acts 12:23), the rich men of Luke 12 and Luke 16, Ananias and Sapphira (Acts 5:1–11), the King of Sardanapolos, the Persian emperor Xerxes, Alexander the Great, and the Roman emperors Nero, Domitian, Diocletian, Hadrian, Maximorus, Maxentius, Julian the Apostate, and others, according to Coelestin, who lumped together illustrations from biblical and classical history which recalled not only greed but other abuses of power. A similar list of those who had abused their callings and their responsibilities in these callings repeated Ananias and Sapphira and added Laban (Gen. 31), Balaam (Num. 22:7–35), Achan (Josh. 7:1–26), Nabal (1 Sam. 25:36–38), Elisha's servant Gehasi (2 Kings 5:19–27), Judas Iscariot (John 18:2–3), Simon Magus (Acts 8:9–24), and Demetrius the goldsmith (Acts 19:23–41).[22] Those who followed in their path in the pursuit of ungodly profits, through the production and sale of printed works that would not promote the common good and the truth of God, would also follow in their path toward hell, suffering terrible deaths—by drowning, by being crushed under their horse and wagon, by becoming mad and taking their own lives, by falling victim to the executioner, by being taken bodily by the devil, and so forth.[23]

---

[21] *Von Buchhendlern*, C4a–C5b. Later, Coelestin quoted Augustine, again against greedy merchants, from Psalm 9 in an appeal for repentance. At this point he also called upon Luther's authority regarding God's punishment upon those who feel themselves secure in their sinning; ibid., C8a–b.

[22] *Von Buchhendlern*, B2b, C3a.

[23] *Von Buchhendlern*, Bb–B4a.

Such fates awaited those who did not carry out the responsibilities of the callings God had given them. Coelestin presupposed a view of human life based upon Luther's doctrine of creation and his understanding of the structure of life as God had designed it in the callings of day-to-day living. Coelestin recognized that God had ordained the activities of daily life in his created order. Even though he feared that concerns of this life could overpower the seed of God's word in the human heart, he affirmed that Christians carry on a trade, sell goods, marry, and use all temporal gifts without sin.[24] This earthly life takes place within the structure Luther had described in his concept of the Christian's calling. He had appropriated the medieval framework for daily living that divided life into three situations or "estates" (*Stände*)—the *Nährstand* (family and economic life), the *Wehrstand* (political life), and the *Lehrstand* (ecclesiastical life). The reformer had, however, provided a new theological framework for understanding life in human society. All human creatures live in these three situations, whether they believe in Christ or not. For believers in Christ, however, Luther taught that human performance in these realms of daily life flows from the Christian's new identity, which God bestows through his word of forgiveness for sinners, a word that frees them for service to him. Serving God, according to Luther, takes form in service to one's neighbor. Christians exercise their new gift of salvation—the restoration of their humanity—through "offices" (*Ämter*), the roles and responsibilities incumbent by God's design on people in each situation of life. While all people have these roles and responsibilities—and may view them as duties or burdens or even opportunities—Christians view them as callings from God, assignments to be a part of the way he provides blessings for his world.[25]

With this paradigm in mind, Coelestin defined the calling of bookdealers and printers. Their calling had as its purpose the production and sale of "books, musical pieces, and tracts" as well as illustrative material.[26] Indeed, people work in the book trade because they must provide for their own physical needs and those of spouse, children, and servants. Nonetheless, the purpose of exercising the calling lies in broader service to the neighbor, to human society, because in this way God may be served. Indeed, printers or bookdealers serve as "vehicles, instruments, gifts, tools, and weapons" of God, where

---

[24] *Von Buchhendlern*, Ba.

[25] On Luther's view of Christian vocation or calling, see Gustaf Wingren, *Luther on Vocation*, trans. Carl C. Rasmussen (Philadelphia: Fortress, 1957); George W. Forell, *Faith Active in Love: An Investigation of the Principles Underlying Luther's Social Ethics* (Minneapolis: Augsburg, 1954); Paul Althaus, *The Ethics of Martin Luther*, trans. Robert C. Schultz (Philadelphia: Fortress, 1972).

[26] *Von Buchhendlern*, A8b, B8a.

Coelestin presumed basic standards of honesty, diligence, and accountability, and added a warning against laziness. Some vocations were more dangerous for the spiritual well-being of the person than others: soldiers, merchants, traveling salesmen, bookdealers, courtiers, lawyers, physicians, pharmacists, and artisans were particularly vulnerable to greed, he thought.[27]

Specifically, he expected printers and typesetters to read and examine what they were printing so that they would not offer the public material that might pervert either morals or the teaching of the Gospel. Like the pharmacist who has in stock a variety of substances but does not sell on demand those that would be harmful, so the printer and bookdealer must avoid dispensing to readers spiritual poison or other harmful materials. To do so is contrary to the fundamental identity of the Christian as a baptized child of God and is also a violation of the calling God gives to those whom he has placed in the book trade. It sells for thirty pieces of silver the souls of believers who are misled by such printed materials.[28] Printers and bookdealers should recognize the names of the authors whose works they publish and exercise caution in the case of notorious writers whose work might be expected to be less than edifying, whether they be religious ravers (*Schwärmer*) or "Epicureans." If printers and bookdealers could not be sure about the content of work, they should turn to the inspectors or censors whom the government provides, and if they give uncertain answers, the printers may turn to local pastors and teachers for a responsible review of the work.[29]

Coelestin's standards for what might constitute the careless sale or production of books that could make bookdealers and printers guilty of leading readers toward damnation were simple but clear. He opposed the printing and sale of books that in any way disturbed church or society: slanderous treatises, slanderous illustrations, libelous verses, idolatrous heathen manuals, pasquils, and the like.[30] He complained that every boy who herded cattle and every girl who cared for children—no matter how young or simple they might be—could sing and repeat godless, shameful ditties and songs far better than the catechism because of their distribution in print.[31] His chief concern focused, however, on false teaching that would lead believers away from the truth of God's word. Coelestin warned against publication of those deviations from Luther's understanding of the biblical message within the Lutheran churches

[27] *Von Buchhendlern*, C4b, E6a.
[28] *Von Buchhendlern*, D8a–D8b, B7b–B8b.
[29] *Von Buchhendlern*, B8b, D3a, D5b–D6a, Eb–E3a.
[30] *Von Buchhendlern*, F2a.
[31] *Von Buchhendlern*, B8a.

that were leading people astray—he enumerated the "Osiandrian,"[32] "adia-phoristic,"[33] "Majoristic,"[34] and "synergistic"[35] heresies, a list that reflected the concerns he and his colleagues at Jena, for example, had in their controversies with other Lutheran parties. He also opposed publication of the ideas of others outside his own church, the "Jews, Papists, Schwenkfeld,[36] Servetus,[37] the Anabaptists, and the Sacramentarians."[38] To contribute to the deception of people by spreading such misconceptions of the truth could only earn God's wrath, Coelestin was certain.

His Melanchthonian training in rhetoric had taught him that he must anticipate objections to his position, and so he rehearsed five excuses that seem to reflect objections he might actually have encountered from printers and bookdealers he knew. First, the argument had been mounted that "Epicurean" bookdealers make more money than those who reject opportunities to print all kinds of books. That suggests that God does not punish those who take advantage of such opportunities. Furthermore, printing such books is neces-sary to support family and servants. Coelestin argued that faithful Christians often have to get along with less of this world's goods, but those who deceive people or damage the public good through their printing will someday con-front God's wrath.

The third objection pleaded that the situation of the printer was no differ-ent from that of the smith who makes knives or guns. Smiths cannot be held responsible for those who misuse their products; neither should printers. Coelestin rejected the comparison. Knives and guns have both proper and

---

[32]Andreas Osiander (1498–1552) had defined saving righteousness as the indwelling divine righteousness of Christ; not Christ's obedience to the Father, his suffering, death, and imputed righteousness, as nearly all other Lutherans taught.

[33]The term applied to defenders of the compromise proposed to stave off a Roman Catho-lic imposition of the recatholicizing "Augsburg Interim" of 1548 through concessions in adia-phora, or things neither forbidden nor commanded in the Bible.

[34]The Wittenberg professor Georg Major (1502–1574) had defended the proposition "good works are necessary for salvation" and was therefore accused of reverting to a medieval view of salvation.

[35]The term applied to those who attempted to affirm the activity of the human will reach-ing out to God in the process of coming to faith in Christ.

[36]Caspar von Schwenckfeld (1489–1561) taught that God brings people to faith only through the internal working of the Holy Spirit and held that "externals," for example the Bible and the sacraments, were unnecessary.

[37]Michael Servetus (ca. 1511–1553) denied the doctrine of the Trinity.

[38]Von Buchhendlern, B4a, B6a, E8a. The last reference included all those who denied the Real Presence of Christ's body and blood in the Lord's Supper.

improper uses, but there can be no proper use of books that teach errors or in other ways undermine the public order.

Against the defense that pleaded ignorance of what was true and false in the materials the bookdealer or printer handled, Coelestin suggested the use of official censors or local pastors and teachers to evaluate the products they were about to print or sell. He also rejected the argument that printing a few bad books among many good ones could not be a terribly great sin. Indeed, a book that contained much good could still lead people away from God on the basis of a little falsehood. God opposes even the smallest of evils.[39]

The final excuse for printing such books raised the question of the relationship between government and the printing trade: What if rulers command production and distribution of works that oppose the proper teaching of God's Word? Coelestin's friend Matthaeus Judex had written against princely censorship of the writings of legitimate theologians only four years earlier, on the basis of their common experience under Johann Friedrich the Middler in Jena.[40] Judex had no concept of freedom of the press. His argument had been based upon the presupposition that the church held competence for public comment on the truth of God's word, the prince did not.

On the basis of the same paradigm Coelestin commented on government and the book trade from several angles. He did not object in principle to princely exercise of responsibility for public order in regard to the printing trade (a principle Judex had also granted in his critique of improper governmental censorship[41]). Christian rulers should remember that God has made them agents of his will for the promotion of good and the prevention of evil. Therefore, they should see to it that their people have good books. They should avoid suppressing good books, as had the Jewish king Jehoiakim, who forbade the prophet Jeremiah to proclaim the truth and spread it through useful and necessary books (Jer. 36:1–32). Their efforts would be frustrated, as were those of Jehoiakim, and they would bring judgment upon themselves.

On the other hand, the issue was not censorship but the propagation of the truth in its continuing battle against falsehood and error. Coelestin recalled that Emperor Constantine had provided a good example for Christian governments when he suppressed the books of the Arians.[42] However, he urged

---

[39] *Von Buchhendlern*, D3a–E4a.

[40] Matthaeus Judex, *De typographia*, 45–84. On the background of governmental censorship and control of the press, see Dieter Breuer, *Geschichte der literarischen Zensur in Deutschland* (Heidelberg: Quelle and Meyer, 1982), 23–47; and Dirk Kruse, *Nachdruckschutz und Buchaufsicht vom 16. bis zum 19. Jahrhundert* (Inaugural dissertation, University of Bonn, 1987), 22–49.

[41] Matthaeus Judex, *De typographia*, 35–44. [42] *Von Buchhendlern*, D7a–b.

printers and bookdealers to defy governmental orders to publish the wrong kind of books. The same principle that guided Judex's argument against princely censorship of "good" books shaped Coelestin's conviction that the authorities must be resisted when they command the printing or sale of materials offensive to the faith or public order. Coelestin's associates in the Gnesio-Lutheran movement had propagated a theory that justified resistance to governmental authority on the basis of the biblical principle that "we must obey God rather than any human authority" (Acts 5:29) and the theology of the Christian's calling: It is not the calling of the prince to interfere with the teaching of the church. Even if government officials command the production or sale of unchristian literature, Christians should recognize what belongs to Caesar and what belongs to God (Matt. 22:21) and follow the example of Benevolus, the pious counselor of the Arian empress Justina, the mother of Emperors Gratian and Valentinian. When she ordered Benevolus to issue an imperial mandate against Bishop Ambrose and other faithful teachers of the church, he refused to do so and resigned his position. Similar resistance to evil commands of rulers can be found in Scripture, among them the Hebrew midwives of Egypt who disobeyed Pharaoh's command to kill Hebrew boys (Exod. 1:17); Daniel, who defied Darius' order not to pray to God (Dan. 6:6–13); and the apostles who rejected the Jewish leadership's attempts to silence them (Acts 5:27–42): It is not the calling of the prince to interfere with the teaching of the church. Christian bookdealers and printers will resist impious commands from rulers in similar fashion, Coelestin insisted. In so doing they would fulfill God's design for their lives.[43]

Martin Luther had emphasized the necessity of pious service to God and neighbor in the vocations or callings of family and economic spheres of life as well as in society and church. His followers had pledged themselves to that understanding of the way God works in human culture through their subscription to the sixteenth article of the Augsburg Confession.[44] Johann Friedrich Coelestin addressed a societal problem that he saw developing in the 1560s with the tool that Luther had fashioned in his doctrine of the Christian's calling. With a variety of rhetorical devices learned from Wittenberg rhetoric (examples, stories, citations from authorities, and so forth) and within the eschatological context of his times he shaped guidance for printers and bookdealers to fulfill their assignments from God. This profile for their profession consisted more of warnings against that which would lead them to abuse

---

[43] Von Buchhendlern, D8a–b, E4b–F3a.

[44] Die Bekenntnisschriften der evangelisch-lutherischen Kirche, 11th ed. (Göttingen: Vandenhoeck & Ruprecht, 1992), 70–71.

their office than of positive instruction, which he apparently presumed they could supply themselves. His concern for public order and proper teaching of God's Word placed upon those in the book trade the obligation of providing printed materials to the reading public that would edify individual readers and society as a whole. In so doing he demonstrated the importance of this vocation for the life of the church and of society in late Reformation Germany.

THE IMAGE OF SPAIN IN THE PAMPHLET LITERATURE OF THE THIRTY YEARS' WAR

William S. Maltby

NATIONAL IMAGES, LIKE RACIAL STEREOTYPES, belong to the murkier realms of popular culture. They may be defined as a set of characteristics generally attributed to the members of a particular ethnic or national group and at their broadest level involve a kind of mythmaking, an attempt to provide a short-hand description of complex phenomena through the creation of an arche-type. Though they do not always possess the deeper linguistic and subconscious elements described by Winthrop Jordan in his study of Anglo-American attitudes toward people of African descent,[1] they are similar in that they are rooted in a series of incomplete or superficial impressions. If these impressions develop in an atmosphere of conflict or exploitation they will almost certainly be negative, and if negative impressions are systematically fos-tered for political or religious reasons over a long period of time, they will result in a negative national or ethnic stereotype. The process resembles thought itself: selection, conceptualization, and the creation of memory through repetition and reinforcement. But it cannot develop widely without an effective means of communication. In a sense, then, the "national image" is yet another gift of the printing press. When an image is deliberately created and disseminated in print, especially in the cruder forms of wartime propa-ganda, it makes an immediate and vivid impression that can be reinforced almost indefinitely through repetition. When the crisis passes, its emotional impact may subside, but a residue remains that can be drawn upon in later conflicts.

In the case of European attitudes toward Spain, this process was complete long before the outbreak of the Thirty Years' War. There is a substantial litera-ture on the resulting "Black Legend" and general agreement that the Euro-pean image of Spain was almost wholly negative by the end of the sixteenth century. This was to some extent an outgrowth of Spain's position as the great-

---

[1]Winthrop D. Jordan, *White Over Black: American Attitudes toward the Negro, 1550–1812* (Chapel Hill: University of North Carolina Press, 1968).

est of contemporary empires. Spain had been involved in hostilities from Germany to Peru and had left in its wake a host of enemies, many of whom were motivated by religious as well as political passions. In denouncing Spanish activities, French, English, and Dutch pamphleteers uncovered a host of unsavory or atrocious incidents that they served up with rich embellishments to readers who already felt threatened by Spanish power. These accounts in turn found their way into formal histories and *belles lettres* through the process of compilation so beloved of early modern authors. The result was a memorable literary portrait of the Spaniard. Cruel, vain, and bigoted, he was as ignorant as he was ambitious and a mortal threat to the well-being of Europe. The proof could be found in three basic sources: Spain's abuse of the Indians as described by Las Casas, the enormities committed by Alba in the Netherlands as described by the Dutch, and the crimes of the Inquisition as described by Protestants. For English readers there was also the Armada and the tribulations of English seamen on the Spanish Main whose tales were often published independently before their collection by Richard Hakluyt.[2]

The pamphlet literature of the Thirty Years' War as it applied to Spain was written against this backdrop, but though it often referred to these earlier sources, its focus had changed. This was due in part to the character of the war itself and secondarily to changes in the conditions under which ephemeral literature was produced. To begin with, the majority of pamphlets and broadsheets written during this period do not mention Spain. The Thirty Years' War was not a single war but a series of conflicts between different opponents in the course of a prolonged diplomatic crisis, and Spanish participation was limited to only a few of its phases. Moreover, when Spain was mentioned it was not always in ways that encouraged the formation of a coherent image. Many of the pamphlets and nearly all of the *corantos* that made this one of the best-reported of early modern wars were little more than brief, unemotional descriptions of events. An image of the Spanish and their intentions emerges only from those publications that sought to influence rather than inform. As such writings inevitably clustered around events or circumstances in which the

---

[2]The term "Black Legend" was first coined by the Spanish author Julián Juderías, *La Leyenda Negra y la verdad histórica* (Madrid, 1914). The literature that developed on the subject is reviewed by Charles Gibson, *The Black Legend: Anti-Spanish Attitudes in the Old World and the New* (New York: Knopf, 1971), which also presents examples of anti-Spanish writing from the earliest times to the present day. For aspects of the Black Legend relating to the present subject, see W. S. Maltby, *The Black Legend in England: The Development of Anti-Spanish Sentiment, 1558–1660* (Durham, N.C.: Duke University Press, 1971), and the article by K. Swart, "The Black Legend during the Eighty Years War," *Britain and the Netherlands* 5, ed. E. H. Kossmann and J. S. Bromley (The Hague: Anglo-Dutch Historical Conference, 1975).

arousal of public opinion might have a political effect, publication was sporadic, and content as well as timing tended to vary from country to country.

In the Netherlands there was a sustained flurry of pamphlets in the years
prior to the expiration of the twelve years' truce. After a predictably high level
of production in 1621 and 1622, interest appears to have fallen off until 1629
when Spain sued for peace, having lost Den Bosch and the Indies treasure fleet
in a single year. The flavor of the pamphleteer's response may be gathered from
a single title: *Tractaet tegen Pays, Treves en Onderhandelinge met den Koningh van
Spaignien*.[3] It was much the same when Spain tried further negotiation in
1632,[4] and again when the peace talks of 1646–48 appeared likely to succeed.
The final burst of pamphleteering accompanied the arrival of Antoine Brun as
Spanish ambassador at the Hague in 1649.[5]

Because censorship in the Netherlands was for the most part a local matter, anti-Spanish pamphlets appeared only in those towns whose *vroedschappen*
favored the war for economic reasons (Leiden, Haarlem, Gouda, and the port
towns of Zeeland and North Holland), but they were clearly intended to be
read by the burghers of Amsterdam, Rotterdam, and the other peace towns.[6]
The quantity of this literature should not be underestimated. Craig Harline has
found that 39.2 percent of all the pamphlets printed in the Netherlands
between 1607 and 1648 reflect anti-Spanish views. Of those defined by him as
"best-sellers" (titles that ran to at least four printings), the percentage is 63.6. If
each printing averaged a thousand to fifteen hundred copies and each copy
was read by several people, this represents a remarkable penetration of the target market.[7]

In England, pamphlets on Spain appeared only to encourage James I to
intervene in the Palatinate or to oppose the Spanish Marriage. In Germany
they cluster around Spinola's invasion of the Palatinate and to a much lesser

[3]The Hague: Aert Meuris, 1629. See also Willem Usselincx, *Waerschouwinghe over den Treves
met den Coninck van Spaenghien aen alle goede Patriotten ghedaen met ghevichtige redenen* (Flushing,
1630), and the anonymous *Discours aengaende Treves of Vrede met de Infante ofte Koning van Hispanien*
(Haarlem, 1629).

[4]A good example is *Allarm Trompet, teghens overgecomen s'Conincx Gedeputeerde in den Haegh*
(Z.n.v.p., v.dr. en z.j., 1632).

[5]*Vrijmoedige Aeenspraeck Aen sijn Hoogheyt de Heer Prince van Orangien* (Middelburg, 1650),
and the anonymous *Lauweren-krans gevlochten voor Sijn Hoocheyt, Wilhelm, de Heer Prince van Oran-
jien* (n.p., 1650).

[6]J. I. Israel, *The Dutch Republic and the Hispanic World* (Oxford: Oxford University Press,
1982), 234–235.

[7]Craig E. Harline, *Pamphlets, Printing, and Political Culture in the Early Dutch Republic* (Dor-
drecht: Nijhoff, 1987), 244–245.

degree, the battle of Nördlingen (1634).[8] The situation in France was different, with the pamphlets of 1621 leaning toward neutrality or even mild approval of Spanish actions. An exception was Fancan's *Dialogue de la France Mourante* (1623), which warned against Spanish plots.[9] It was not until the French occupied the Valtelline in 1624 that anti-Spanish tracts began to appear whenever Richelieu's policies seemed to demand them, notably at the time of the Mantuan War (1628–31) and of the French intervention after Nördlingen.

This pattern reflects the other main circumstance that affected pamphleteering in the Thirty Years' War: the increased ability of governments to control the press. Both James I and Cardinal Richelieu were able to gain a large measure of control over what was published in their respective countries.[10] Unapproved works could be printed elsewhere and smuggled in, but most bootleg pamphlets came from the Netherlands, and the Dutch press lost much of its exuberance after the triumph of Maurits of Nassau and his Contra-Remonstrant allies in 1619.[11]

The effect of this restriction was to reduce the total number of pamphlets devoted to political matters and to cause those that remained to adhere more closely to the government's line, even in the relatively free atmosphere of the Dutch Republic. It is especially visible in France where the rich controversial literature of the early 1620s gave way to the meager and almost entirely official production of the 1630s. The other consequence was to raise the literary and intellectual quality of the pamphlets to levels rarely achieved in earlier times. Neither the Stuarts nor Richelieu nor the House of Orange (after achieving its goals in 1619) had much to gain from exciting the rabble. Perhaps because of this the majority of pamphlets written against Spain during the Thirty Years' War appear to have been intended for a relatively well educated audience. They are longer, more literate, and politically more sophisticated than the anti-Spanish tracts of the sixteenth century. There remained what might be called a second level, best typified by that epitome of Dutch folksiness, the

[8]The pamphlet literature on Nördlingen is covered in depth by Göran Rystad, *Kriegsnachrichten und Propaganda während des Dreissigjahrigen Krieges: Die Schlacht bei Nördlingen in den gleichzeitigen gedruckten Kriegberichten* (Lund: C. W. K. Gleerup, 1960).

[9]F. Langlois, sieur de Fancan, *Dialogue de la France Mourante* (n.p., 1623), 9, 17, 59–60. Fancan became one of Richelieu's favored publicists in spite of his tendency to favor the Huguenots and a genuine phobia about Spain. See W. F. Church, *Richelieu and Reason of State* (Princeton: Princeton University Press, 1972), 98–99.

[10]For an analysis of censorship under Richelieu, see Church, *Richelieu*, 112–114.

[11]Publications could be banned by towns, provinces, the States General, or the Court, and publishers were often subjected to crippling fines and the closure of their shops; see Harline, *Pamphlets, Printing, and Political Culture*, 125–127.

Ghespreck van Langhe Piet met Keesje Maet,[12] but examples are few and there is little of the overt rabble-rousing found in such earlier works as *Ghe Patriotten Thans: Kijck uyt, Kijck uyt, Kijck uyt.*[13]

In terms of content, the result was predictable. Whereas sixteenth-century pamphleteers had sought to create outrage in support of a resistance movement or other broad-based national goal, their seventeenth-century counterparts usually tried to justify specific policies to a more sophisticated minority. This absolved them from having to retail stomach-churning atrocities and forced them instead to develop a coherent if not necessarily accurate picture of Spanish intentions. Because of this, the anti-Spanish pamphlets of the Thirty Years' War are largely variations on a single theme. Almost without exception they portray Spain as the center of a gigantic conspiracy aimed at world domination.

The chief vehicle for this accusation is a type of pamphlet that constitutes a literary genre in itself: the exposé of the "Spanish council." Though their actual construction varied widely, all of these works claimed to reveal the inner deliberations of the Spanish court in its endless quest to rule the world. The *Cancellaria hispanica*, published by the Palatine chancellor Ludwig Camerarius in 1622, has been regarded as a prototype, but the idea itself was much older. Three pamphlets in at least nine editions had been published in Holland on the *Spaenschen Raedt* in 1617 and 1618.[14] What made Camerarius unique was that instead of conjecturing about Spanish plans, he actually published 173 pages of documents taken from various Catholic chanceries. The resulting sensation led the Catholics to publish a collection of Protestant documents,[15] but this did nothing to dampen the enthusiasm of anti-Spanish writers. In France the Valtelline crisis called forth a pamphlet entitled *La Caballe Espagnole* in 1625. It was reprinted in 1626 and 1632 and supplemented by several other works that warned the princes of Europe against "the designs of the Spaniards."[16] In England, several works by the energetically anti-Spanish Thomas Scott, includ-

[12]*Ghespreck van Langhe Piet met Keesje Maet, belanghende den trevens met den Spaigniaert* (Z.n.v.pl., v.dr. en z.j., 1629).

[13]A typical *blauwboekje*, or little blue book, published without place of publication in 1615. For a discussion of the audience for whom Dutch pamphlets were intended, see Harline, *Pamphlets, Printing, and Political Culture*, 57–71.

[14]*Spaenschen Raedt, Homen de vereenichde Nederlanden alderbest wederorn sal konnen brengen order t'gebiedt van den Coninc van Spagnien* (Z.n.v.p.l., v.dr. en z.j., 1617), *Practycke van den Spaenschen Raedt* (n.p., 1618), and *Ontdeckinge vande valsche Spaensche Jesuijtische Practijcke* (n.p., 1618). All three were issued in multiple editions.

[15]Geoffrey Parker, *Europe in Crisis, 1598–1648* (London: Fontana, 1979), 182.

[16]*Dessein perpetuel des Espagnols a la monarchie universelle* (n.p., 1624), and Jeremie Du Ferrier, *Advertissements a tous les estats de l'Europe, touchant les desseins des Espagnols* (n.p., 1625).

ing *Vox Populi* and its sequel, were based on this theme,[17] and as late as 1658 a thirty-chapter pamphlet called *The King of Spain's Cabinet Council Divulged* appeared to justify the anti-Spanish policies of Cromwell's Protectorate.[18]

All of these works revolve around the idea that Spanish arms and the gold of the Indies were the sinews of a great strategy that involved the pope, the Jesuits, and the Catholic princes of the empire. The actual identity of the participants varied somewhat from tract to tract, but their purpose was always the destruction of Protestantism, or so Spain's coconspirators had been led to believe. In reality, said the pamphleteers, religion had little to do with it. The Spaniards with reptilian subtlety were using their allies in the service of political ends for which religion was only a pretext. This charge was especially popular in France where Cardinal Richelieu wished to maintain his reputation as a Catholic while supporting Protestants,[19] but it was echoed elsewhere on the theory that Protestants needed no convincing, whereas something really had to be done to bring Spain's dupes to their senses. There were also local variations of some interest. The best are from the Netherlands where several pamphlets tarred the Arminians with the Spanish brush. This is the theme of *Langhe Piet*, but there are other, less picturesque examples.[20]

Regardless of content, the mode of argumentation in these pieces is always historical. Some follow the lead of Camerarius and publish extracts of documents dating back to Commines or Paolo Giovio as evidence of Spain's imperial ambitions.[21] Most simply describe the history of Spain's involvement in world affairs from the Sack of Rome (1527) onward, and relate it to Spanish designs on the Palatinate, the Valtelline, or whatever concern happened to be uppermost at the moment. In the process there was a tendency to fall back upon the Black Legend of the sixteenth century with reference not only to the theme of Spanish ambition, but to the crimes and atrocities that resulted from it. The difference is that where the pamphlets of the sixteenth century dwell on these horrors with unconcealed and almost pornographic delight,

[17]Thomas Scott, *Vox Populi, or Newes from Spayne, translated according to the Spanish coppie, which may serve to forewarn both England and the United Provinces how far to trust the Spanish pretences* (n.p., 1620) in *Somers Tracts* 2:508–524. The sequel is *The Second Part of Vox Populi, or Gondomar appearing in the likeness of Matchiauell in a Spanish Parliament* (n.p., 1624). For Scott and his career, see Maltby, *The Black Legend in England*, 102–108.

[18]*The King of Spain's Cabinet Council Divulged; or a Discovery of the Prevarications of the Spaniards*, by J. H. for J. S. to be sold by Simon Miller (London, 1658).

[19]It was the chief theme of Du Ferrier, *Advertissements*, but see also *La Caballe Espagnolle entierement discouuerte, a l'auancement de la France et contentment des bons François* (n.p., 1626), 4.

[20]See *Spaensche ende Jesuitische Practijcken: Ofteer Arminiensche Brandene Liefde* (n.p., 1623) and *T'Vrije Nederlandtsche Gesangh Over de Spaensche Roomsche ende Arminiaensche Vriede* (n.p., 1623).

[21]See, for example, *Dessein perpetuel des Espagnols*.

those of the seventeenth century refer to them only in passing as though the reader's assent could be taken for granted. A reference to "their monstrous and new devised cruelties which these devilish and tyrannous Spaniards have inhumanly practised amongst the simple and innocent people, as appeareth by Don Bartholomew de Las Casas,"[22] was usually sufficient, and there is almost no mention of contemporary outrages. The fact is that in the Thirty Years' War the Spanish behaved rather well, at least by comparison with the soldiers of Tilly or Christian of Brunswick.

In addition to the exposés of Spanish ambition, there were older, related themes. One that was especially popular was to portray Ambrosio de Spinola, commander of the Spanish army of Flanders and chief minister of the archdukes in Brussels, as a spider spinning his webs over Europe. The obvious play on words proved a useful convention for political cartoonists, but it was really no more than a graphic variation on the theme of conspiracy.[23] In fact, the idea of conspiracy was so pervasive that it influenced even those pamphlets whose purpose was largely reportorial. An otherwise innocuous piece on Spain's defeat in the Valtelline was called *Les Desseins et entreprises de l'armée espagnole descouverte* (n.p., 1625).

Perhaps most interesting of all were the pamphlets in which Spanish designs were uncovered by the illustrious dead. England was forewarned, through the agency of Thomas Scott, by Sir Walter Raleigh and by *Robert Earl of Essex his Ghost,* [24] while Louis XIII had to endure an *Advertissement de Henry le Grand* in which his departed father likens the Spaniards to gangrene.[25] The most elaborate of the genre were those in which the dead meet as a committee. Thomas Scott's *Vox Coeli, or Newes from Heaven* involves such English notables as Henry VIII and Queen Elizabeth,[26] but *Les Entretiens des Champs Elizies* (1631) is truly international in scope. In addition to a cast of French, Dutch, and Italian worthies, the reader is treated to the complaints of Alba, his court rival Ruy Gómez de Silva, and Gonsalvo de Córdoba, the "Great Captain" of

---

[22]*An Experiemental Discoverie of Spanish Practises, or The Counsell of a well-wishing Souldier for the Good of his Prince and State* (n.p., 1623), 31.

[23]William A. Coupe, *The German Illustrated Broadsheet in the Seventeenth Century* (Baden-Baden: Heitz, 1966/7), 1:156, and for example, "Spanische Spinnstuben oder Rockenfahrt," in ibid., vol. 2, plate 83.

[24]Thomas Scott, *Sir Walter Raleigh's Ghost: or England's Forewarner: Discovering a secret Consultation, newly holden in the Court of Spain* (Utrecht, 1626), and idem, *Robert Earl of Essex his Ghost, sent from Elizian: To the Nobility, Gentry and Communalitye of England: Printed in Paradise* (1624) in *Somers Tracts,* 2:596–603.

[25]*Advertissement de Henry le Grand au Roy sur les affaires de ce temps* (n.p., 1623).

[26]Printed in *Somers Tracts,* 2:555–596.

Ferdinand of Aragon. All of them claim to have been cozened by the king of Spain.[27]

But was any of this true? The answer is both yes and no. Spanish policy did not seek world domination, but it did hope to regain the Netherlands and this meant holding the "Spanish Road," a long, inconvenient supply route that meandered through several principalities. The need to keep this corridor open, even more than the desire to aid Catholicism, ensured that Spain would be deeply enmeshed in imperial politics. The same concern, centered on the Palatinate but reinforced by the never-ending struggle in the West Indies, involved Spain's ministers in the affairs of England. Control of the Palatinate offered a viable alternative to the Spanish Road, but it was ruled by the son-in-law of James I whose election as king of Bohemia in 1619 began the Thirty Years' War. English intervention on behalf of the Winter King, as he was called, was to be avoided at all costs and in securing the neutrality of James I, the Spanish ambassador Gondomar aroused legitimate fears of subversion. As Spain's military and financial strength declined, it became more and more necessary to rely on the kind of secret diplomacy that creates such fears and Spain's unquestioned adherence to the Catholic church together with the dynastic ties of Philip IV made the conspiracy hypothesis credible.

Against this must be set the fact that if there was a plot it was a very unsatisfactory one from the Spanish point of view. The supposed coconspirators, from the pope to Ferdinand of Styria, were not always willing to play their lines as written. They may have been Catholics, but they had political interests of their own and would support Spain only when it suited them. As far as the Catholic clergy was concerned, it remained as it had always been, a heterogeneous group with chronically divided loyalties. Olivares and a host of Spanish viceroys might have wished that they were part of a grand conspiracy, but they had no illusions that it was so, and even fewer about the limits of Spain's wealth and power. Recruiting for the army had become a problem as early as the 1580s and the appalling condition of Spanish finances is too well known to require further comment.

Spain's formidable image was thus the final irony in her decline as a major power. The vision of a great conspiracy was fashioned by Spain's enemies for their own ends, but by exaggerating Spanish might, they contributed to the illusion that sustained it. It has been argued, notably by C. H. Carter, that the false perception of Spanish power increased the exertions of her enemies,[28] but

---

[27]*Les Entretiens des Champs Elizies* (n.p., 1631), 14–15.

[28]C. H. Carter, *The Secret Diplomacy of the Habsburgs, 1598–1625* (New York: Columbia University Press, 1964), 1–42.

this is unlikely. The hostility of France, the Netherlands, or the English Puritans was rooted in causes far deeper than the fantasies of pamphleteers. When those governments restrained their hostility it was only through fear of Spanish reprisals, and if the pamphlets of the Thirty Years' War were taken seriously, their fears were out of all proportion to reality.

It is of course impossible to gauge the impact of the press on policy then or now, especially when the press serves as a conduit for official views. There can, however, be little doubt about its impact on Europe's image of Spain and the Spanish. The pamphlets printed during the Thirty Years' War reinforced the negative view of Spain that had emerged in the sixteenth century, but above all they provide a measure of their predecessor's success. It was no longer necessary to tell new stories of Spanish violence and perfidy. Readers in the seventeenth century could be expected to remember the old ones.

Schnucker in his combined academic-editorial office, ca. late 1980s.

Printing the Metaphor of Light and Dark

From Renaissance Satire to Reformation Polemic

James V. Mehl

The importance of the printing press for humanist reform and for the spread of Reformation ideas is well established.[1] A less well known side of the reform movements of early-sixteenth-century Germany is the adaptation of the popular metaphor of light and dark in certain written and visual texts that were published in the second and third decades of the sixteenth century. Transitional applications can be seen in some effective uses of this metaphor during the Reuchlin controversy in pre-Reformation Germany by Reuchlin's humanist supporters, who aligned themselves on the side of the enlightened while disparaging their traditionalist opponents as unenlightened "obscure men." The *viri obscuri*, on the side of "darkness," were portrayed as ignorant and morally corrupt. This metaphor was adapted most creatively by the humanist authors of the satirical *Epistolae obscurorum virorum* (*Letters of Obscure Men*) and then appropriated, in a more serious and cutting way, by the religious proponents of the new evangelical cause.

While the metaphor of light and dark has deep historical roots in ancient Greek (e.g. Plato's *Republic*) and in Judeo-Christian thought (e.g. the Gospel of John), to mention only two well-known western sources, it took on a specific Renaissance meaning in the course of the Reuchlin controversy. The publication in 1514 of a collection of letters in support of Reuchlin, the *Epistolae clarorum virorum*, gave rise to the famous *Epistolae obscurorum virorum* in 1515–17. There the metaphor was designed to lampoon the scholastic opponents of Reuchlin. Later, in the "Triumphus Capnionis," the addressee of the satirical letters, Ortwin Gratius, is even portrayed with a blindfold. The metaphor is

---

[1]See, for example, Elizabeth L. Eisenstein, *The Printing Press as an Agent of Change: Communications and Cultural Transformations in Early-Modern Europe*, 2 vols. (Cambridge: Cambridge University Press, 1980), part 2.

Epistolae obscurorum virorum (Letters of Obscure Men), 1st ed., pt. 2. From Eduardus Böcking, ed., *Ulrichi Hutteni equitis Operum supplementum: Epistolae obscurorum virorum cum illustrantibus adversariisque scriptis,* 2 vols. (Leipzig, 1864–70).

then adapted, for purposes of religious propaganda, in a number of early Reformation pamphlets and broadsheets. Just as the humanist supporters of Reuchlin had characterized their opponents as being blind to the truth and thus in intellectual darkness, so too the religious promoters of Luther cast their opponents in spiritual darkness. Several pamphlet illustrations of the period indicate the polemical transformation of this metaphor, depicting Luther and his followers on the side of "light" and the Catholic antagonists on the side of "darkness."

The oppositional metaphor of light and dark is an example of a "root paradigm" as defined by Victor Turner.[2] Like other root paradigms, the contrasting images of light and dark have been used in a number of cultural contexts, both in western and nonwestern traditions. Among the more familiar western uses are Plato's "Allegory of the Cave" and the Christian Bible. In his fictional description of *The Republic* Plato inserted the "Allegory of the Cave" as book 7 in order to clarify the metaphysical and political class-bound assumptions of his ideal state. There the lower or "worker" class is bound at the bottom of a cave, where they mistake the shadows and sound reverberating from the cave wall as realities. Only the prisoner who escapes to the upper world, adapting gradually to the shadows of natural things, to the real objects of nature, to the stars and moon, and eventually to the sun itself is able to grasp the true meaning of reality by contemplating the pure forms or essences. Thus Plato relies on the darkness of the cave and the light of the sun to symbolize the respective intellectual levels of the workers and the philosophers and to demonstrate the role of the philosopher-king for his ideal state.

The gospel writers also relied on the metaphor to express the new spiritual realities and hope for those baptized in Jesus' name. John began his gospel with the concept of the Logos, or Word, which has both Greek and Jewish origins. For example, in John 1:1–5 Jesus is treated as a figure of light:

> In the beginning was the Word, and the Word was with God: and the Word was God. He was in the beginning with God. All things were made through him, and without him was made nothing that has been made. In him was life, and the life was the light of men. And the light shines in the darkness; and the darkness grasped it not.

[2]As argued by R.W. Scribner, *For the Sake of Simple Folk: Popular Propaganda for the German Reformation*, 2d ed. (Oxford: Clarendon Press, 1994), 58; the term "root paradigm" is defined by Victor Turner, *Images and Pilgrimage in Christian Culture* (New York: Columbia University Press, 1978), 248–249.

And Paul relied on the metaphor in his instructions to the Christian community in Ephesus (Eph. 4:17–20):

> This, therefore, I say and testify in the Lord, that henceforward you
> are not to walk as the Gentiles walk in the futility of their mind, hav
> ing their understanding clouded in darkness, estranged from the life
> of God through the ignorance that is in them, because of the blind
> ness of their heart. For they have given themselves up in despair to
> sensuality, greedily practising every kind of uncleanness.

Thus we have in these early Christian texts an association of light with the
Christ and with faith in God and virtuous living, while darkness, blindness,
ignorance, and despair are the characteristics of the world and the fallen
Gentiles.

This Christian tendency to associate their own age as one of light in contrast to the spiritual darkness of the pagans before them continued as an
important motif through medieval culture, until Petrarch reversed the meaning
of the metaphor in the mid-fourteenth century. As Theodor Mommsen
argued more than half a century ago, the Italian humanist Petrarch was the first
to invert the metaphor to indicate that he was living at the end of a long
period of *tenebrae* or darkness, a cultural darkness suggested by corruption in
the Church and by the decline of political conditions in Italy. The years from
1337 to 1342/3 were crucial in the evolution of a new concept of history, as
Petrarch was narrowing the focus of his major historical work, *De viris illustri-
bus*.[3] Citing passages in the *Secretum* and letters, Mommsen traced the development of Petrarch's changing view of ancient Roman history by demonstrating
how he had narrowed the focus of his work to include only the lives of famous
men from the time of Romulus to Emperor Titus. Thus Petrarch's increasing
interest in the classical pagan period, as opposed to Christian Rome, served as
the basis for his inversion of the metaphor to interpret the ancients as living in
a period of "light." And it was this spirit of the ancient Romans that he
invoked for the *renacita* or renewal of Italian culture during his own time. The
intervening period became a *medi aevum*, a middle age of "barbarian" decline
and darkness.[4]

During the Reuchlin controversy the oppositional metaphor took on an
interesting new twist of the Renaissance meaning. Both in Renaissance Italy
and in the North there had been a long series of controversies in which con-

---

[3]Theodor E. Mommsen, "Petrarch's Conception of the 'Dark Ages,'" *Speculum* 17 (1942):
226–242, esp. 229–230.
[4]Ibid., 228, 237–239.

servative clerics, usually mendicant friars, had accused the humanists of encouraging a lascivious lifestyle by reviving the pagan texts of Ovid and other "immoral" ancient authors. On their side the humanist poets had countered with various defenses of their revival of ancient Roman and Greek authors, sometimes showing their compatibility with Christian faith.[5] In the North there were also intellectual disputes regarding the proper burial of condemned criminals, the number of Mary Magdalens, and other pre-Reformation controversies waged primarily through the exchange of pamphlets. When critical humanists, such as Lorenzo Valla, Erasmus, and Lefèvre d'Etaples, began to apply the new method of philology to religious texts, however, serious conflicts and debates erupted with scholastic theologians in the late medieval universities.[6] In Germany such humanist-scholastic disputes were accompanied by a growing wave of popular anticlericalism during the fifteenth and sixteenth centuries.[7] At the beginning of the sixteenth century the efforts of a converted Jew, Johannes Pfefferkorn, to restrict the use of Hebrew books, especially the Talmud, were countered by the humanist scholar Reuchlin. The controversy that followed, the Reuchlin affair, is well known.[8] Of interest here is the appearance of several works during the dispute that rely on the metaphor of light and dark: the *Epistolae clarorum virorum*, the *Epistolae obscurorum virorum*, and the *Triumphus Doctoris Reuchlini*.

The metaphor is applied with particular intentions, and therefore takes on specific meanings, within the context of the exchanges during the Reuchlin affair. At the time of the Speyer decision in 1514, which was favorable to Reuchlin, the Hebrew scholar published a volume of letters that had been written in his support, the *Epistolae clarorum virorum*. These *Letters of Illustrious Men* relied on the Latin adjective *clarus* to distinguish Reuchlin's proponents from his adversaries. The word *clarus* has several possible meanings: "bright" or

[5]These controversies are traced for Renaissance Italy by Concetta Carestia Greenfield, *Humanist and Scholastic Poetics, 1250–1500* (London: Associated University Presses, 1981). For an example of a humanist defense in the North, see Mehl, "Hermann von dem Busche's *Vallum humanitatis* (1518): A German Defense of the Renaissance Studia Humanitatis," *Renaissance Quarterly* 42 (1989): 480–506.

[6]Erika Rummel, *The Humanist-Scholastic Debate in the Renaissance and Reformation* (Cambridge: Harvard University Press, 1995); Charles G. Nauert, *Humanism and the Culture of Renaissance Europe* (Cambridge: Cambridge University Press, 1995).

[7]Peter A. Dykema and Heiko A. Oberman, eds., *Anticlericalism in Late Medieval and Early Modern Europe* (Leiden: E.J. Brill, 1993).

[8]On the Reuchlin affair, see Hans Peterse, *Jacobus Hoogstraeten gegen Johannes Reuchlin: Ein Beitrag zur Geschichte des Antijudaismus im 16. Jahrhundert* (Mainz: Philipp von Zabern, 1995); James H. Overfield, *Humanism and Scholasticism in Late Medieval Germany* (Princeton: Princeton University Press, 1984), 247–297.

"shining" when referring to sight; "clear" when referring to the mind; and "illustrious," "distinguished," or "famous" when referring to a person. So the references to the various *viri clari* who had written in Reuchlin's defense express a somewhat complex but specific meaning: they were a group of "famous" men who were also enlightened in their vision and "clearheaded" in their arguments supporting Reuchlin's cause. Since Reuchlin and many of his defenders were humanists, there was an implied opposition to the scholastic theologians and other opponents as being less than famous, enlightened, and clearheaded. Thus the characterizations of intellectual and personal "obscurantism," of being on the side of darkness, are increasingly emphasized in the texts directed against Reuchlin's clerical opponents.

Two of these texts take on a particular satirical form in their rhetorical appeal. Perhaps the most famous satire in pre-Reformation Germany is the *Epistolae obscurorum virorum*. The first installment of these anonymous fictional letters (known at Part I), which were printed in 1515 and attributed to Crotus Rubeanus, was followed with additional letters the next year and with a second installment (Part II) in 1517. These later letters are attributed primarily to Ulrich von Hutten, with the likely involvement of Hermann Buschius and other humanist supporters of Reuchlin. Their title suggests a satirical takeoff on the earlier letter collection, the *Epistolae clarorum virorum*. The *Epistolae obscurorum virorum* is an original mimic satire written by Crotus Rubeanus, Hutten, and other humanists to mock Jacob Hoogstraten, Arnold Tongern, Ortwin Gratius, and other real-life opponents of Reuchlin.[9] The Cologne arts professor Gratius is the addressee of most of the letters and is thus treated as the mentor of the *viri obscuri*, while Hoogstraten (as Jacobus de Alta Platea) and Tongern (as Arnoldus de Thungaris) and several other scholastic theologians make appearances in the correspondence. However, most of the correspondents are entirely fictional, crafted to satirize Reuchlin's opponents as intellectually arrogant, stupid, and morally degenerate. As I have argued elsewhere, a number of the fictional correspondents are actually references to common peasants and village laborers, meant to associate the elite university professoriate (the obscure men) with the lowest classes in sixteenth-century German society.[10] Such satirical usages relied on the oppositional metaphor of light and

[9]On the *Epistolae obscurorum virorum*, see James V. Mehl, "Characterizations of the 'Obscure Men' of Cologne: A Study in Pre-Reformation Collective Authorship," in Thomas F. Mayer and D. R. Woolf, eds., *The Rhetorics of Life-Writing in Early Modern Europe: Forms of Biography from Cassandra Fedele to Louis XIV* (Ann Arbor: University of Michigan Press, 1995), 163–185.

[10]James V. Mehl, "Language, Class, and Mimic Satire in the Characterization of Correspondents in the *Epistolae obscurorum virorum*," *Sixteenth Century Journal* 25 (1994): 289–305.

dark as embodied in the characterization of obscurantism. Just as Reuchlin's name meant "smoke" in the vernacular (*Rauch*), his enemies were ironically dismissed for their intellectual obscurity, for their academic pretensions, and for their preoccupation with wine and women.

The characterization of the *viri obscuri* was first formulated in the *Triumphus Doctoris Reuchlini* (The Triumph of Doctor Reuchlin). An initial draft of the *Triumphus* was probably circulated by Buschius in 1514. A revised and expanded copy was published in 1518, probably under the direction of Hutten.[11] The edition included a large woodcut illustration, the "Triumphus Capnionis," showing a triumphant Reuchlin being greeted at a city's entrance.[12] He is preceded in the triumphal parade by Hutten leading a band of defeated obscurantists. The *viri obscuri* include Hoogstraten, Tongern, and a blindfolded Gratius, among others. Similar satirical characterizations may be found in the written text of the *Triumphus Doctoris Reuchlini*, where, for example, the reader is admonished to blindfold Gratius, "lest he cast a spell over all men."[13] The blindfolding could also be an allusion to Gratius's opposition to Reuchlin's *Augenspiegel* (Eyeglasses). How could a sightless Gratius condemn the very thing that would clarify vision? Such satirical treatment of Gratius is representative of the characterizations of the obscurantists in both the written and visual texts of Reuchlin's "Triumph."

The transformation of such humanist satire for use in early Reformation propaganda can be seen in the *Triumphus Veritatis* (1524). A comparison of the woodcut illustrations of the two triumphs indicates how the band of Reuchlin's obscurantist opponents has been replaced by a similarly chained group of Luther's defeated adversaries.[14] The captured enemies include members of the ecclesiastical hierarchy and various Catholic theologians who had expressed most vociferously their opposition to the new evangelical cause. In the front line there are a pope and a bishop, both with broken staffs and with their traditional symbols of office falling off their heads. Behind them are two obscured cardinals and the theologians, the most prominent of whom are represented with animal heads. Hoogstraten, who is the only holdover from the earlier "Triumph," is depicted wearing a crown with a rat on top, mocking him as

[11] On the authorship of the *Triumphus*, see Thomas W. Best, *The Humanist Ulrich von Hutten: A Reappraisal of His Humor* (Chapel Hill: University of North Carolina Press, 1969), 48–53.

[12] The foldout woodcut illustration is reprinted in Ludwig Geiger, *Renaissance und Humanismus in Italien und Deutschland* (Berlin: G. Grote, 1882), opposite 522.

[13] Eduard Böcking, *Ulrichi Hutteni, equitis Germani, opera … omnia*, 5 vols. with 2 suppl. vols. (Leipzig, 1859–70; reprinted, Aalen: O. Zeller, 1963), 3:434: "Lictor, ades, frontemque liga, ne fascinet omnes!"

[14] The foldout woodcut illustration is reprinted in Scribner, *For the Sake*, 64, fig. 46.

the "rat king." Such binary images carried over from the pre-Reformation controversies were further reinforced in Reformation polemics through the use of the metaphor of light and dark.

This point is illustrated with several early Reformation woodcuts borrowed from R. W. Scribner's *For the Sake of Simple Folk: Popular Propaganda for the German Reformation.* While Scribner has recognized the use of the metaphor of light and dark in these examples, he has often not associated their meanings with the pre-Reformation applications as discussed here. Just as the creator of the *Triumphus Veritatis* adapted the layout, imagery, and meaning of "The Triumph of Reuchlin" for the new polemical purposes of the evangelical Reformation, so too the images of light and dark are used to reinforce the new spiritual message of Luther and his followers. Several of the woodcuts rely on specific scriptural references for their propaganda value. In a 1524 broadsheet, "Luther Leads the Faithful from Egyptian Darkness" (1524), Luther leads the Christian faithful out of the bondage and spiritual darkness of the Roman Church, symbolized by the dark cave at the left bottom, as Moses had led the Jews from their Egyptian masters.[15] Luther, wearing his doctor's cap, directs his lay followers into the sunlight where they assemble around the crucified Christ. Behind Luther an emperor and a king turn back into the darkness of the cave, suggesting the lack of political support by the emperor and other Catholic heads of state for the evangelical cause. Standing above the cave, attempting to distract the faithful, are a pope, Church officials, and various theological opponents of Luther.

Another woodcut, Hans Holbein the Younger's "Christ the Light of the World," relies on a passage from Matthew's gospel: "the people who sat in darkness have seen a great light, and upon those who sat in the region and shadow of death, a light has arisen."[16] Christ, of course, was that new spiritual light, as he proclaims his word to the group of peasants and burghers on the left. On the right side of the lamp, members of the Catholic clergy, including a pope, a cardinal, a bishop, monks, and canons, turn away from the light and are led into a dark pit (similar to the cave in the previous example) by two figures labeled Aristotle and Plato.[17] Not only are there strong implications that the Church had fallen into the errors of the pagan philosophers, perhaps as a result of scholastic theological speculations, but that their intellectual and religious blindness had directed them away from the true source of spiritual salvation, Christ and his Word as expressed in the gospels. This woodcut is also

[15]Ibid., 30, fig. 21.
[16]Matt. 4:16–17.
[17]Scribner, *For the Sake of Simple Folk*, 46–47, fig. 33.

important because it places to the left of the lamp those accepting Christ as the new light of the world, while the traditional Church is condemned to an eternal darkness on the right. This binary or oppositional characteristic can be seen in a number of other polemical woodcuts of the period, such as the title page illustration for *Die Luterisch Strebkatz* (1524).[18]

The metaphorical themes of blindness, darkness, and light are especially well represented on the title page of a pamphlet by Haug Marschalck, *Ein Spiegel der Blinden* (A Mirror for the Blind) (1523).[19] Although the general theme, layout, and message are like those in the Holbein piece, the particular emphasis on blindfolds, blindness, and a mirror evoke the images of the humanist satire during the Reuchlin controversy. Recall how Gratius had been portrayed in Reuchlin's "Triumph" as an enemy with menacing eyes requiring a blindfold, in part because he had rejected the *Augenspiegel*. The mendicant preacher on the left, who is identified as the scholastic Duns Scotus, is himself blindfolded and holding a blindfolded mirror. Facing the pulpit are a blindfolded bishop and canon, suggesting the total folly of the situation. Not only is the scholastic message of the preacher clouded in darkness, but the ecclesiastical hierarchy is so blinded by arrogance that they could not see the scholastic message (let alone themselves as the fools they really are) even if they desired to do so. The message for the German laity is clear: Turn away from such foolishness and receive the true Word from the Lord who is risen above.

The final woodcut summarizes, rather nicely I believe, the points that I have made regarding the metaphor of light and dark. The polemical illustration, "Pope and Cardinal as Wolves, with Luther and Christ," incorporates the biblical symbolism of Christ as the Shepherd, now dying on the cross, with a binary layout reinforced with the metaphor of light and dark.[20] On the left, showered in sunlight, is the crucified Christ. Below the cross we find the sheep (the faithful) grazing peacefully in a lush pasture. A short fence is unable to restrain the large wolves in the foreground, representing a pope and a cardinal, from carrying the unsuspecting sheep to the right (possibly to devour them). The right side of the woodcut is barren and clouded in darkness. At the top right are a goat and a wolf symbolizing the damned who have been separated from the sheep, a spiritual message of the Last Judgment alluded to by the two saints at the top (perhaps Peter and Paul). One points his finger to the particular biblical passage, while the other motions toward the crucifixion. At the right bottom corner, beyond the reach of the wolves, we see Luther holding a Bible and a pen. The hand with the pen, which he had used to translate

[18]Ibid., 60, fig. 43.   [19]Ibid., 47–48, fig. 47.
[20]Ibid., 27, 29, fig. 20; see also a version of this woodcut without Luther on 56, fig. 40.

the Scriptures and to argue his theology of *sola scriptura*, directs our attention back to the crucified Christ.

The use of the oppositional metaphor of light and dark, then, was an important rhetorical element in some of the early Reformation pamphlets and broadsheets. Although direct links cannot be established between every Reformation woodcut and earlier pre-Reformation texts where the metaphor had been employed, examples such as the title page illustration for Marschalck's *Ein Spiegel der Blinden* suggest more than a coincidental borrowing. The elements of blindness, blindfolding, and a mirror on the side of the Catholic opponents are among the same motifs that had been developed by the humanist supporters of Reuchlin to satirize and to castigate his scholastic antagonists. The specific image of Gratius' blindfolding in Reuchlin's "Triumph" is replicated in the satirical treatment of the blindfolded scholastic preacher and Church authorities in the Reformation polemic "A Mirror of the Blind." And the mirror or *Spiegel* in the woodcut had been a playful image and book title during the earlier Reuchlin affair.

The Renaissance meaning of the metaphor of light and dark was also developed in more general and complex ways during the course of the Reuchlin controversy, as may be seen in the satirical characterizations of the *Epistolae obscurorum virorum* and the *Triumphus Doctoris Reuchlini*. The humanist supporters of Reuchlin saw themselves on the side of "light," while the scholastic enemies were cast on the side of "darkness." During the early years of the evangelical reform, the defenders and promoters of Luther appropriated this powerful root metaphor as a polemical device in their pamphlet warfare. Some of these pamphlets included woodcut illustrations that emphasized the new religious message that Luther was on the side of Christ and "light," while the Catholic clergy, caught up in arrogance and ignorance, were condemned to "darkness." If we are to understand more clearly the success of the early Reformation message in Germany then we need to explore more thoroughly the complex interrelationship and textual exchange between the pre-Reformation and Reformation controversies. The metaphor of light and dark was an important part of the rhetorical appeals, used first by the humanist elite in defending Reuchlin and then adapted for broad popular support of Luther's reform movement.

THE PRINTED CATECHISM AND RELIGIOUS INSTRUCTION IN THE FRENCH REFORMED CHURCHES

Raymond A. Mentzer

A CRITICAL FEATURE OF THE REFORM and supervision of communal religious life during the Reformation was the process by which churches, both Protestant and Catholic, sought to edify and instruct the laity through the use of the printed catechism. For centuries Christians had transmitted the truths of the faith within a largely oral tradition. Excepting the members of a small educated elite, most people's knowledge of Christianity derived from lifelong participation in the liturgy. The experience meant, above all, sharing in the sacraments and other rituals, memorizing basic prayers, and by the later Middle Ages, listening attentively to the preacher. Only with the invention of printing did this educational process come to involve a concise, printed summary of core beliefs. While scholars have long acknowledged the value of studying the catechism, few have examined the interactive nature of these printed texts. How did literate and educated religious authorities attempt to shape ordinary people's understanding of religion? What was the reaction of common folk? What, in short, was the place of the printed text in the monumental Reformation effort at religious indoctrination? To better appreciate these issues, let us turn to the example of the Protestant effort in France.

On an elementary level, the French Reformed churches required congregants to commit to memory and recite certain prayers and confessions of faith, notably the Lord's Prayer and the Apostles' Creed. The faithful also learned to sing French translations of the Psalms, which Calvin and others had incorporated into the liturgy.[1] Perhaps most important were the pastor's regular sermons—detailed and orderly explanations of Scripture that, in the French churches, took place each Sunday and Wednesday. Finally, ecclesiastical officials provided catechism lessons for the religious education or, in the early

---

[1]Francis Higman, *La diffusion de la Réforme en France, 1520–1565* (Geneva: Labor et Fides, 1992), 117.

years, reeducation of generally illiterate and unlearned congregants. Still, standardized catechism instruction, a prominent feature within the routine religious experience of almost every French Protestant, remains a neglected and poorly understood subject. Despite its considerable place in the ongoing life of the church, the nature, scope, and effect of catechism instruction for the body of the faithful are not understood in anything approaching a systematic and exacting fashion.

Both Martin Luther and John Calvin penned brief vernacular catechisms early in their movements. Luther had drafted two catechisms—a Small and a Large—by 1529. The shorter version was an elementary text of no more than a dozen pages and included several illustrations. Addressed to an uneducated, often youthful, and rural audience, it contained a series of questions and answers, which, according to the preface, teachers were to read and students memorize without changing "a single syllable." Pupils learned about the Ten Commandments, the Apostles' Creed, the Lord's Prayer, and the sacraments. There were additional sections on morning and evening prayer, grace at meals, and even a "Table of Duties" based on various scriptural passages.[2]

Calvin published a *Formulaire d'instruire les enfants en la Chrétienté* in 1542,[3] after his return to Geneva the previous September. It was, in fact, his second French catechism. Five years earlier during his initial tenure at Geneva, he had written an *Instruction et confession de foi dont on use en l'Eglise de Genève*. The later *Formulaire*, a more developed text, reflects the experience at Strasbourg and the influence of Martin Bucer as well as the continuing elaboration of his own theological position.[4] Calvin unquestionably attached great importance to catechism and, for example, insisted upon a free hand in establishing both "catechism and discipline" as a fundamental condition for his resumption of ministerial duties at Geneva.[5]

In all of this, the objective was to inculcate the rudiments of the faith and to do so with precise and intelligible theological language. According to Luther, common people had "no knowledge whatever of Christian teaching"

[2]Jean-Claude Dhotel, *Les origines du catéchisme moderne d'après les premiers manuels imprimés en France* (Paris: Aubier, 1967), 21; Mark A. Noll, ed., *Confessions and Catechisms of the Reformation* (Grand Rapids: Baker Book House, 1991), 62.

[3]Olivier Fatio, ed., *Confessions et Catéchismes de la Foi réformée* (Geneva: Labor et Fides, 1986), 29–110.

[4]Dhotel, *Catéchisme*, 25–27, 36–38; Elisabeth Germain, *Langages de la foi à travers l'histoire* (Paris: Fayard-Mame, 1972), 36–38.

[5]John Calvin, *Ioannis Calvini Opera quae supersunt omnia*, ed. G. Baum, E. Cunitz, E. Reuss, 59 vols. (Brunswick: C. A. Schwetschke, 1863–1900), 9:894; François Wendel, *Calvin: Sources et évolution de sa pensée religieuse* (Paris: Presses Universitaires de France, 1950), 52–54.

and even many pastors were "incompetent and unfit for teaching" the truths of Christianity.[6] French Protestant pastors frequently echoed these sentiments in lamenting the religious ignorance and "superstitious" beliefs of their congregants. On the other hand, Protestant reformers set their catechisms as father-child dialogues, intending them ideally for patriarchs, who would provide instruction to wives, children, and servants within a domestic context. Yet heads of households, even pious ones, were often incapable or uninterested in this educational role.[7] At the very least, literacy was essential. Family devotions, moreover, tended not to be overly didactic and explanatory. They were more ceremonial and ritual affairs, concentrating upon routine recitation of prayers, common singing of the Psalms, and familiar readings from Scripture, assuming again that the head of household could read. Catechizing duties fell consequently to ecclesiastical authorities.

Historians have long supposed that the clergy "naturally" dominated this indoctrination of the faithful through basic explanations of religious belief and obligation. Preliminary examination of practice suggests, however, that this may not have always been the case, at least not in France. The lay persons who staffed and often controlled the French Protestant consistories played a crucial role in carrying out all facets of reform. Their intense, sustained involvement in the religious schooling of children and adults, men and women, is conspicuous. Even a cursory reading of the consistory minutes makes clear that pedagogical responsibilities within the local church frequently fell to deacons and elders. Pastors may have set the tone or laid down guidelines, but the laity often had charge over actual instruction.

To begin, we might ask what the substance of the lessons given to villagers and townspeople was. John Calvin's printed catechism was widely used in France through the first decades[8] and a brief look at his text is an obvious starting point. It also provides a rough notion of the beliefs and behavior deemed essential. The very title, *Formulaire,* suggests the content; this was a carefully edited, authoritative summary of the Christian faith for the entire community. The *Formulaire* contains fifty-five lessons or "Sundays," which frame a series of brief questions and answers. Divided into four major sections,

---

[6]Noll, *Confessions and Catechisms,* 61.

[7]Ibid., 59–60. John Bossy, *Christianity in the West, 1400–1700* (Oxford: Oxford University Press, 1985), 118–119; Marc Venard, "Le catéchisme au temps des Réformés," *Quatre fleuves* 11 (1980): 48.

[8]Gaston Serr, *Une église protestante au XVIe siècle, Montauban* (Aix-en-Provence: La Pensée Universitaire, 1958), 116; Janine Garrisson-Estèbe, *Protestants du Midi, 1559–1598* (Toulouse: Privat, 1980), 232.

Calvin's catechism begins with a lengthy examination of the essential "Articles of Faith." Having established the orthodox tenets of belief, the text then moves to explanations of the "Law" (i.e., the divine will that we must obey), the "Prayer" by which all persons honor and revere God, and finally the "Sacraments," those fundamental rites in which Christians participate.[9] Altogether, the catechism sought to present Christian dogma and piety in a form accessible to a plain and unsophisticated audience.

At the Pyrenean town of Le Carla in the seventeenth century, the pastors Jean and Jacob Bayle, a father and son team, followed Calvin's plan closely. The substance of their regular catechism lessons, especially those for children, centered on elementary explanations of the Decalogue, learning the Lord's Prayer, and understanding the reasons behind observances like singing the Psalms. The pastors drilled children in the various articles contained in the national Confession of Faith. They also carefully explained the meaning and practice of the Reformed liturgy.[10]

The design of Calvin's catechism and its instruction as practiced by the pastors at Le Carla convey a good sense of how the educated minority viewed the larger community and people's capacity for comprehension. Catechism promoted learning by rote, a method that church officials thought appropriate for unlettered persons belonging to the oral culture. Delegates to the National Synod meeting at Sainte-Foy in 1578, for example, advised pastors to be succinct and avoid long-winded explanations in teaching catechism. Officials thought "simple and familiar questions and answers" were best, given the "coarseness of the people."[11]

At the same time, printed catechisms were more than doctrinal and moral primers. Many doubled from the outset as textbooks for teaching children their ABCs. They were used in primary schools and in this manner contributed to the spread of literacy.[12] The very language of the catechism also bears noting. In southern France where Protestantism was perhaps strongest, most people spoke not French but Occitan. Still, the vocabulary of the Reformed churches was French. Here and elsewhere in the kingdom, French language catechisms contributed to the formation of a national linguistic culture. There were broad cultural reverberations in the attempt to inculcate uniform doctrine and devotion.

---

[9]Dhotel, *Catéchisme*, 38–50.

[10]Bibliothèque Interuniversitaire de Toulouse, ms. 267, pp. 17, 18, 48, 65, 68, 69, 74, 77.

[11]Jean Aymon, *Tous les synodes des Eglises réformées de France*, 2 vols. (The Hague, 1710), 1: 127; Garrisson-Estèbe, *Protestants du Midi*, 232–233.

[12]Rodolphe Peter, "L'abécédaire genevois ou catéchisme élémentaire de Calvin," *Revue d'histoire et de philosophie religieuses* 45 (1965): 11–45.

Close examination of the church records can help to resolve a number of other, more focused queries. Who, to return to an earlier question, taught catechism lessons? Pastors were the preferred instructors and many did catechize on a regular basis, even if they were not always enthusiastic.[13] Pastoral responsibilities were considerable and some clergymen may have balked at the prospect of drilling illiterate or at best semiliterate parishioners. As educated persons, they surely took greater pride in their sermons. Still, pastoral participation was strong, especially in the larger towns. During the 1590s, the pastors of Montauban assumed responsibility for the general adult catechism that invariably preceded the celebration of the Lord's Supper. On the other hand, the church hired a local bookseller to serve as cantor, reader, and catechist for the weekly lessons given to the town's children. His familiarity with the printed word apparently made him a good choice for the position.[14]

Local churches, in keeping with the federative nature of the French Reformed movement, had a strong measure of autonomy in designating catechism teachers and many congregations seem to have relied heavily upon their elders and deacons. In addition, there had been a close identification of deacon and catechist within French Reformed circles from the beginning of the movement.[15] The Church of Nîmes, likely suffering from a shortage of pastors, confined catechism instruction to the deacons, assisted by the elders, during its earliest years. Only later did the pastors assume catechizing duties. Even then, elders appear to have instructed people living in the outlying suburbs.[16] The consistory of Saint-Amans typically selected three of its elders to conduct catechism. The Church of Saint-André-de-Sangonis similarly appointed two elders to catechize the faithful. Catechism lessons at Troyes also took place under the direction of deacons and were apparently held in private homes. The consistory of Layrac initially divided the town into three quarters and then secured a house in each for the elders to teach catechism. Not until much later did the pastor take charge and move the instruction into the temple.[17]

---

[13]Garrisson-Estèbe, *Protestants du Midi*, 229–232.

[14]Archives Départementales (hereafter AD), Tarn-et-Garonne, 1:1, fols. 39 r–v, 63 r–v, 199 r–v, 207v, 221.

[15]*Histoire ecclésiastique des églises réformées au royaume de France,* ed. G. Baum, E. Cunitz and R. Reuss, 3 vols. (Paris, 1883–89), 1: 927, 929.

[16]Philippe Chareyre, "Consistoire et catéchèse: L'Exemple de Nîmes, XVI–XVIIe siècles," in *Catéchismes et Confessions de foi: Actes du VIIIe Colloque Jean Boisset,* ed. M.-M.Fragonard and M. Péronnet (Montpellier: Université de Montpellier III, 1995), 404.

[17]AD, Gers, 23067, 3 mars 1579, 22 février 1587, 18 mars 1588, 4 février 1603, 6 mars 1618. AD, Tarn, 1:8, 21 mars 1593. Archives Nationales (hereafter AN), TT 268, dossier 9, fol.

Naturally enough, for catechism to be effective it had to be taught
methodically and systematically. French Protestant churches generally had uniform schedules of instruction, though much depended on the target audience
and specific purpose. The Protestants pitched catechism at two levels: children
and adults. The goal was that children receive weekly schooling and some
churches appear to have made a genuine effort along these lines, imitating the
example of Geneva, where catechism was taught each Sunday at noon. The
pastor of Layrac, for example, held a "service on the small catechism" every
Sunday. He expected the children to attend and answer the questions put to
them.[18] Other, larger towns—La Rochelle, Montauban, and Nîmes, for
instance—had Sunday afternoon catechism, too. At Nîmes the so-called *petit
catéchisme* took place following the midday meal and before the afternoon sermon service; at La Rochelle, it was set for two o'clock. In both towns, children were examined and asked to "respond by turn."[19] The Sunday "small
catechism" lessons at Nîmes may have also included women and servants, a
pattern consistent with practice elsewhere in the Reformed world. In still
other locales, the Sunday catechism included the entire congregation.[20] How
many churches worked diligently at this sort of training and how successful
they were remains unknown. A pastor from Mas-Grenier complained that
many in his church, after thirty years of religious instruction, were still ignorant of basic prayers.[21] Most people, on the other hand, appear to have been
able to recite the Lord's Prayer and a few sacred songs from memory, even
though it is difficult to gauge how well they understood the meaning.

Adults participated in catechism, too. Some were recent converts or back-
sliders who, like the children, needed to learn basic beliefs and prayers.
Churches tended, moreover, to view catechism as a basic religious obligation
for all persons, not unlike the requirement to attend sermon services. There

---

647; Penny Roberts, "The Demands and Dangers of the Reformed Ministry in Troyes, 1552–
1572," in *The Reformation of the Parishes*, ed. A. Pettegree (Manchester: Manchester University
Press, 1993), 167.

[18]AD, Gers, 23067, 3 mars 1594. Gregory Hanlon, *Confession and Community in Seventeenth-Century France: Catholic and Protestant Coexistence in Aquitaine* (Philadelphia: University of
Pennsylvania Press, 1993), 133–134; Higman, *La diffusion*, 117.

[19]Chareyre, "Consistoire et catéchèse," *Catéchismes et Confessions de foi*, 404–405, 410;
Etienne Trocmé, "L'Eglise Réformée de La Rochelle jusqu'en 1628," *Bulletin de la Société de
l'Histoire du Protestantisme Français* (hereafter *BSHPF*) 98 (1952): 177–178. Serr, *Montauban*, 115–
116.

[20]Garrisson-Estèbe, *Protestants du Midi*, 233–236.

[21]AN, TT 252, dossier 5, 1 septembre 1590, 13 avril 1591.

was, in connection with this concept, a general adult catechism, sometimes known as the *grand catéchisme*, which was closely tied to the life of worship and the communion service that took place four times annually, on Easter, Pentecost, early September, and at Christmastide. To avoid profanation of the Eucharist, the elders and deacons in their role as religious watchdogs distributed metal entry tokens or *méreaux* to those members of the faithful whom they deemed qualified by virtue of correct belief and proper conduct. No one could participate in the Lord's Supper without presenting her or his token at the temple door.

This control mechanism usually meant that Protestant men and women had to attend catechism lessons in the week or so preceding the communion service.[22] The custom at Montauban, for instance, was that the faithful were catechized and afterwards the elders distributed the communion tokens. The same was true at La Rochelle and Nîmes. The pastor at the small village of Durfort held a general catechism with the approach of each communion service and made a point of questioning the adult members of the congregation.[23] Elders of the Church of Montdardier, to cite another example, regularly notified all members of the congregation of their obligation to attend catechism in preparation for the celebration of the Lord's Supper. Instruction took place on Tuesday about two weeks before the communion service. These same elders also refused to allow persons from outlying villages, despite their distance from town, to receive the sacrament unless they had presented themselves for catechism at least once during the preceding year.[24] Ecclesiastical officials viewed attendance at catechism lessons as an absolute prerequisite for the Lord's Supper.

Some churches went further and drew up long lists of the catechized, which is to say, persons qualified to join in the sacramental meal. The deacons at Nîmes composed elaborate rosters and even made annotations regarding those whose understanding of the faith was satisfactory and, conversely, those whose catechism responses were inadequate.[25] Other churches were content merely to keep track of attendance. In 1584, church officials at Aimargues counted 324 persons (151 men and 173 women) who received catechism

---

[22]AD, Gers, 23015, 20 mai 1594, 25 mai 1595, 24 novembre 1596, 24 février 1596, 25 novembre 1596. Bibliothèque de l'Arsenal, Ms 6563, fols. 54, 64; Bibliothèque de la Société de l'Histoire du Protestantisme Français, Ms 222/1, fol. 34v.

[23]Béatrice Ducret, *Le consistoire et la communauté réformée de Durfort au XVIIe siècle (1634–1667)* (Mémoire de maîtrise: Université Sorbonne–Paris I, 1994), 77–78.

[24]AD, Tarn-et-Garonne, 1:1, fol. 358; "L'Ancienne Eglise Réformée de Montdardier," *BSHPF* 22 (1873): 67.

[25]Chareyre, "Consistoire et catéchèse," *Catéchismes et Confessions de foi*, p. 404.

instruction. The figure roughly corresponded to the number of persons who participated in the Lord's Supper.[26] Throughout the 1570s, the Reformed Church ofVendémian maintained analogous lists of those "who had been catechized" and were thereby eligible to receive the sacrament.[27] The Vendémian rosters, however, listed far more men than women, suggesting that the church tended to count heads of household rather than individuals. Catechism may have been, in this sense, yet another obligation for which the Reformed consistory held the *paterfamilias* responsible. In addition, formal education of any kind was a traditionally masculine reserve. Children's catechism instruction at Le Carla, for example, was heavily weighted toward boys. They consistently outnumbered girls, sometimes by three or four to one.[28]

Failure to attend catechism not only barred a person from reception of the Lord's Supper, but the consistory considered it a moral fault, deserving of punishment. A married woman from Saint-André neglected to partake of the Lord's Supper. When questioned by members of the consistory, she pleaded that she had not attended catechism and the subsequent communion service because she was not "well trained in the catechism." She feared that she would not know how to "respond properly." Church officials were unsympathetic.[29] The pastor and elders of Layrac, in like manner, scolded several married couples for their failure to attend catechism; and men from Saint-Amans were pointedly told to show better attendance at catechism.[30]

In the end, perhaps the most striking features of this attempt at mass education are the concentration on instruction for adults and the involvement of lay instructors. All catechism aimed at teaching the simple and unlearned. Reformed churches took it a step further in underscoring the obligatory nature of instruction for adults, perhaps even more than for children, and conditioning reception of the Lord's Supper upon attendance. In truth, catechizing adults as well as children was not unique to French Protestants. English and German reformers were also vigorous and dedicated in this regard.[31] Accordingly, it may be misleading to think of catechism as directed principally at the young. Despite much of the rhetoric of the age, the practical insistence was upon adults. The Church of Nîmes, for example, complained about the noise

[26]Ibid., 408–409; Archives Communales, Aimargues, GG 30, fols. 25–30.

[27]AN, TT 275A, dossier 3, fols. 39–44.

[28]Bibliothèque Interuniversitaire de Toulouse, ms. 267, pp. 17, 18, 24, 28, 39, 54, 81, 83.

[29]AN, TT 268, dossier 9, fol. 651.

[30]AD, Gers, 23067, 27 et 29 décembre 1617; AD, Tarn, 1:8, 12 janvier 1592.

[31]Ian Green, *The Christian's ABC: Catechism and Catechizing in England, c. 1530–1740* (Oxford: Clarendon Press, 1996), 45–92; Gerald Strauss, *Luther's House of Learning: Indoctrination of the Young in the German Reformation* (Baltimore: Johns Hopkins University Press, 1978), 158.

that (presumably younger) children made at the *petits catéchismes* and urged mothers to leave them at home. As a practical matter, children in some communities may have only started catechism at about the age of twelve, which was the time when the church permitted them to receive the bread and wine in the Sacrament.[32]

Secondly, the participation of the laity as instructors and pupils differs not only from medieval religious tradition in which rudimentary catechism instruction for ordinary people was virtually nonexistent,[33] but it also contrasts with practice among Catholic Counter-Reformers. Catholic bishops imposed catechizing duties primarily upon parish priests.[34] The heavy responsibilities accorded Reformed deacons and elders underscores the "lay culture" that the Protestant Reformation fostered. An emerging middle group of lay persons from professional and mercantile backgrounds—men who could read, write, and who owned books—increasingly dominated the French Reformed churches, to include formal religious education for the faithful, both young and old.

These catechistical approaches bespeak, of course, a model to which churches aspired. Although the printed catechism provided a common text and national as well as provincial synods attempted to standardize procedures, there was a good deal of local variation regarding whom and how often, when and under what circumstances church leaders taught the faithful. Furthermore, catechism was more than the repetitious learning of prayers. It was also a widespread disciplinary device to instill confessional conformity and correct behavior. Simply getting people to attend, listen attentively, and respond when called upon was a major challenge. Eradicating old ways and laying down moral boundaries, teaching new prayers, and instilling the rudiments of the faith proved an arduous and unending task.

[32]Chareyre, "Consistoire et catéchèse," *Catéchismes et Confessions de foi*, 410; Serr, *Montauban*, 116.

[33]Jean Delumeau, "Prescription and Reality," in *Conscience and Casuistry in Early Modern Europe*, ed. E. Leites (Cambridge: Cambridge University Press, 1988), 147.

[34]John Bossy, "The Counter-Reformation and the People of Catholic Europe," *Past and Present*, no. 47 (May 1970): 64–69.

Detail from *The Holy Family,* Lucas Cranach, 1509.

Erasmus' Spiritual Homeland

The Evidence of His 1527 Will

Charles G. Nauert

ALTHOUGH ERASMUS OF ROTTERDAM explicitly declared himself a citizen of the world,[1] the question of how he conceived his identity in regional or national terms has elicited a number of studies, notably the much-cited article by James D. Tracy and a more recent piece with rather different conclusions by István Bejczy.[2] Both authors are aware that neither Erasmus nor any of his contemporaries had a national identity in the modern sense of the term. Yet the question of how he defined his own identity is of considerable importance, for it did much to determine where he chose to reside, how he regarded the church hierarchy at Rome, and how he interpreted the contemporary movement for religious, cultural, and educational reform in which he became one of his generation's most important figures. His clearest "national" or geographical self-identification was as a Hollander, for he was born and reared in the county of Holland and regularly affixed the name of his native city to his baptismal name (Erasmus) and the extra name that he added, Desiderius: Desiderius Erasmus of Rotterdam. Yet being born a Hollander meant that he was also born a German, since Holland was part of the German empire and was directly ruled by the imperial Habsburg dynasty. Since Holland was also one of the provinces ruled by the Burgundian dukes and their Habsburg successors, Erasmus also sometimes referred to himself as a Netherlander. The whole point of Bejczy's recent article is that the meaning of these national terms was vague and changeable, and in particular that the many years that Erasmus spent living in Upper Germany changed his sense of his own identity and his usage of the terms "Hollander," "German," and "Netherlander." Indeed, occasionally

---

[1]Roland H. Bainton, *Erasmus of Christendom* (New York: Charles Scribner's Sons, 1969), 114; Margaret Mann Phillips, *Erasmus and the Northern Renaissance* (London: Hodder & Stoughton, 1949), 3.

[2]James D. Tracy, "Erasmus Becomes a German," *Renaissance Quarterly* 21 (1968): 281–288; István Bejczy, "Erasmus Becomes a Netherlander," *Sixteenth Century Journal* 28 (1997): 387–399.

Erasmus even toyed with the idea that since in Roman antiquity the people of the Netherlands had been called Gallo-Germans, he might even be defined as a Gaul—a Frenchman.[3] Some light is shed on the question of Erasmus' view of his own place in the world by the distribution of copies of his collected works as he planned this distribution in the will he composed in 1527.

In general, Erasmus thought of himself more as a citizen of the total Christian society than as a citizen of any political entity. He traveled widely and lived in many places; and even during his years in Basel (1521–29), his longest stay in one place, he never sought citizenship, but was content to live as a respected resident alien. What determined his place of residence was the requirements of his scholarly work and a determination to avoid any obligations that might compromise the personal independence and international fame that he had attained through great exertions and careful crafting of his public image.[4] From about 1514, he had become famous and was constantly besieged by offers from princes and prelates urging him to settle in their territories. Leaving aside offers from places where there was no chance that he would ever settle for a long period, there were several offers he did consider. Always, of course, there was his native Netherlands, where he had a fixed residence from 1517 to 1521 at Louvain, where he had many highly placed friends, and which he acknowledged as his homeland. After his move to Basel, he gradually realized that unless he returned to the Netherlands, he would never receive any further payments of his imperial pension.[5] There were many reasons behind his failure to come back after he settled in Basel to work with the Froben press in 1521, notably his desire not to be drawn into the imperial policy of repressing heresy by force; but still he always thought of the Netherlands as home, as a place to which he might return.

England was another place where he had lived for a considerable period (1509–13) and where he had loyal and influential friends. An English benefice granted by the archbishop of Canterbury was one of his most reliable sources of income. In 1509, upon learning of the accession of Henry VIII to the throne, he had rushed from Italy to England, assured by his English friends

[3] *The Collected Works of Erasmus: The Correspondence of Erasmus* (Toronto: University of Toronto Press, 1974–), 3:303–309, ep. 421; henceforth cited by epistle (ep./epp.) number(s) as *CWE*. The same numeration system is valid for the standard Latin edition of Erasmus' letters, P. S. Allen et al., eds., *Opus epistolarum Des. Erasmi Roterodami*, 12 vols. (Oxford: Clarendon Press, 1906–58); see also Bejczy, "Erasmus Becomes a Netherlander," 341.

[4] The determination of Erasmus to create and project his own persona is the central theme of Lisa Jardine, *Erasmus, Man of Letters: The Construction of Charisma in Print* (Princeton: Princeton University Press, 1993).

[5] *CWE*, epp. 1408, 1582, esp. n. 1 of the English-language edition of *CWE*, ep. 1582.

that the new reign would provide munificent patronage. Experience, however, had taught him that except for a few men attached to the personal service of the king, no foreigner would receive a lucrative and permanent position. His many close friendships with leading men did not disappear, but by 1516, when he was deciding where to reside if he did not accompany Prince Charles to Spain, England never entered the picture as a place to settle. Although he was invited to accompany the Burgundian court to Spain, he never had an inclination to go there. The country was too far away, too alien.

But there were two contenders that he had to consider seriously as alternatives to Louvain and then to Basel. One of these was Rome. Both he and his defenders against his critics pointed out that three consecutive popes had endorsed his biblical and patristic scholarship and had invited him to settle in Rome and put his talents at the service of the Holy See. Leo X graciously accepted the dedication of the first edition of his Greek New Testament in 1516 and in 1518 issued a papal brief publicly endorsing his biblical scholarship, a document that Erasmus printed at the head of the second edition.[6] Adrian VI, a Netherlander who had known him at Louvain, sent him two warm, friendly letters of invitation, promising not only financial security but the company of other scholars and access to the city's rich libraries.[7] Clement VII sent him a friendly letter and a substantial gift of money.[8] Both Leo and Clement granted him valuable dispensations that further regularized his status as a former monk authorized to live in the secular world and to hold ecclesiastical benefices.[9]

The other serious offer that Erasmus did consider came from Francis I, king of France. In 1517, both Guillaume Budé, the most learned of all French humanists, and Guillaume Cop, personal physician to the king, wrote to inform Erasmus that Francis would grant him a valuable benefice if he would move to that country.[10] Erasmus replied politely but vaguely and did not move. A few years later in 1523, after he had settled in Basel, the king renewed his invitation. This time he made a far more specific offer, engaging to appoint Erasmus to a valuable sinecure that would ensure him freedom to pursue his scholarly work under royal patronage. The king even signed a personal letter

[6]*CWE*, ep. 384; CWE, ep. 864, dated December 10, 1518, and printed on the reverse of the title page of the second edition; see also CWE, epp. 832, 835, for evidence of Erasmus' efforts to secure this papal brief.

[7]*CWE*, epp. 1324, 1338. Adrian also sent a verbal message by Erasmus' friend Johannes Fabri, whom he was sending back to Germany to participate in negotiations on the religious crisis.

[8]*CWE*, epp. 1443B, 1466 (n. 3).

[9]For Leo's dispensation, *CWE*, ep. 518; for Clement's, *CWE*, ep. 1588.

[10]*CWE*, epp. 522, 523.

and sent a friend of Erasmus to deliver the letter and explain the details.[11] Budé chided Erasmus for his hesitation to accept such a munificent offer.[12] Erasmus responded by dedicating to King Francis his paraphrase on the gospel of Mark, but he did not come, partly because of the wars and partly because he felt that as a born subject and sworn councillor of Charles V he should not enter the service of the emperor's principal enemy.[13]

So Erasmus politely but definitively rejected both the offers from Rome and the offers from France. His reasons were complex. Reservations about the corruption of the Roman curia and about papal policy in Germany were among them. In addition, his letters clearly show that he did not much like Italy or Italians, even though he respected certain individuals and maintained a network of correspondents who kept him informed of developments at the curia.

In the case of France, he rejected a country where he had lived during his studies at Paris and where he felt more at home than he ever did in Italy. But though he had many friends and connections to influential individuals, he had never formed a close bond with the country's leading Christian humanist, Jacques Lefèvre d'Étaples, and his disciples. In 1516–17, Erasmus had reacted with fury to a publication of Lefèvre that implied that his textual notes to one New Testament passage (Heb. 2:7, an echo of Ps. 8:6) were not only mistaken but unspiritual and perhaps heretical.[14] Erasmus responded with an *Apologia* so devastating (and so clearly unanswerable) that Lefèvre did not even attempt to respond, though he let the offensive passage stand in his next edition.[14] Budé and other mutual friends smoothed over the conflict, but a residue of ill will remained. Furthermore, although Erasmus conducted an extensive correspondence with Budé and publicly acknowledged his erudition, an undercurrent of reserve and veiled hostility marked their relations.[15] Besides, though Erasmus

[11] *CWE*, ep. 1375.   [12] *CWE,* epp. 1439, 1446.

[13] The dedication to King Francis is *CWE*, ep. 1400, and a separate letter transmitting the gift is ep. 1403. Cf. ep. 1386 to Theodoricus Hezius, secretary to Pope Adrian VI, and ep. 1484 to François du Moulin, bishop of Condom; also ep. 1411 and ep. 1408, both of which express his sense of obligation to the emperor.

[14] Helmut Feld, "Der Humanistenstreit um Hebräer 2,7 (Psalm 8,6)," *Archiv für Reformationsgeschichte* 61 (1970): 5–35.

[15] André Stegmann, "Érasme et la France (1495–1520)," in *Colloquium Erasmianum: Actes du Colloque International réuni à Mons...* (Mons: Centre Universitaire de l'État, 1968), 275–297; Marie-Madeleine de la Garanderie, "Les relations d'Érasme avec Paris, au temps de son séjour aux Pays-Bas méridionaux (1516–1517)," in J[oseph]. Coppens, ed., *Scrinium Erasmianum*, 2 vols. (Leiden: E.J. Brill, 1969): 1:29–53; and Garanderie's introduction to her annotated French translation of the whole Erasmus-Budé correspondence, *La correspondance d'Érasme et de Guillaume Budé*, "De Pétrarque à Descartes," vol. 13 (Paris: Vrin, 1967). The relationship with France is also

in his younger years had been glad to publish works with Paris printers, none of them was the equal of his Basel publisher Johannes Froben.

So Erasmus never returned to Italy or to France, despite the lure of papal support and the "mountains of gold" dangled by the French king.[16] His original homeland, the Netherlands, still remained a possibility, but in fact he remained in Basel until after the Reformation gained control of Basel in 1529, when he left for Freiburg.

One influence on these decisions was how he perceived the relationship between his own values and the spirit of the various societies in which he might settle. England was friendly, but not a place where he could live. Italy was alien and in general not very friendly at all—and in his opinion its intellectual elite were not very deeply Christian, either. France was less alien but still a place where he deliberately chose not to live. The Netherlands was his native land, but also a place where he would inevitably have to become embroiled in all the conflicts of the Reformation.

His own spiritual or cultural relation to these regions is reflected with remarkable clarity in an important document that has long been known but has never been applied to an analysis of his regional or "national" affinities. In January 1527 at Basel he executed his first will. This will was replaced in 1533 by a second that has not survived and in 1536 by a third and final will.[17] The original will contains a unique provision directing that his trustee Bonifacius Amerbach and the three executors should use part of his wealth to publish an edition of his collected works, a plan that was actually carried out in 1540. In the present context, the most significant part of the will is the section that provides that twenty sets of the *Opera* should be specially bound and presented to specific recipients. The persons named, and also the persons not named, go far to reveal what Erasmus thought were his true spiritual, intellectual, and "national" affinities; and they certainly help to explain why despite his polite words, he never agreed to settle in Rome or in France. The list reflects his long-standing ties to England, even though he chose not to reside there. Six of the twenty copies were to go to England: to William Warham, archbishop of

---

treated in several excellent biographies of Erasmus, including the older ones by Preserved Smith, Johan Huizinga, Margaret Mann Phillips, and Roland H. Bainton, and recent ones by R. J. Schoeck, Léon-H. Halkin, and James D. Tracy.

[16]*CWE*, ep. 539.

[17]Allen, *Opus epistolarum*, 6: 503–506 (appendix 19); R. J. Schoeck, "Erasmus' Wills," appendix D in his *Erasmus of Europe*, 2 vols. (Edinburgh: Edinburgh University Press, 1990–93), 2:384–386.

Canterbury, his most reliable English patron; to three other English bishops, clearly (in his opinion) the best of the lot: Cuthbert Tunstall of London, John Longland of Lincoln, and John Fisher of Rochester; one to "Thomas More, English baron"; and one to the library of Queens' College, Cambridge, where he had lived during his last residence in England. Rather surprisingly, two copies were destined for Spain, a country he regarded as totally alien. But one of these was for the imperial library, and thus was really an acknowledgment of his obligations to the emperor, whose court just happened to be in Spain rather than in Germany. The second copy was for the archbishop of Toledo, Juan de Fonseca, whom his correspondents identified as the most powerful of his Spanish admirers. With one significant exception, all of the other copies went to Germany or the Netherlands. The two German copies went to representatives of Habsburg power in Germany: Archduke Ferdinand, brother of the emperor and direct ruler of the Austrian duchies and of the Habsburg territories in southwestern Germany, a prince who admired Erasmus; and to Cardinal Bernhard von Cles, bishop of Trent and Ferdinand's closest adviser. Three copies went to educational institutions in the Netherlands: Busleyden's College at Louvain, the famous Trilingual College of which Erasmus himself had been one of the original trustees and organizers; the College of the Lily at Louvain, where Erasmus had resided while living in Louvain; and a new humanistic college that a wealthy humanist, Pierre Cotrel, was trying to establish at Tournai.[18] The other Netherlands copies were for Franz van Cranevelt, a friend of long standing who was a judicial officer in the central law court at Mechelen; Lieven Huguenoys, abbot of the Benedictine abbey of St. Bavo's in Ghent, who had made manuscripts available for Erasmus' scholarly work; Marcus Laurinus, dean of the church of St. Donatian at Bruges, another old friend who had helped to arrange payment of Erasmus' income from a benefice at Courtrai; Nicolaas Everaerts, an old friend and sympathizer with humanistic church reform who was lord president of the Council of Holland; Herman Lethmaet, a Paris-trained theologian whose career at the imperial court and in the church Erasmus had assisted with letters of recommendation; and finally, the library of the monastery of Egmond, the oldest Benedictine abbey in the county of Holland. The one exceptional gift was a copy for Giambattista Egnazio of Venice, one of the scholars who had assisted Erasmus with the expanded edition of the *Adagia* published by Aldus in 1508. This was one of the few close scholarly relationships that Erasmus had maintained after

---

[18]Henry de Vocht, *History of the Foundation and Rise of the Collegium trilingue Lovaniense,* 4 vols. (Louvain: Bibliothèque de l'Université, 1951–55), 1:521–523. This bilingual college opened in 1525 but was not successful and closed again in 1530.

leaving Italy in 1509, and the intended gift appears to have been a mark of admiration for a talented classicist and a personal friend.[19]

This last gift to Egnazio underlines the intention of Erasmus to give presentation copies to those who shared his own values. It also impressively indicates how (at least in 1527) Erasmus conceived his own identity. Egnazio's is the only copy destined for Italy, the homeland of Renaissance humanism and nerve center of late medieval Catholicism. No copy was intended for any of the other prominent Florentine, Venetian, and Roman humanists, the group whom Erasmus would soon make the principal target of his *Ciceronianus* on account of their religious attitudes as well as their narrow stylistic purism.[20] Erasmus thought of Rome as an alien and unfriendly country in spiritual and intellectual terms as well as in nationality. So there was to be no presentation copy of Erasmus' *Opera* in the Vatican Library, even though Erasmus upheld papal authority over the church. Aside from the copy for one learned Venetian friend, there would be no copies at all for Italy.

And none for France! The lack of even a single presentation copy for anyone in France is striking—not the king, not his close friend Nicolas Bérault, not any of the wealthy and powerful bishops associated with the court—no one in France was to get Erasmus' collected works. Erasmus had a very clear sense of the parts of Latin Christendom with which he shared a common set of values. These regions were where he found true friends whose support for his life's work—the work collected in the planned edition—was reliable and durable. Italy and France and Spain were not among those regions; and this perception must have been one of the deeper, half-unconscious reasons why he did not settle there. His spiritual and intellectual affinities were with the countries to which he intended to present sets of his collected *Opera*: England, his native Netherlands, the Habsburg regions (and only those regions) of Germany. These lands were at the center of Erasmus' identity, with the single addition of Basel itself, the place where he freely chose to reside. Basel received none of the presentation copies, but the work of printing and editing was to

---

[19]M. J. C. Lowry, "Giambattista Egnazio," in *Contemporaries of Erasmus: A Biographical Register of the Renaissance and Reformation*, 3 vols. (Toronto: University of Toronto Press, 1985–87), 1:424–425.

[20]Erasmus' criticism of the pagan attitudes of the Italian and especially the curial humanists is expressed candidly, even in letters to hostile figures like Noël Béda (*CWE*, ep. 1581, lines 121–126) and, with somewhat more circumspection, to an influential curial humanist, one of the few whose moral integrity and spiritual seriousness he respected and admired, Jacopo Sadoleto (ep. 1586, lines 5–14). For the attitudes expressed in his *Ciceronianus*, see the introduction by Betty I. Knott to her translation of *Dialogus Ciceronianus*, in *Collected Works of Erasmus*, 28:324–336, esp. 328–331.

be done there, and the trustee and all of the executors of the will were living or had lived there, as did nearly all recipients of specific bequests of money or valuable objects. These regions and no others were Erasmus' true homeland.

Portrait of Erasmus, by Johann Eberlin von Günzburg, 1521

The Revenge of Titivillus

Paula L. Presley

TECHNOLOGY HAS BEEN BOTH CURSED AND PRAISED by scholars. Each significant technological development seems to act as a magnet: on one end are those repelled by newfangled changes; on the other, those who are keenly drawn by the attraction of new tools. Adaptability seems to be the key to survival among the ever-changing methods and tools. Any scholar of publishing may profit from a look at the long life of a Master Adapter: Titivillus. Evidence of the magnificent adaptability and durability of Titivillus abounds today in scholarly works.

Titivillus was born of monastic wit in the early centuries of Christianity, probably in Europe, as a demon who influenced worshippers to neglect their religious duties, especially the recitation of prayers and psalms. He was more extensively developed in the Middle Ages in *exempla,* short illustrations to demonstrate or elaborate a religious or moral truth or a theological doctrine.[1] His childhood antics and adolescent capriciousness were well recorded in the twelfth and thirteen centuries. Some of his early adulthood, apparently while he was seeking to "find himself," was spent in England. In the fifteenth and sixteenth centuries he reappeared in Germany and other European areas. Little is heard of him after that, but there is an abundance of evidence attesting to his continued existence and his splendid adaptation to technological advances in his field. Lately, in his more mature years, he seems to have become a specialist rather than a general practitioner of his craft.

In *Tractatus de Penitentia* (ca. 1285), John of Wales discusses prayer in church and tells of "titivillum" who appeared in a choir collecting "minucias et particulas psalmorum." John warned his readers against such negligence and its dire consequences. John of Wales' *Tractatus* preserves the first-known text to use the demon's name (rendered "Tutivillus"), although he admittedly depended upon an earlier source.[2]

---

[1] Margaret Jennings, "Titivillus—The Literary Career of the Recording Demon," *Studies in Philology* 74 (1977): 5–7.

[2] Jennings, "Titivillus," 17.

In Titivillus' younger years he had the task of collecting fragments of words dropped, skipped, or mumbled by either laity or clergy in the recitation of divine services. John of Wales' *Tractatus* and other documents warned the slothful:

> Fragments of words
> Titivillus collects,
> He burdens himself
> With a thousand a day.[3]

In his *Sermones Vulgares,* Jacques de Vitry (ca. 1220) describes the demon in an exemplum as having a bag into which he put his collected fragmina.[4] Titivillus was required to bring a thousand sacksful of such errors to the devil every day to be recorded for use on Judgment Day against the transgressors.[5]

Once Titivillus became old enough to write, he replaced his weighty sack with parchment and pen. It is recorded that as early as the beginning of the seventh century the abbot Aicardrius was hindered in his prayers by the demon, who was hiding in a corner with some sort of parchment.[6] After practice among the laity with his new scribal skills, Titivillus reappeared in divine services. There he recorded the gossip, mumbled prayers, poorly recited masses, and other "jangling" right on the spot. He especially liked to pick on slothful churchgoers uttering idle words[7] and choristers who were "janglers, cum jappers, nappers, galpers, quoque drawers, momlers, forskippers, overenners, sic overhippers ..." (see fig. 1).[8]

---

[3]"Fragmina verborum / Titivillus colligit horum. / Quibus die mille / Vicibus se sarcinat illle"; John of Wales, *Tractatus* or *Summa,* B. M. Royal 10, A, IX, fol. 40 vb, etc., cited by Jennings, "Titivillus," 16 n. 21; see also the anonymous "Versus de musica," from S. A. van Dijk, "Saint Bernard and the Instituta Patrum of Saint Gall," *Musica disciplina* 4 (1950): 109: "Fragmina verborum titivillus colligit horum. / Sicque die mille vicibus resarcinat ille. / Cantemus Domino. socii. cantemus honore. / Dulcis amor et personat ore pio," available for viewing at http://www.music.indiana.edu/tmo/12th/.

[4]Thomas F. Crane, ed., *The Exempla or Illustrative Stories from the Sermones Vulgares of Jacques de Vitry* (London, 1890).

[5]Drogin, *Medieval Calligraphy,* 18.

[6]Jennings, "Titivillus," 4; Titivillus had plenty of time to keep records if he wrote quickly: "A Pater Noster is twenty seconds. I say three when blanching almonds, to know when to take them out of the boiling water. An Ave is about 13 seconds. This is recited at a good speed, but not dropping any syllables for Titivillus to pick up"; see at www.pbm.com/~lindahl/rialto//measures-msg.htm.

[7]Jennings, "Titivillus," 10.

[8]British Museum, *A Catalogue of Lansdowne Manuscripts in the British Museum* (London, 1819), cited by Drogin, *Medieval Calligraphy,* 18.

Fig. 1. Titivillus recording the "jangling" of nuns right on the spot.

Titivillus' new ability to record immediately the errors of worshippers was attended with serious problems, however. In 1303 Robert of Brunne wrote about one kind of problem in his *Handlying Synne*. He tells of a "holy man hys messe songe." While the holy man was reading the Gospel, his deacon "lough a grete laghter an hy." When the celebrant took the deacon to task for laughing in the church service, the deacon explained that he had seen a demon sitting in the congregation between two women, busily noting their gossip on a "rolle." To make his roll large enough to write all the sins the women were committing, he tugged at one end of it and gnawed at the other. All the tugging and pulling caused the parchment to split apart and Titivillus banged his head on a nearby wall. Thereupon the deacon laughed because the demon had lost his newly recorded list of sins.[9] Titivillus, having lost the list, slunk away in embarrassment. In other versions of the story we find that when chorister sang more slowly and carefully or when a bold cleric laughed at Titivillus, the

[9]Robert Mannying (fl. 1288–1338), "Robert of Brunne's *Handlying synne* A.D. 1303, with those parts of the Anglo-French treatises on which it was founded ..." (London: Paul, Trench & Truebner for Early English Text Society, 1901), EETS o.s., no. 119.

parchment was immediately erased. As we will see, Titivillus never forgot this
phenomenon.

Titivillus acquired a good deal of experience in writing and eventually
became qualified to move into another area of religious life. His big opportunity came when Charlemagne, with the aid of the English monk Alcuin,
sought to establish a single script that would be recognizable throughout his
European empire. Charlemagne ordered all liturgical and classical works
recopied in the new Carolingian minuscule instead of their former "pagan"
scripts. According to Frederic W. Goudy, Charlemagne ordered that "every
abbot, bishop, and count should keep in permanent employment a qualified
copyist, who must write correctly, using the Roman letters only, and that
every monastic institution should maintain a room known as a scriptorium."[10]
Imagine the twinkle in his eye when Titivillus found work in these new build-
ings! The recopying of that many classical and liturgical works opened a new
phase of Titivillus' career.

Monks who were copyists had seemingly escaped major influence by
Titivillus since their work was scribal instead of oral. Now, however, things
would change. The monks labored with as much diligence as they could sum-
mon. Scribal accuracy was so important that copyists or scribes were forbidden
to change the copy before them, even when such copy was obviously in error.
For safety's sake, artificial light such as candles and lamps was forbidden in the
scriptorii.[11] No doubt this made Titivillus' work a good deal easier than it had
been when he worked near an altar or in another area of a church lit with candles. He could lurk in dark corners and under tables and benches, waiting for
a bored scribe's mind to wander. In this setting he combined his sack-carrying
duties with his scribal skills and accomplished his tasks so that they would be
recorded for the world to discover in centuries to follow, and yet he could
deliver the required sacksful of errors for their proper accounting.

Apparently Titivillus' powers grew so great that careful proofreading of
the newly written manuscripts did not render perfect copies, even when
proofread by more experienced monks. Some types of scribal errors of the
Middle Ages have been catalogued.[12] Besides mistakes induced by handwriting
styles, transposition, and changes in spellings and pronunciations, the largest

[10]Frederic W. Goudy, *The Alphabet and Elements of Lettering* (New York: Dover Publications, 1918), 53.

[11]Douglas C. McMurtrie, *The Book: The Story of Printing and Bookmaking* (London: Oxford University Press, 1943), 79.

[12]L. D. Reynolds and N. G. Wilson, *Scribes and Scholars: A Guide to the Transmission of Greek and Latin Literature* (Oxford: Clarendon, 1974), 200ff.

class of errors was omissions (the special domain of Titivillus). Thus we see the
demon busily afoot, snatching away parts of the new texts before the monks
had them inscribed. Sometimes he snatched away only a few letters, especially
if he could remove them from a place where a sequence of letters should have
been written more than once or repeated but was written only once (haplog-
raphy). On other occasions, if the same word was repeated close together with
a few intervening words, the poor scribe's eyes would skip from the first location of the word to the next, only a few inches across the page, and the intervening words would be omitted (homoarcton). If two words were in close
proximity and had the same beginning or ending (homoeoteleuton), Titivillus
could snatch away a few words or syllables without notice of the scribe. Aging
scribes with faulty eyesight were influenced to omit whole lines of text. L. D.
Reynolds remarks, "It should be added, however, that a large number of omissions occur *for no apparent reason* except the carelessness of the scribe; this is
particularly common in small words."[13] Knowing the wiles of Titivillus and his
sack-carrying task we can have no doubt about the disposition of those omissions. As if to make fun of the scribes, Titivillus sometimes caused errors of
addition (dittography). He was judicious in this jest, however, allowing only a
few letters or syllables to be added at a time.

As the years passed, Titivillus began to wax bolder. The *Cloisters Manuscript*
of 1325–28 was written with fifteen saints misplaced in the calendar and the
names of more than thirty saints misspelled.[14] A few hundred years of experience produced even more unbelievable errors. In 1561 a certain monk edited
the manuscript of *Anatomy of the Mass.* Fifteen pages of errata had to be added
to the 172-page work! The monk rightly attributed the omission to "the work
of the devil."[15]

Even while enjoying all this devilment among the scribes, Titivillus may
have felt pangs of what is now termed "job burnout" because as early as 1445
he was meddling with the newer developments of block and plate printing. In
that year an abbot of the Netherlands sent to Bruges for two copies of a doctrinal *gette en molle* from a scribe vendor, and when it arrived it was full of
errors.[16] One would think that a work produced by the slow process of block

---

[13] Ibid., 204 (emphasis added).

[14] Drogin, *Medieval Calligraphy,* 18.

[15] I. Disraeli, *Curiosities of Literature,* 3 vols. (Boston, 1834). This same incident is mentioned
by Geoffrey Ashall Glaister, *An Encyclopedia of the Book* (Cleveland: World, 1960), 325, where
Glaister explains the origin of the term "printer's devil."

[16] Glaister, *Encyclopedia,* 325.

or plate printing would have far fewer errors than a hastily inscribed book, but that was not the case.

Not only did he meddle with block and plate printing, but he followed many a European to the new universities that began to pop up all over the Continent. The demand for textbooks was so great that more and more scribes began to write faster and faster to keep up. Titivillus was comfortable among the professional copyists, mostly laymen, who appeared on the edges of the new university towns. The academic and theological milieu pleased him and he bustled among this new group of lay scribes, influencing them differently than he had the monks. Instead of committing only simple omissions or additions, these scribes in their haste developed an abundance of abbreviations, which are now almost impossible to decipher. All the parts of words omitted via the abbreviation system could be carried off in Titivillus' sack without causing a twinge of the lay scribes' consciences. Titivillus grew comfortable with book production in an academic atmosphere, never lost his attraction to scholarship and scholarly publications.

Even so, like many a university student who fancies himself a thespian, Titivillus was tempted to seek an acting career. We find him in England in the fifteenth century, typecast in a number of morality plans. In *Myroure of Our Ladye* he goes "bysely" about a choir gathering the "faylynges that eny made," and putting them into the "longe and greate poke hangyng about hys necke."[17] He also appeared in *Mankind*[18] and Towneley's *Judicum,* and he made appearances in other morality plays in Germany and France.[19] In *Mankind* the staging directions indicate that Titivillus is to have "a large head, probably a devil's mask, a net, a board and weeds."[20] He tries to thwart the good work of Mankind by placing the board under the earth. Mankind begins to dig in the earth to plant, finds he cannot dig very far, becomes discouraged, and leaves his work. Later Titivillus is seen scattering weeds among Mankind's garden. The lure of the theater and its unfamiliar roles didn't last long for Titivillus, perhaps because he could see no future recognition in such a profession, and he returned his more familiar and lasting work among scribes and European block and plate printers.

[17]Jennings, "Titivillus," 36.

[18]Mark Eccles, *The Marco Plays: The Castle of Perseverance; Wisdom; Mankind* (London: Oxford University Press for Early English Text Society, 1969), xli.

[19]Jennings, "Titivillus," appendix 2, p. 91.

[20]*Mankind* was presented by the Workshop Theatre in Camerino, Italy, in June 1996. See a photo of the characters, including Titivillus, at http://www.leeds.ac.uk/theatre/photos/mnknd-ph.htm.

New developments in the reproduction of written material intrigued Titivillus. The invention of moveable type was the greatest technological development to affect his profession and he adapted amazingly well. He confidently found an entrance into the new area of technology through his familiar field of religion. The Roman Catholic Church contracted in 1454 with Johann Gutenberg for multiple printed copies of the famous Mainz indulgences. Apparently Titivillus visited Gutenberg's printing establishment. Douglas C. McMurtrie tells us that there is evidence of at least three printings of this job because "although differing in slight details of spelling," the printing is otherwise identical.

One might speculate that if Gutenberg had not made his typefaces to resemble scribal hands, Titivillus might have been discouraged from influencing printers, but the talented and adaptable demon could accomplish his assignment against anyone using an art or skill that involved the visual reproduction of words. By now Titivillus was an adult, but he couldn't resist one adolescent prank in 1631. Aware as he must have been of Christian admonitions against sexual excesses and promiscuity, he succumbed to the temptation to snatch away one little word from that year's edition of the Authorized Version of the Bible. Such a simple omission as he had in mind could cause great distress in Puritan-influenced England if it were made in a selected verse. Hence we find that the removal of the little word *not* leaves the Holy Scriptures saying in Exod. 20:14, "Thou shalt commit adultery."

In the 1780s an English printer named Isaiah Thomas ordered some metal type from London's Fry Foundry, which was to be used for his "standing Bible." To thwart Titivillus, Thomas had the type set up, proofed, and then kept that way in order to print and reprint perfect copies of the Bible." No doubt other diligent men were able to escape the machinations of Titivillus, for we can find many beautifully set printed works of this period that are free from error. In the early centuries of Christianity many holy men escaped Titivillus' tricks, too, but as the demon became ever more skillful, fewer and fewer clerics remained faithful to their oral recitations. When he began to influence scribes there were fewer errors than in the scribal heyday of the university textbook. As printing replaced hand inscription, the more skilled Titivillus became in his ability to influence the work of printers.

This master of adaptation met challenges of printing with moveable type. Printers developed more and better high-speed printing devices; they also designed beautiful functional typefaces in the years following the birth of the printing profession. Instead of simply influencing the apprentices (who were called "printer's devils" early in the history of printing) as they set up type,

Titivillus learned how to influence the actual casting of the metal type, especially type that resembled handwriting since his experience had been with handwritten words.[21]

The next significant technological advance to affect Titivillus' career was the arrival of the computer and its use in typesetting. Again, his talent for adaptability met the new challenges and this technology even permitted him to exercise a certain degree of revenge to make amends for some embarrassment in earlier ages. Instead of slinking around with a worn sack or unwieldy parchment and leaky inkpen, Titivillus, in the waning decades of the twentieth century, can work anonymously alongside modern text compositors who use computerized typographic systems. Titivillus' *coup de maître* in the pursuit of revenge was a well-known and respected scholarly journal produced in the Heartland region of the United States whose editors were academic holy men, Protestants, at whose expense Titivillus could have a laugh. There, the pages of the journal were hand-keyed on disks. The disks were hand-carried to the phototypesetting machine that produced long strips of galleys on phototypesetting paper, which were developed in a darkroom in a chemical bath. The galleys were photocopied and to authors for proofing. Meanwhile, the galleys were run through a machine that spread a thin coat of wax on the back of each strip. The waxed strips were cut in the appropriate places with a sharp knife, and the pieces were arranged on layout boards that were aligned on a light table (fig. 2). When author's emendations were made, new lines or paragraphs were typeset, developed, and composed on the layout.

On one occasion, after the editor had sent galleys of a journal article to its author, Titivillus secretly erased the computer disk on which the article was stored. That deftly executed act netted him at least three sacksful of words to register against the editor, not counting the erased footnotes which filled another one or two sacks to be registered against the typesetter. Undaunted, the editor (apparently forgetting the origin of the term "printer's devil" for apprentice typesetters) had the type hastily reset on another disk by a student typographer. Because time was short and the camera-ready copy of the journal had to be delivered to the printer, the proofreader missed Titivillus' additional sally—accomplished by way of the same jest used in centuries past: dittography.

Titivillus had never disposed of the little word *not* which he had extracted from the 1631 "adulterous Bible." Perhaps he remembered the words of Rev. 12:12, "for the devil is come … having great wrath, because he knows that he

[21]For example the typeface used by Aldus Manutius' Aldine Press for Pietro Bembo's *De Aetna* (1495) was modeled on the handwriting of the Renaissance scribe Giovanni Tagliente.

Fig. 2. Layout table from the 1980s, used by Titivillus.

has but a short time," and he swiftly inserted *not* on the newly reset disk—in the most effective place he could find to accomplish his wrathful revenge: the author's thesis sentence—thus negating the remainder of a carefully crafted work. Titivillus now became heady with revenge. He was not finished with that author, the holy editor, nor the "printer's devil." When the editor graciously provided an errata sheet for the next edition of the journal, Titivillus slyly inserted an extra letter *t* in the word *errata*. Now he would see if a holy man would laugh at him again![22]

The technological age has allowed Titivillus time to play, and he can be found on the World Wide Web as a character in an electronic game called *In Nomine*. The game's designer claims, "For *In Nomine*, I'd say Titivillus has had a hand in the recent popularity of internet communications. Although not responsible for the creation of the internet, he immediately saw the potential

[22]The citation for this article shall remain anonymous; it is well known to its author, the journal editors, and the typographer.

to further his Word. Titivillus has spawned newsgroups, mailing lists, IRC discussion, and MU's. In the past few years his records (which have long since been transferred to computer) have swelled at an incredible rate."[23]

Scholars and publishers, beware! Titivillus may play around, but his work is never finished.

[23]Steve Jackson, on http://www.sijgames.com/in-nomine/articles/INChar/.

Reader, how can you wish to see,
Each proof from errors always free!
When next in gall you dip your pen,
Reflect, that Printers are but men!
Why then expect in them to trace,
What's not found in the human race?
Should Providence this blessing send,
From that hour must your bus'ness end.

OUT OF PRINT

The Decline of Catholic Printed Sermons in France, 1530–1560

Larissa Juliet Taylor

DURING THE INCUNABULAR PERIOD, the printing of sermons reached astonishing proportions as churchmen and preachers began to comprehend the almost limitless possibilities it offered for teaching clergy and, indirectly, the laity. Lawrence Duggan has shown that more than five thousand volumes of sermons and preaching aids were printed in Europe in the years between 1460 and 1500;[1] at least one quarter of all books printed in Strasbourg before 1500 were sermons.[2] My own research on French sermons suggests that the printing of sermon editions attained a peak between 1510 and 1520 that was not matched at any point later in the sixteenth century.[3] Most of the demand for printed sermons came from other preachers, who were encouraged to use these books to improve their preaching skills. They would have been of little value to the laity, as sermons were translated into Latin for printing to make them accessible to preachers all over Europe.

If sermon printing in pre-Reformation France was big business, the same cannot be said after the Reformation. Although editions continued to be printed in lower numbers in the 1520s, there was a dramatic decline in the printing of sermons after 1530 that suggests a paradox. Why, just as the Lutheran and Swiss evangelicals began to spread their message even in Paris, did Catholic preachers lose interest in publishing their sermons? Did Catholic churchmen, as David Nicholls has suggested in his study of Rouen, fail to recognize the seriousness of the threat?[4] Did they assume that a religion that had

---

[1]Lawrence Duggan, "The Unresponsiveness of the Late Medieval Church: A Reconsideration," *Sixteenth Century Journal* 9 (1978): 19.

[2]Miriam Chrisman, *Lay Culture, Learned Culture* (New Haven: Yale University Press, 1982), 84.

[3]Larissa Taylor, *Soldiers of Christ: Preaching in Late Medieval and Reformation France* (New York: Oxford University Press, 1992), figs. 1, 5.

[4]David Nicholls, "Inertia and Reform in the Pre-Tridentine French Church: The

endured for more than fifteen hundred years was invulnerable? Some preachers may have failed to apprehend the dangers of the situation, but the connection that Nicholls and others make between the preaching of sermons and
their publication is unwarranted.[5] Archival evidence proves that preaching
continued as much as before; it was the printing of sermons that declined pre-
cipitously. The printing history of other religious books in France does not
match that of sermons. In a preliminary tabulation of all religious books
printed in sixteenth-century France, the St. Andrews Reformation Institute
found the following:[6]

Table 1: Preliminary Tabulation of French Sixteenth-Century Printed
Religious Books

Decade	Books Printed
1500–09	221
1510–19	261
1520–29	287
1530–39	446
1540–49	726
1550–59	1,171
1560–69	2,893
1570–79	1,656
1580–89	2,693
1590–99	2,201

This shows that when sermons were reaching their peak of publication before
1520, they comprised a much more substantial part of the whole than in later
years. It should be noted that while religious publications generally reached
their peak in the later decades,[7] there was a consistent increase in such publications from 1530 to 1560. Sermons were the exception.

Response to Protestantism in the Diocese of Rouen, 1520–1540," *Journal of Ecclesiastical History*
32 (1981): 196.

[5]Nicholls, "Inertia and Reform," 191; see also Marc Venard, "L'église d'Avignon au XVIe
siècle" (Ph.D. diss., Université de Paris IV, 1977), 1:441.

[6]St. Andrews Reformation Studies Institute, "The Sixteenth Century French Religious
Book Project: Annual Report 1996–97" (Sept. 1997): 4.

[7]See also Francis M. Higman, "Theology in French: Religious Pamphlets from the
Counter-Reformation," *Renaissance and Modern Studies* 23(1979): 130.

In *Soldiers of Christ,* I offer several possible explanations for this sudden decrease in the printing of Catholic sermons. The very enthusiasm that had initially greeted the production of sermon editions may have been partially responsible for their decline. So many sermons had been printed in the six decades before the Reformation that few monasteries or convent libraries would have been without at least some collections of classical and contemporary sermons. By midcentury, some preachers active in France had vast personal libraries that included substantial collections of sermons.[8] By 1530, most preachers had either personal or collective access to numerous volumes. Anne Thayer, studying model sermon collections throughout western Europe, situates the decline in sermon printing even earlier:

> Although my data for the first two decades of the sixteenth century is not as complete as it is for the fifteenth, there seems to be a real falling off in the production of model sermon collections in the last twenty year period [1500–20]. This overall picture is confirmed by Chrisman's study of printing in Strasbourg where there were 106 editions of sermon collections between 1480 and 1500, but only thirty-five in the next twenty years.... There is also some indication that the market was becoming saturated at this time. In 1503, the printer Anton Koberger wrote to his associate Johannes Amerbach, "One has the priests so completely trained with books, and so drained of money, that they no longer want to buy them."[9]

This glut on the market would have only become worse over time. The decline in the printing of sermons may also relate to censorship. Although censorship had been instituted almost immediately after Luther's Ninety-Five Theses reached France, its implementation was relatively uncommon in the early decades of the Reformation. From 1520 to 1540, eleven printed books and twelve manuscripts were condemned by the Sorbonne; only after 1540

---

[8]Claude Guilliaud (1493–1551) amassed a library of some fifteen hundred volumes over his lifetime. Less than one third were still extant in the late nineteenth and early twentieth centuries when two sets of investigators catalogued the books. See Marie Pellechet, *Catalogue des livres de la bibliothèque d'un chanoine d'Autun: Claude Guilliaud, 1493–1551,* new ser. (Autun: Mémoires de la société Éduenne, 1890); A. Gillot and Charles Boëll, *Supplément au catalogue des livres de la bibliothèque d'un chanoine d'Autun: Claude Guilliaud, 1493–1551,* new ser. (Autun: Mémoires de la société Éduenne, 1910). Among the sermons owned by Guilliaud were volumes by contemporaries, including Guillaume Pepin (c. 1465–1533) and Jean Raulin (1443–1515).

[9]Anne Thiel Thayer, "Penitence and Preaching on the Eve of the Reformation: A Comparative Overview from Frequently Printed Model Sermon Collections, 1450–1520" (Ph.D. diss., Harvard University, 1996), 45–46.

was censorship consistently employed to control heretical literature.[10] Even the draconian measures ordered against printing by Francis I in the wake of the Affair of the Placards were soon relaxed. The edicts of July 1542 and June 1551 marked an important turning point toward the efficient and systematic censorship of books.[11] Yet, as Francis Higman remarks, "The year 1536 marks a curious hiatus in the evolution of religious printing in French. All the major printers so far involved in Reformed or evangelical texts disappear almost simultaneously...."[12] While censorship was obviously aimed at heretical works, the resultant delays and perhaps even the fear of inadvertently printing a heterodox opinion may have had a chilling effect on both authors and publishers. This is not far-fetched. As early as 1525, when the publisher Claude Chevallon tried to reprint Michel Menot's 1519 *Carême de Tours,* he was told by a representative of the Faculty of Theology that he could do so only if he omitted statements that condemned excommunication for temporal matters.[13]

Royal policy may also have discouraged Catholic preachers from printing their sermons. Before the Affair of the Placards, Catholic preachers such as François Le Picart (1504–56) suffered exile and imprisonment for their incendiary Lenten preaching against the reformers.[14] If the delivered sermons could cause serious problems for orthodox preachers, how willing would they be to commit them to print?

All of these possibilities—a glut of the market, censorship, and fear of royal reprisals—may well have inhibited the printing of Catholic sermons between 1530 and 1560, but there is a stronger reason. A clue may be found in the attitude of many French-speaking Protestant preachers. Perhaps because of their faith in a preacher's inspiration by the Holy Spirit, Calvinists did not for the most part share the interest of pre-Reformation preachers in preserving their sermons:

> The reformers showed a certain indifference toward the sermons pronounced by their pastors. Thus during an entire century ... they hardly thought at all about publishing them. From Farel and Viret we have no sermon printed during their lifetime. Beza only published his

---

[10]Francis M. Higman, *Censorship and the Sorbonne: A Bibliographical Study of Books in French Censured by the Faculty of Theology of the University of Paris, 1520–1551* (Geneva: Droz, 1979), 49.

[11]Ibid., 52, 64.

[12]Francis Higman, *Piety and the People: Religious Printing in French, 1511–1551* (St. Andrews: Scolar Press, 1997), 16.

[13]James Farge, *Biographical Register of Paris Doctors of Theology, 1500–1535* (Toronto: Pontifical Institute of Medieval Studies, 1980), 386–387.

[14]Taylor, *Soldiers of Christ,* 218.

sermons at the end of his career. In German Switzerland it was the same. There were only two exceptions to this rule: Bullinger and Calvin.[15]

Among the only Catholic sermons from this period that found their way into print were those delivered by Le Picart, but even they were not printed until after his death. The first volume of his sermons was printed by the Reims' publisher Nicolas Bacquenois in 1557,[16] but most appeared after 1560.[17] The provenance of these sermons offers clues to the thinking of the most popular Catholic preacher in Paris, beliefs that may link him to the thought of many of the reformers. René Benoist, Le Picart's successor at Saint-Germain l'Auxerrois, investigated the proliferation of sermons reputedly by Le Picart:

> I considered how by his grace I had familiar access to him and often saw his library, yet I never heard him say one word to the effect that he had written, or proposed to write, anything, nor did I see any sign of writings among his books. What really dissuaded me from receiving these sermons as his work was that during the year that it pleased God … to call him to Him, in the last three months of his life, that is, June, July and August [1556], he was in Reims in Champagne, where he had been sent … by Monseigneur the Most Illustrious Prince and Most Reverend Cardinal Charles of Lorraine. I was charged to preach in his stead at Saint-Germain l'Auxerrois on Sundays and feast days. I stayed in his room, and used his books, among which I saw no sign of composition or even compilation for the purpose of printing. Similarly, upon his return, in the short time that preceded his death, I was often with him and neither by words nor any other sign did he indicate he had something to publish, or even that he had any desire to do so. Considering all these things, I was completely unwilling to believe that these written sermons were his, and I disdained to read them.[18]

---

[15]Edmond Grin, "Deux sermons de Pierre Viret, leurs thèmes théologiques et leur actualité," *Theologische Zeitschrift* 18 (1962), 116.

[16]François Le Picart, *Instruction et form de prier Dieu en vraye & parfaite oraison, faite en forme de sermons, sur l'Oraison Dominicale, par M. François le Picart, Docteur en Théologie* (Reims: Nicolas Bacquenois, 1557).

[17]The first work by Nicolas Chesneau appeared in 1560, with later volumes and editions in 1562, 1563, 1565, 1566, and 1574; Farge, *Biographical Register*, 265–266.

[18]René Benoist, "Preface" in François Le Picart, *Les sermons et instructions chrestiennes, pour tous les iours de Caresme, & Feries de Pasques: Enrichis d'un sermon pour le iour & feste de l'annonciation de la vierge Marie* (Paris: Nicolas Chesneau, 1566), fols. 3–4.

Benoist's suspicions were heightened by the rapidity with which successive volumes appeared: "soon they were seen in the hands of sincere and faithful Christians, both learned and unlearned, who held them in great esteem, saying that they had found great consolation and edification in reading them. ..." Benoist flipped through the pages and skimmed a few passages, but felt confirmed in his initial opinion. His cursory examination forced him to admit the sermons were sound in doctrine, so he decided to spend some time reading them. "After a short time, I began to develop a taste for them, and feeling the passion for the faith contained in them, slowly I began to change my mind."[19] But the excellence and purity of doctrine in the sermons did not prove they were the work of Le Picart. Benoist was impressed, however, that they had been published by a longtime acquaintance, Nicolas Chesneau, the future canon and dean of Saint-Symphorien in Reims.[20] Chesneau was a man known for his faith, prudence, and probity. Moreover, the care with which the sermons had been collected, edited, and printed fit what Benoist knew of the character of the man. Still in some doubt, Benoist decided to speak directly with Chesneau about the matter.

> In view of my belief that Le Picart had written nothing, I wanted to know how he had come into the possession of these sermons. Chesneau explained everything to me—how he had gathered them from those who regularly attended the sermons of this learned man. They had taken the sermons down as diligently as possible, without changing (or only very little, as sometimes happens) a sentence or a word. Chesneau then showed me diverse examples of the said sermons, gathered from several people who had been frequent auditors, and who had assiduously written down and collected them. It simply could not be denied.[21]

Benoist, however well he came to know Le Picart at the end of his life, had had fewer opportunities than many to hear his sermons, as he had only entered the Collège de Navarre for advanced theological studies in 1556,[22] the year of Le Picart's death. As Benoist began a close reading of the sermons, he

---

[19]Benoist, "Preface," *Caresme*, fol. 4.

[20]Also known as Querculus, Chesneau had studied and taught at the Collège de la Marche in Paris. An author of poems in Latin, Chesneau specialized in printing works of piety and ecclesiastical history in translation. In 1557, the cardinal of Lorraine appointed him as a preacher for the stations of Lent in Reims, and in 1574 he was given the post at Saint-Symphorien; see Pierre Desportes et al., *Histoire de Reims* (Toulouse: Privat, 1983), 231.

[21]Benoist, "Preface," *Caresme*, fol. 5.

[22]Émile Pasquier, *René Benoist: Le Pape des Halles (1521–1608)* (Paris: Picard, 1913), 42.

was struck by their popular nature, surprising to him in view of Le Picart's erudition and reputation as both a preacher and teacher. Then he remembered the criticisms he had heard voiced by heretics, who mocked Le Picart for his simple style, failing to understand that the mark of an excellent preacher was his ability to accommodate himself to the capacity of his listeners.

> My friends, I saw nothing there that persuaded me that the sermons belonged to anyone but the man to whom they were attributed. To prove this to those who want to be more certain, I ask them to refresh their memory about Le Picart's manner of preaching and then read these sermons, and I promise that then they will say these are his true and own works, and will praise God to have given them this good and grace. No longer able to hear the clear sound of this Evangelical Trumpet, they can now read them at their ease and in comfort in their own homes, participating in the same Word of God preached by this learned and virtuous man.... It should not be thought that these sermons have less authority for having been written down by someone else and not by him..., for just as the words of a president of *parlement* are written down by several clerks after being pronounced by the said president, they have no less authority and efficacy than if he had written them personally. And just as the president signs the document to verify the writing of the clerk, so these present sermons have been signed and approved as Christian and Catholic by the doctors of the Faculty of Theology. They have decided not to change even some statements that appear puerile, in order that the sermons should live on in their own form, and be truly represented as they were given and faithfully collected, not by one or two only, but by several learned and diligent men. As the writings and reports were sometimes slightly different..., they have been compared and the one closest to what was preached was chosen.[23]

Benoist offers a hypothesis about Le Picart's reluctance to publish the sermons himself:

> The greatest and most knowledgeable men customarily have written nothing or only a few things, unless they have been practically constrained to do so, thinking it enough, in fact even more important, to engrave their knowledge on the spirits of men and not amuse themselves by committing it to insensate paper. Because to teach, retain

[23]Benoist, "Preface," *Caresme,* fol. 5.

and persuade men by words is a much greater thing than to write
something down without resistance at one's convenience. So it was
with the great and divine philosopher Socrates. So too with our
heavenly doctor Jesus Christ, who didn't write down or give anything
to his Apostles to write down, but preached and announced the gospel.... But God, the author of this knowledge and virtue, wanted
these gifts and grace to multiply and profit others, so he would not
permit their memory to be effaced.... [A]nd so God did not want the
memory of this holy and virtuous person our master François Le
Picart who, in the judgment of all who knew him, had led a Christian and irreproachable life and edified the Church of Jesus Christ by
the preaching of the Word of God, to be extinguished or even less-
ened by his death.[24]

Benoist said that it was God's will that the people of Paris and indeed of all
Christianity could still hear Le Picart preach through his works.

At the beginning of this essay, the question was posed as to why, at the
most critical juncture for the Catholic faith in France, preachers lost interest in
printing their sermons. The answer to this enigma can be found in the question itself. It was precisely because the faith in France had approached a cross-
roads—printing sermons, fixing forever their form, content, and structure,
would have been the least effective means of responding to the Protestant
threat. Before the implantation of a Calvinist church in Paris in 1555 there was
simply no unified heretical threat. Sermons needed to be fluid and responsive
to changing circumstances. Le Picart's apparent total lack of interest in printing his sermons shows that (1) he felt he had more urgent and pressing
demands on his time—preaching correct belief and warning his listeners
against heresy; (2) he did not feel it was especially important to publish his sermons, for during his lifetime he had seen conditions in the capital change dramatically; and (3) he may have been in agreement with the reformers on the
subject of printing sermons, believing that the inspiration of the Holy Spirit
was more important to an effective preacher than ready-made sermons. Had
conditions not fluctuated so much between 1530 and 1556, and had the threat
been less serious, he might have felt differently.

Finally, a major linguistic shift occurred during Le Picart's lifetime that
would have an impact on sermon language and structure as well as on printing. Francis Higman's study of all religious books printed in French from 1511

---

[24]Benoist, "Preface," *Caresme*, fols. 5–6.

to 1551 confirms the absence of Catholic sermon printing in these years,[25] which may relate to dramatic changes in language usage. Earlier sermons had all been printed in Latin, and are not included in his study, which is limited to the vernacular; the years between 1511 and 1551 mark the period of transition from Latin to French in the printing of religious books. Sermons were caught in this transition, for it was not until the 1560s that Catholics seem to have realized the potential for propaganda offered by printing popular sermons in French. Le Picart's sermons printed in the 1560s constituted the first major collection of Catholic sermons printed in French. This dramatic change from earlier publishing efforts marked not only the progress of the vernacular, but the perceived need to deal with heretics on an equal footing. The structure of Le Picart's sermons bears no resemblance to that found in sermons of only a generation earlier, which followed the elaborate method of division and subdivision known as the modern method. This was undoubtedly a response to the heretical threat as well as changing Catholic homiletic theory and practice being explored in Rome and elsewhere. With so many changes in their own lifetimes, how could Catholic preachers confidently publish sermons that would be useful to later preachers and lay men and women?

[25]A tabulation of all the sermons, homilies, and postils adds up to only forty-four editions (C70, C111, E54–56, E58–59, F3–4, G26, G58, H10, H12–14, I3–4, L92, L110, L120–122, M58, O4, P25–34, Q1, S14–15, T8–9, V49–53). Of these, most are by German and Swiss reformers or Church Fathers. Among the only Catholic sermons by contemporary preachers were those by Jean de Gaigny and Thomas Illyricus, which were individual sermons rather than collections; see Higman, *Piety and the People*.

INDEX LIBRORVM
PROHIBITORⱯVM

*CVM REGVLIS CONFECTIS PER
Patres à Tridentina Synodɔ deleƈtos, authori-
tate Sanƈtiſſ. D. N. Pij IIII. Pont.
Max. comprobatus.*

F. *Pet. Quintianus Inq.Pap.cōceſſit licentiä reimpri.*

Impreſſum P A P I AE *in AEdibus S.* Petri in Cœlo
Aurco. M D LXVII.

MERETRIX EST STAMPIFICATA

Gendering the Printing Press

Raymond B. Waddington

IN TYPICAL ORACULAR STYLE, Marshall McLuhan once proclaimed, "The printing press was at first mistaken for an engine of immortality by everybody except Shakespeare."[1] His easy collapsing of the century between Gutenberg's Bible and Shakespeare's birth oversimplifies considerably the historical evidence. Elizabeth Eisenstein correctly observes, "For at least fifty years after the shift [from manuscript to print] there is no striking evidence of cultural change; one must wait until a full century after Gutenberg before the outlines of new world pictures begin to emerge into view."[2]

During that first half-century or so, reactions to the Gutenberg era were as thoroughly mixed and contradictory as are the responses to the shift from print to electronic culture in our own time. Polydore Vergil saluted the invention with unstinting praise for its efficiency and reliability:

> Truely the commodity of Libraries is very profitable and necessary; but in comparison of the Art of Printing, it is nothing; both because one man may Print more in one day, then many men in many years could write: And also it preserveth both Greek and Latine Authors from the danger of corruption.[3]

Predictably, however, a litany of stock complaints rapidly emerged in response to mechanical printing. On the one hand, the printers themselves were suspect in character, motives, and competence; on the other, the proliferation of previously inaccessible works in cheap editions fostered fears that

[1]Marshall McLuhan, *The Gutenberg Galaxy* (Toronto: University of Toronto Press, 1962), 202.

[2]Elizabeth Eisenstein, *The Printing Press as an Agent of Change* (Cambridge: Cambridge University Press, 1980), 33.

[3]Thomas Langley, trans., *An Abridgement of the Works Of the most Learned Polidore Virgil, Being an History of The Inventors* (1546; London, 1659), 85.

both texts and readers would be corrupted—indeed, that knowledge itself would be debased as the demography of readership changed. Gargantua's letter to Pantagruel (1532) celebrates the "elegant and accurate art of printing" as an invention "of divine inspiration" and describes its rather unsettling consequences: "I find robbers, hangmen, freebooters, and grooms nowadays more learned than the doctors and preachers were in my time. Why, the very women and girls aspire to the glory and reach out for the celestial manna of sound learning."[4]

Less convinced than Rabelais of the accuracy, Johannes Murmellios swore that the devil himself must be responsible for the printing errors that undo all the good of this marvelous invention.[5] Pietro Aretino sourly observed that "you would sooner find a chaste and sober Rome than a book without misprints."[6] The humanists who supplied or prepared manuscripts for the press frequently looked down upon printers as illiterate vulgarians, motivated only by avarice, whose miserly unwillingness to pay "correctores" resulted in the continual degeneration of texts.[7] Printers defended themselves by charging that authors and editors supplied them with bad copy.[8] Even an Aldo Manuzio, who presided over an establishment that Martin Lowry has described as a "now almost incredible mixture of the sweat shop, the boarding house, and the research institute,"[9] was not invulnerable to criticism, as his relations with Erasmus prove.

In October 1507 Erasmus wrote an obsequious letter to Aldo, asking that he publish a new edition of Erasmus' Euripides translation and saying that his work would be immortal if it were printed by the Aldine Press. The next year Erasmus came to Venice, living from March or April through December as a guest in the house of Andrea Torresani, Aldo's father-in-law and senior partner. During this time Erasmus prepared copy for an expanded edition of his *Adagia*,

---

[4] *The Histories of Gargantua and Pantagruel*, trans. J. M. Cohen (Bungay, Suffolk: Penguin, 1955), 2:8, 194. For Rabelais' own relations with printers, see Michael B. Kline, *Rabelais and the Age of Printing*, Études Rabelaisiennes, vol. 4 (Geneva: Droz, 1963).

[5] Cited by Gilbert Tournoy, "Juan Luis Vives and the World of Printing," *Gutenberg Jahrbuch* 69 (1994): 129–148, at 147.

[6] To Jacopo Barbo (December 10, 1537), trans. Thomas Caldecot Chubb, *The Letters of Pietro Aretino* (n.p.: Archon Books, 1967), 118.

[7] See Brian Richardson, *Print Culture in Renaissance Italy* (Cambridge: Cambridge University Press, 1994), 11–13.

[8] See Tournoy, "Juan Luis Vives," 147–148, and Richardson, *Print Culture*, 12–13. For the workshop process of printing a book from movable type, see Johan Gerritsen, "Printing at Froben's: An Eye-Witness Account," *Studies in Bibliography* 44 (1991): 144–163.

[9] Lowry, *The World of Aldus Manutius* (Oxford: Blackwell, 1979), 94.

published in September. An immediate response to the visit is recorded in the revisions to *Festina lente* in which he describes the Roman coin given to Aldo by Pietro Bembo, with the reverse that became the mark of the Aldine Press (fig. 1). He praises Aldo's implementation of the motto in troubling to seek

Mark of Aldus Manutius' Aldine Press

out superior manuscripts: "to call back the dead, to repair what is mutilated, to correct what is corrupted in so many ways, especially by the fault of those common printers who reckon one pitiful gold coin in the way of profit worth more than the whole realm of letters." He concludes that "Aldus is building a library which knows no walls save those of the world itself."[10]

For the sixth edition of 1526, Erasmus added five new paragraphs, still treating the Aldine Press as a standard of excellence and reminiscing about the community of humanist scholars who encircled this primum mobile, contrasting their generosity to the selfishness of Germans:

> When I, a Dutchman, was in Italy preparing to publish my book of *Proverbs*, all the learned men there had offered me unsought authors not yet published in print who they thought might be of use to me and Aldus had nothing in his treasure-house that he did not share with me.[11]

---

[10]Quoted from *Collected Works of Erasmus* (*CWE* hereafter), 33: 2.1.1–2.6.100, trans. R. A. B. Mynors (Toronto: University of Toronto Press, 1991), 10.

[11]*CWE*, 33:14.

Now, however, the lonely excellence of the Aldine Press is an ineffectual counterweight to the general depravity of Venetian printing: "the name of Venice is so misused by certain sordid printers, that scarcely any city sends us more shamelessly corrupt editions of the standard authors." Such printers, he scolds, are

> men so ill-educated that they cannot so much as read, so idle that they are not prepared to read over what they print, and so mercenary that they would rather see a good book filled with thousands of mistakes than spend a few paltry gold pieces on hiring someone to supervise the proof-correcting. And none make such grand promises on the title-page as those who are most shameless in corrupting everything.[12]

Erasmus' scorn for "these swarms of new books" promising accuracy but "stuffed with blunders" causes him to call for the strict regulation of the press with "a big stick" to punish unscrupulous offenders.[13]

Another version of his Venetian days was provoked by the 1529 publication of *Ciceronianus,* which—despite its exemption of Bembo from criticism— was calculated to offend contemporary Ciceronians by its accusations of paganism. The ambitious Julius Caesar Scaliger took on the task of answering Erasmus:

> … you hid yourself at the house of Aldus like a bear who has escaped from his chains, the Italians employed you in correcting proofs, furious to see you sleeping off your wine, detesting both your compan-

---

[12]*CWE*, 33:11. The high-mindedness of the complaint needs to be counterpoised by Erasmus' habitual practice of undercutting his publishers ruinously by offering a revised edition to a rival before the first had sold out. See, for example, the 1516 plea of the Paris printer Josse Bade: "even if you have added nothing new, they will think the old edition worthless; and losses of this kind have been forced on me in respect of the *Copia,* the *Panegyricus,* the *Moira,* the *Enchiridion* (I had undertaken for 500 copies), and the *Adagia,* of which I had bought 110. It would thus be greatly to our advantage if you would assign each individual work to a single printer, and not revise it until he has sold off all the copies." *CWE* 4:88; quoted by Paul F. Grendler, "Printing and Censorship," in *The Cambridge History of Renaissance Philosophy,* ed. C. B. Schmitt and Quentin Skinner (Cambridge: Cambridge University Press, 1988), 34.

[13]In 1552 Girolamo Ruscelli quoted a cynical trade proverb that bad books sell as well as good books and echoed Erasmus' plea for strict state regulation. See Richardson, *Print Culture,* 12. Eisenstein, *The Printing Press,* 108–110, plausibly argues that, although for a time the speed of the new medium accelerated and compounded the existing process of manuscript corruption, so it also remedied that process as printers learned to exploit technological superiority in a rapid sequence of improved editions.

ionship at the tables and your eagerness to desert your labors, could scarcely keep themselves from laying hands on you. I think you are now attempting, by mocking their taste for Cicero, to get even with those you did not dare attack then.... Some of the learned men who were at the house of Aldus were my teachers and told me all that I've said about you. Being of noble birth, eloquent and sober, they were incapable of being envious of you who hated eloquence and loved wine.[14]

This stung Erasmus, provoking an immediate, oblique riposte in the colloquy *Opulentia sordida*, with its thinly fictionalized account of his stay in Venice.[15] Despite the fact that both Andrea and his son-in-law Aldo were now dead and could have had nothing to do with Scaliger's accusations, they bear the brunt of the attack. Antronius (Andrea) is assailed for his penuriousness and avarice, accused of freezing, starving, and, in particular, depriving Gilbert (Erasmus) of drink; Orthrogonus (Aldo), is dismissed with contempt as a feeble yes-man, acquiescent in his father-in-law's miserliness, and pathetically transparent in his efforts to convince Gilbert that he endangers his health by overindulgence in food and drink. Gilbert concedes that diet is a matter of custom and that the Italians were healthy enough, maintaining, instead, that "it was too late to change" his habit of "heavy eating and drinking." Rather, for him, the issue was the miserliness of his host: "His fortune amounted to not less than 80,000 ducats, I believe, and there wasn't a single year in which he failed to increase it by a thousand ducats at least." [16]

There is a curious blindness to the considerable expense of supporting a household of thirty people, making an always risky commercial enterprise pay, and Aldo's equivocal position as the financial subordinate in the collaborative venture, let alone any awareness of the inconvenience and expense of having a houseguest for the better part of a year. Indeed, if anything, Erasmus' dialogue lends credence to Scaliger's charge of drunkenness. Whether in truth or only in fiction, however, Erasmus conforms to a well-established cultural stereotype for northern humanists: "The fifteenth century saw a profusion of Italian plaints, in elegant Ciceronian Latin, about the Germans' loutish behavior and

[14]Scaliger, *Oratio pro M. Tullio Cicerone contra Des: Erasmum Roterodamum* (written March 1529 and published September 1531), trans. Vernon Hall, Jr., *Life of Julius Caesar Scaliger (1484–1558),* Transactions of the American Philosophical Society, n.s. 40.2 (Philadelphia, 1950): 101.

[15]Craig R. Thompson, trans., *The Colloquies of Erasmus* (Chicago: University of Chicago Press, 1965), 488–490, summarizes the circumstances of composition.

[16]Quotations are from Thompson, *Colloquies of Erasmus*, 499.

propensity to drink, not to mention their curious liberties, oral and written, with the Latin language."[17]

In his anti-Ciceronianism and in his excessive thirst for wine, the Italians saw mutually confirming symptoms of Erasmus' pathology. He, in turn, realized bitterly that his confident assumption of acceptance as an equal had been a delusion; moreover, he had been tarred with the character popularly assigned to printers—that of a drunken foreigner. This realization must have been rendered the more frustrating because he was deprived of using the corresponding stereotype for Italian humanists: he could not hurl back the standard charge of sodomy.[18] The insistently familial circumstances of the household rendered it implausible; moreover, his sojourn among "Italian perverts" was far too extended to pass without raising questions about his own character. He had to make do, instead, with a substitute form of unnatural behavior, parsimonious diet, peculiar enough to the mind of a well-fed "German." In the sour ending of this episode, Aldo's attempts to dignify the trade of printer by enveloping it with the garment of a humanist academy failed.

The ease with which Erasmus' long-declared veneration for Aldo could be transformed into contempt for an undignified commercial enterprise illustrates the equivocal status of even the most illustrious Venetian printer. How much more questionable, then, the stature of frankly commercial printers.[19] The Aldine Press in the lifetime of its founder was notable primarily for its austere editions of classical authors. When Aldo ventured into the area of vernacular publication, he turned first to the classics of Trecento Tuscan, extend-

---

[17]Ingrid D. Rowland, "Revenge of the Regensburg Humanists, 1493," *Sixteenth Century Journal* 35 (1994): 307–322; quotation, 308.

[18]It seems likely that this was a subtext to the charge of "paganism" in *Ciceronianus*. Erasmus uses erotic, mythological art—Ganymede, inevitably—to illustrate his complaint: "In paintings … we get far more delight from Ganymede snatched up by the eagle than from Christ ascending into heaven; our eyes dwell on the representations of Bacchus and Terminus, full of vice and obscenity, rather than on Lazarus recalled to life or Christ baptized by John. These are the mysteries which lurk under the veil of Cicero's name"; Betty I. Knott, trans., *CWE* 28 (1986): 396; and see 438 for a mosaic of "the rape of Ganymede." For the German perception of Italian pederasty, see Rowland, "Revenge," 309–315; and, for Ganymede, Leonard Barkan, *Transuming Passion: Ganymede and the Erotics of Humanism* (Stanford: Stanford University Press, 1991).

[19] For the formative stage of the vernacular book trade, and the hazards entailed, see Susan Noakes, "The Development of the Book Market in Late Quattrocento Italy: Printers' Failures and the Role of the Middleman," *Journal of Medieval and Renaissance Studies* 11 (1981): 23–55. David R. Carlson, *English Humanist Books: Writers and Patrons, Manuscripts and Print, 1475–1525* (Toronto: University of Toronto Press, 1993), esp. 102–141, quotation, 130, agrees: "The salient concern of business life for printers in the early period was marketing." Printing did not immediately supplant manuscripts, only complicated the publications options.

ing to Petrarch and Dante the same aura as their Greek and Latin predecessors; as his line expanded to living Italian authors, it emphasized "high" literary culture, Bembo's *Asolani* and Sannazaro's *Arcadia*. By the end of the 1520s, however, the market had changed with the democratization of the reading public that Rabelais ironically celebrates—robbers, hangmen, freebooters, grooms, even women and girls—and printers emerged to satisfy this market.

Rather than the clear-text Aldine octavos, aimed for cultivated courtiers and ladies, printers now produced editions designed to aid a less formally educated readership with notes, glossaries, commentaries, as well as simplified and modernized texts.[20] Popular books took on an identifying format and look.[21] As the demand for popular books burgeoned, so specialists arrived to meet that need; a new class of professional writers, the *poligrafi,* fed the presses of vernacular publishers, such as Francesco Marcolini and Gabriele Giolito.[22] Marcolini commenced operation slightly earlier than the Giolito family and followed the example of Aldo in dignifying his press with the aura of an academy, the "Bottega della Verità." Praising Giolito's 1542 edition of the *Orlando furioso,* printed "as if by a prince rather than by a bookseller," Aretino effused, "one can say that you are in business for honour rather than profit."[23] But such gestures would have fooled no contemporary. Giolito and Marcolini were in business for profit just as much as were Aretino and the other *poligrafi.*

"Is the pen a penis?" a pair of feminist critics once asked, with intent to outrage. Were it possible to imagine a dialogue across the centuries, they might be surprised by the answer from Filippo de Strata, a late-fifteenth-century monk, master of theology, and scribe. About four years after printing was introduced to Venice by John of Speyer in 1469, Strata addressed to the doge, Nicolo Marcello, a diatribe attacking the innovation and urging its banishment from the republic. Strata's sixty-nine-line Latin poem anticipates many of the

[20]See Richardson, *Print Culture,* 90–109.

[21]See Grendler, "Form and Function in Italian Renaissance Popular Books," *Renaissance Quarterly* 46 (1993): 451–485.

[22]On the *poligrafi,* see Paul Grendler, *Critics of the Italian World, 1530–1560* (Madison: University of Wisconsin Press, 1969); and Claudia Di Filippo Bareggi, *Il Mestiere di scrivere: Lavoro intellettuale e mercato librario a Venezia nel Cinquecento* (Rome: Bulzoni, 1988). Most helpful on Marcolini and Giolito are a pair of studies by Amadeo Quondam: "Nel Giardino del Marcolini: Un editore Veneziano tra Aretino e Doni," *Giornale storico della letteratura italiana,* 157 (1980): 75–116; and "'Mercanzia d'onore,' 'mercanzia d'utile.' Produzione libraria e lavoro intellettuale a Venezia nel Cinquecento," in Armando Petrucci, ed., *Libri, editori e pubblico nell'Europa moderna: Guida storica e critica* (Rome: Editori Laterza, 1977), 53–104.

[23]To Gabriele Giolito (June 1, 1542); trans. George Bull, *Aretino: Selected Letters* (Harmondsworth: Penguin, 1976), 213.

soon-to-be stock complaints raised against the press: the printers—drunken, ignorant, and immoral louts, interested only in profit—take advantage of their inexpensive product and achieve large-volume sales by printing anything that is sexually titillating, thereby corrupting the morals of the young, as well as the craft that Strata, a manuscript copyist, had proudly represented.

> They shamelessly print, at a negligible price, material which may, alas, inflame impressionable youths, while a true writer dies of hunger. Cure (if you will) the plague which is doing away with the laws of all decency, and curb the printers. They persist in their sick vices, setting Tibullus in type, while a young girl reads Ovid to learn sinfulness. Through printing, tender boys and gentle girls, chaste without foul stain, take in whatever mars purity of mind or body; they encourage wantonness, and swallow up huge gain from it. (23–32)

> They basely flood the market with anything suggestive of sexuality, and they print the stuff at such a low price that anyone and everyone procures it for himself in abundance. And so it happens that asses go to school. The printers guzzle wine and, swamped in excess, bray and scoff. The Italian writer lives like a beast in a stall. The superior art of authors who have never known any other work than producing well-written books is banished. (36–42)

Warming to the theme of his sermon, Strata reaches new heights of invective, thundering:

> Writing indeed, which brings in gold for us, should be respected and held to be nobler than all goods, unless she has suffered degradation in the brothel of the printing presses. She is a maiden with a pen, a harlot in print. Should you not call her a harlot who makes us excessively amorous? Governed only by avaricious gain, will not that most base woman deserve the name of prostitute, who saps the strength of the young boy by fostering wantonness? This is what the printing presses do: they corrupt susceptible hearts. (45–53)[24]

Est virgo haec penna: meretrix est stampificata. In Strata's striking figure, writing itself is gendered as a woman; the pen is a virgin and only the press a whore. In his anxiety to defame a new invention, Strata overturns the traditional masculine gendering of most tropes for writing—for example, stylus as

---

[24]Filippo de Strata, *Polemic against Printing,* trans. Shelagh Grier and intro. by Martin Lowry (Birmingham: Mayloft Press, 1986). This edition has Latin and English on facing pages.

weapon, either sword or knife, and stylus as plough, in which parchment becomes a white field and ink the black seed sowed by the ploughman.[25] Apparently inventing the debasement trope of writing for the press as female prostitution, the printing house itself as brothel, Strata created a figure that spoke resonantly in the early phases of print culture. Erasmus, in 1526, flayed the degenerate Venetian printers who fill the world with "foolish, ignorant, malignant, libellous, mad, impious and subversive" books:

> When caught out, the printers reply, "Give me something to buy food for my household, and I will cease to print books like this." You might get the same answer, but with rather more excuse, from any thief, any confidence-trickster, the keeper of any brothel....[I]s it perhaps a lesser crime.... to prostitute your own body or another person's for gain without using violence, than to attack someone else's way of life and the reputation that is dearer than life itself?[26]

Until he arrived in Venice (March 1527), Pietro Aretino largely had written as a court poet, serving his patrons in the customary way, using his pen to praise, blame, and amuse; flattering those whom he served or with whom he hoped to ingratiate himself in *canzoni*, epigrams, even a never-completed epic; attacking their enemies in pasquinades, satiric sonnets, and *giudizi;* circulating comedies in manuscript. Despite his contempt for the court that he had forsaken and his endless boasting about the freedom and honesty of his new life, Aretino's attitudes toward authorship were imprinted by the court poet's principle of indirect compensation; and he never entirely overcame his ambivalence about earning his living by writing.

Sixteenth-century authors and printers worked together in several ways: first, the printer might require the author to subsidize complete publication costs, either through a patron or out of his own pocket. Second, the printer and author might share printing costs, with the author agreeing to buy a predetermined portion of the edition. Third, the printer might publish at his own

---

[25]On these, see Ernst R. Curtius, *European Literature and the Latin Middle Ages,* trans. Willard R. Trask (New York: Pantheon, 1953), 311–314. Strata's sense of mechanical printing as profoundly different and threatening is highlighted by more ordinary attempts to adapt the book trades to the new technology. See, for example, Sheila Edmunds, "From Schoeffer to Vérard: Concerning the Scribes Who Became Printers," in Sandra Hindman, ed., *Printing the Written Word: The Social History of Books, circa 1450–1520* (Ithaca: Cornell University Press, 1991), 21–40. On adapting the vocabulary of writing to printing, see David Shaw, "'Ars formularia': Neo-Latin Synonyms for Printing," *The Library,* series 6, 11 (1989): 220–230.

[26]*Festina lente,* CWE 33:13.

risk, compensating the author with a fixed number of copies. Fourth, the printer might pay the author directly a small sum for his manuscript.[27] In this ascending scale of market confidence, all but the last option leave the author with books to dispose of; a small number of copies—say, twenty to fifty—could go to friends and potential patrons; any larger number would need to be sold.[28]

Probably Aretino had personal experience of each of these arrangements. On the brink of his greatest success, Aretino delivered to his printer and friend Marcolini the manuscript of the *Lettere,* including a letter declaring these a gift:

> It is reward enough that you proclaim that I gave them to you.... As for having printed at one's own expense and one's own urging the books that a man has drawn forth from his imagination, that seems to me to be like feasting on one's own limbs, and he who every evening visits the bookstore to pick up the money earned by the day's sales, to be like a pimp who empties the purse of his woman before he retires to bed. For that reason, I hope God will grant that the courtesy of princes rewards me for the labor of writing, and not that small change of book buyers.

Aretino concludes by asserting that anyone who writes for profit should "Frankly call yourself a book pedlar, and lay the name of poet aside."[29] Presumably, Marcolini is publishing Aretino at his own risk, compensating him for the manuscript with copies that will go first to prospective patrons, "the courtesy of princes," and, if that does not pay off, the remainder for sales, "the small change of book buyers."

Aretino finds particularly debasing and humiliating the least attractive option, printing "at one's own expense" and then selling the run—cannibalizing himself, in his vivid image—and visiting the bookstore "like a pimp who empties the purse of his woman before he retires to bed" ("del roffiano che, prima che se ne vada a letto, vòta la borsa de la sua femina"). The uncertainties of court service were bad enough—indeed, nearly costing Aretino his life—

---

[27]See helpful summary in Grendler, "Printing and Censorship," 31–33; also Carlson, *English Humanist Books*, 108–109. For a finely detailed account of the printing trade at midcentury, see Paul Grendler, *The Roman Inquisition and the Venetian Press, 1540–1605* (Princeton: Princeton University Press, 1977), 3–24.

[28]A press run of one thousand copies was standard for Venetian imprints throughout the century; see Lowry, *The World of Aldus*, 257, and Grendler, "Printing and Censorship," 28.

[29]June 22, 1537, trans. Chubb, 66.

but the continual anxiety of living by the response to one's books, whether in patronage or copies sold, may be worse.

Throughout the Renaissance, genius, intellectual creativity, was gendered as a male attribute;[30] therefore the extended analogy—bookstore as brothel, book as prostituted child, author as pimp—spells out literary prostitution as a sex transformation. Socrates' distrust of a new technology, writing, was expressed in the metaphor of infertile planting (*Phaedrus* 274–277); other ancients developed the metaphor as human infertility: writing was stigmatized as female and a form of prostitution.[31] Only after its acceptance did the tropes for writing convert its gender to masculine. That the transition from scribal to print culture was a paradigm shift comparable to that from oral to literacy is attested by the resurrection of feminine gendering and the prostitution metaphor. With the historical precedents in mind, we may want to scrutinize the language with which the age of electronic communication has been greeted.

[30]On the Cinquecento vocabulary of genius—*virtù, ingegno, divino*—see Martin Kemp, "The 'Super-Artist' as Genius," in Penelope Murray, ed., *Genius: The History of an Idea* (London: Blackwell, 1989), 32–53. For the persistence of propagation metaphors to describe intellectual creativity, see, on the language of copyright law, Mark Rose, "Mothers and Authors: *Johnson v. Calvert* and the New Children of our Imaginations," *Critical Inquiry* 22 (1996): 613–633.

[31]On the "Typically Greek ... disparagement of writing and books," see Curtius, *European Literature*, 304–305. For the misogynistic association with female sexuality, see Charles Segal, "Greek Tragedy: Writing, Truth, and the Representations of the Self," in *Mnemai: Classical Studies in Memory of Karl K. Hulley,* ed. Harold J. Evjen (Chico, CA: Scholars Press, 1984), 55–59, 63.

Robert V. Schnucker, 1989, with plaque to recognize Pickler Memorial Library of Truman State University (then Northeast Missouri State University) as one of thirty-two libraries with complete microform holdings of the *Early English Books: 1475–1640* series. Schnucker was instrumental in the library's acquisition of this valuable resource.

Kinder, Kirche, Landeskinder

Women Defend Their Publishing in Early Modern Germany

Merry Wiesner-Hanks

Though learned men in early modern Europe disagreed about many things, they were united in their view that women should be silent. With exceptions one can count on one hand, Italian, English, and German; Protestant, Jewish, and Catholic men agreed that the ideal woman was, to use the title of Suzanne Hull's collection, "chaste, silent, and obedient."[1] That ideal changed little throughout the many centuries of the late Middle Ages and early modern period when so much else about European culture changed dramatically. Those of us who have explored women's history in this period for the last several decades are so used to this ideal that we sometimes forget its pervasiveness. I was reminded of this last spring when I taught an undergraduate seminar entitled "Gender and Power in the Renaissance" and the students first got angry and then got bored with all the injunctions to female chastity, silence, and obedience. Their anger led to the question "Why did women put up with this garbage?" (a good beginning of feminist consciousness, and a question asked by the male students as well as female) and their boredom to the question, as one put it: "Didn't any guy ever have an original thought?" The easy answer to the second question involves, of course, a discussion of the reverence for standard authorities and the practice of frequent citation on *all* issues in this period; the harder answer, and one many of us have been looking for over the last several decades, is why ideas about women were so much

---

[1] Suzanne Hull, *Chaste, Silent and Obedient: English Books for Women, 1475–1640* (San Marino, Cal.: Huntingdon Library, 1982). Other studies or collections of male opinion include: Ian Maclean, *The Renaissance Notion of Woman* (Cambridge: Cambridge University Press, 1980); Margaret R. Sommerville, *Sex and Subjection: Attitudes to Women in Early-Modern Society* (London: Arnold, 1995); Kate Aughterson, *Renaissance Woman: A Sourcebook: Constructions of Femininity in England* (London: Routledge, 1995).

slower to change than ideas about anything else, including the best form of government or the best way to get into heaven.

That is the subject of a far different—and far longer—paper, however. I wanted to bring up the issue to emphasize the power and durability of the cultural injunctions to women's silence, which explains why most early modern women who wrote felt the need to justify and explain their actions. I have explored these justifications for writing in an earlier article, and they have also been examined by, among others, Margaret Hannay, Gerda Lerner, Jean Woods, and Barbara Becker-Cantarino.[2] In this paper I investigate a few examples, all from the collections of the Herzog August Bibliothek, of women who did something even *more* audacious, who published their works or agreed to their publication during their own lifetimes. Though some texts by women do not include a justification, many do, and these generally include one of three reasons, or some combination of these: their children, their faith, or their duty to their subjects, what I have termed *Kinder, Kirche, Landeskinder.* This paper explores a range of texts by female authors from the sixteenth and seventeenth centuries and analyzes the authors' justifications for publishing. Though in some ways placing the justification for publishing outside themselves allows the authors to conform to expectations for women, I argue that it also allows them to go beyond those expectations, both in the act of publishing itself and in their claims to an authorial voice which transcends gender.

The first text is Katharina Zell's *Ein Brieff an die ganze Burgerschafft der Statt Straßburg* published in 1557.[3] This is a long pamphlet criticizing Ludwig Rabus, a Lutheran pastor in Ulm who had previously been in Strasbourg, for his rigid Lutheran confessionalism and denunciations of spiritualists such as Caspar von Schwenkfeld. Its author, Katharina Zell, was the widow of Matthias Zell, one of the moderate Strasbourg reformers, and most of the text is an argument for toleration, based to some extent on Sebastian Castellio's

[2]Merry E. Wiesner, "Women's Defense of Their Public Role," in Mary Beth Rose, ed., *Women in the Middle Ages and the Renaissance: Literary and Historical Perspectives* (Syracuse, N.Y.: Syracuse University Press, 1986), 1–27, and reprinted in *Gender, Church and State in Early Modern Germany: Essays by Merry E. Wiesner* (London: Longmans, 1997), 6–29; Margaret Hannay, ed., *Silent But for the Word: Tudor Women as Patrons, Translators and Writers of Religious Works* (Kent, Ohio: Kent State University Press, 1985); Gerda Lerner, *The Creation of Feminist Consciousness: From the Middle Ages to Eighteen-Seventy* (Oxford: Oxford University Press, 1993), esp. chaps. 3–6; Jean M. Woods, "'Die Pflicht Befihlet mir/ zu Schreiben und zu tichten': Drei litterarische tätige Frauen aus dem Hause Baden-Durlach," in Barbara Becker-Cantarino, ed., *Die Frau von der Reformation zur Romantik: Die Situation der Frau vor dem Hintergrund der Literatur- und Sozialgeschichte* (Bonn: Bouvier, 1980), 3 6–57; Barbara Becker-Cantarino, *Der lange Weg zur Mündigkeit: Frau und Literatur 1500–1800* (Stuttgart: J. B. Metzler, 1987).

famous text, *De hereticis,* which had been published a few years earlier in German and French as well as Latin. This was not Zell's first venture into publishing, for decades earlier she had published several short works, including a pamphlet in defense of her own marriage and of clerical marriage in general. This so horrified the Strasbourg city council that they ordered Matthias to forbid his wife to publish anything further. She honored their request, and did not publish again until after her husband was dead.

Zell had originally criticized Rabus in a personal letter, which he had returned unopened twice, saying that he was too busy to read it but that he knew it was "heathen, unchristian, stinking and false" (Bi*v*). She then decided to print her original letter, Rabus' letter, and her lengthy reply, directing the pamphlet to "the whole citizenry of Strasbourg," and noting, in the very long full title, that she wanted "one and all to be able to read and judge impartially without hatred, but simply avail themselves of the truth." The "truth," in Katharina's eyes, was one which the increasingly Lutheran Strasbourg clergy in 1557 did not want to hear, involving as it did a reminder of Strasbourg's earlier toleration of divergent religious viewpoints. This truth was so controversial, in fact, that the pamphlet was printed without publisher or date of publication, and Miriam Chrisman notes that it was most probably *not* published in Strasbourg, for the publisher of Zell's earlier works was dead and no Strasbourg printer would by this date have touched something so critical of a Wittenberg-trained theologian. [4]

What led Zell to publish something this incendiary, at a point decades after most lay pamphleteers, male or female, had ceased printing works of religious controversy? (It is so late, in fact, that Paul Russell does not include this work of Zell's in his study of lay pamphleteers, though he does include her earlier works, because there is nothing with which to compare it.[5]) Zell's justification is a complex one. In part it is her duty to her deceased husband, as a

---

[3]Katharina Zell, *Ein Brieff an die ganze Burgerschaft der Statt Strassburg* ... (n.p., 1557), Herzog August Bibliothek (HAB) shelf number K61, Helmst. 4° (5). For a longer discussion of this see Merry Wiesner-Hanks, "Katharina Zell's *Ein Brieff an die ganze Burgerschaft der Statt Straßburg* as Theology and Autobiography," *Colloquia Germanica* 28 (1995): 245–254, and Elsie Anne McKee, "The Defense of Zwingli, Schwenkfeld, and the Baptists, by Katharina Schütz Zell," in *Reformiertes Erbe: Festschrift für Gottfried W. Locher zu seinem 80. Geburtstag,* ed. Heiko A. Oberman, et al., (Zurich: EVG, 1992), 1:245–264. Professor McKee is currently working on a biography of Katharina Zell and a critical edition of her writings, to be published by Brill in 1998 in their Studies in Medieval and Reformation Thought series.

[4]Miriam Chrisman, personal communication, September 26, 1989.

[5]Paul Russell, *Lay Theology in the Reformation: Popular Pamphleteers in Southwest Germany 1521–1525* (Cambridge: Cambridge University Press, 1986).

"piece of the rib of the blessed man Matthias Zell" (Aiv*v*), with whom "in matters of belief [she] had never disagreed" (Giv*v*). In part it is that God has called her, expecting more of her than he does of other women because he has given her more talents and gifts. Only if she lets people know about these matters will God give her peace of mind and a clear conscience.

Zell's religious justification for publishing is quite different from those of many female authors, however, for she never views herself as God's passive mouthpiece or talks about visions or voices. Her duty is not simply to God, but to the church, and specifically the church in Strasbourg, which she feels has forgotten its past and is moving in a dangerous direction. Zell writes not as an external critic but as one who has "done more work with my life and mouth than any helper or chaplain of the church" (Gii*v*). She knows the words in 1 Timothy (2:12) about women's keeping silent in church, but interprets them very narrowly; "I haven't stood in the pulpit because I didn't need to in order to carry out my duties, so I have followed the rule that St. Paul set for believing women of his time" (Gii*v*). Thus Zell's religious justification for her publishing blends into what we might term a civic justification, a call to the laity of "my beloved Strasbourg" to remember their role in a church that was becoming increasingly dominated by the clergy.

Zell's addressing the "whole citizenry" of Strasbourg as her equals is unique, as far as I know, in the writings of sixteenth-century women, for no other woman claims membership in the civic community in the same way. It fits well with the south German tradition of civic pride and patriotism which we know so well from many studies of urban Reformation, but Zell's contemporaries did not see this. Though she wanted them to judge her pamphlet "not according to the standards of a woman, but according to the standards of what God through his Spirit has given to me" (Aii*r*), they did not. It provoked only one pseudonymous reply, whose author stated that he had not bothered to read the whole thing, but only the preface, and it was never cited in later arguments for toleration.[6]

My second text had a much different fate because it was written, not by someone her contemporaries considered primarily a troublemaking pastor's widow, but by a ruler. In 1556, Elisabeth of Brandenburg, the duchess of Braunschweig/Lüneburg, published a book of consolation for widows—she had been widowed sixteen years earlier and served as regent for her son for six years—which included many biblical and historical examples of how terrible it

[6]Robert A. Kolb, *For All the Saints: Changing Perceptions of Martyrdom and Sainthood in the Lutheran Reformation* (Macon, Ga.: Mercer University Press, 1987), 43.

was to be a widow and how God will punish those who treat widows badly.[7] She dedicated it to her sister-in-law and to all widows in Braunschweig and Hannover, bitterly noting that God often treats widows better than the world does, so that they should learn "that it is good to trust in God and not in people." Her 1556 edition was reprinted in 1557 by Georg Coelestinus, who included an additional dedication to five noble widows and comments that he is reprinting it because Elisabeth wanted it to be available to many widows to help them. It was reprinted again in 1598, "for the special consolation of all Christian widows of high and low status," with the reprint paid for by five noble widows, who are all named.

My third text has also been reprinted several times, although, like many early modern texts, it is difficult otherwise to judge its impact. Anna Sophia of Quedlinburg was the abbess of the free imperial canoness house of Quedlinburg, which had become Protestant in the 1540s. In 1658 she published a book of spiritual meditations, *Der treue Seelenfreund Christus Jesus / mit nachdenklichen Sinn-Gemahlden,* which was initially regarded as theologically suspect by some Lutheran theologians, who thought she stressed the ubiquity of Christ's presence too strongly in her comments that women could feel this

---

[7]Elisabeth of Braunschweig, *Der Widwen Handbüchlein durch eine hocherleuchte fürstliche Widwe/vor vielen Jahren selbst beschrieben und vefasset/ Jetzt aber wiederumb auff newe gedruckt/Allen Christlichen Widwen/ hohes und nieder Standes/ zu besonderem Trost* (Leipzig: 1598). HAB shelf number YJ 130 Helmst 8°. Elisabeth also wrote an advice manual for her son and one for her daughter, both of which went unpublished during her lifetime but saw publication later; the book for her son, the *Unterrichtung und Ordnung,* has been reprinted in Friedrich Karl von Strombeck, *Deutscher Fürstenspiegel aus dem 16. Jahrhundert* (Braunschweig: Friedrich Vieweg, 1824), 57–130. The HAB also holds a number of other mirrors of princes written by noblewomen for their sons, including those of Anna Maria of Brandenburg/Prussia and Benigna Solms-Laubach. Many of these women had been regents, so they offer practical advice about ruling as well as general religious and moral guidance; they are directed to the author's children (or one of them at least) so they fit with one of the standard justifications for female authorship, but because they were not published during the authors' lifetimes they have not been included here. They do often include a specific discussion about why the author wrote, such as Elisabeth of Braunschweig's comments to her son: "I have written this book for you myself with my own hand, from the beginning to the end; therefore you should not stick it under a bench, but should read it often ... so that you are not burdened with such danger, trouble, and work as I have been, and are not taken in as normally happens with young princes ... so I have written this for your benefit, out of motherly love and good intentions, and have taken on the trouble and work gladly and with good will.... [D]o not scorn what I have said here, for to scorn your mother, as it says in Jesus Sirach, is your own shame." (In this case we know directly about "reader response," for shortly after Elisabeth's son Erich took over rule at age eighteen he joined the Catholic princes and banished the Lutheran ministers.)

presence equally with men, but was later judged acceptable.[8] Anna Sophia uses a fairly standard religious justification for her work: "the cause that impels us to the construction of this little book may not be suppressed, but is itself first and foremost God's command. His authority obliges all people, women as well as men, to his love and praise" (67). Because Anna Sophia was in the somewhat unusual position of being both a Lutheran and an abbess, she also feels compelled to defend her choice of a virginal life and explain why virgins should publish:

> Young women, said David, should fully praise the name of the Lord even as other people should. (This does not stem from their own gratification but is commanded of them.) They have sufficient cause for that praise since they are created as well by God the Father, redeemed by God the Son through his priceless rose-colored blood, and sanctified by the Holy Spirit through grace. Women carry their heads on high [i.e., at the top of their bodies] just as much [as men], which means that they should look to heaven and honor the creator of the heavens no less than other people, that they are therefore no less born to high and heavenly considerations than other people are. They must put a check on their natural weakness and occupy their idle minds, says the well-known Netherlander, Anna Maria von Schurman, in her explanation of the female sex's capacity for studies. St. Augustine also exhorted women to such praise when he said: "Praise, (O virgins,) more sweetly, [him] to whom your thoughts are more fully devoted." ... Virgins of Christ will rejoice over Christ, in Christ, with Christ, through Christ, and because of Christ. Why should we therefore not want to praise our true soul's friend, Christ Jesus, with such joy? Second, the Christian example of so many holy and most praiseworthy women has led us to this work. One generally is accustomed to think, that nothing better reminds a person, or can move him or her to do something, than an example. This is held both in deed and in truth. Because of this, when we consider the mother of all the living, Eve, she is the first next to God in holy Scripture who reacted and called out from her mouth to honor the promised

---

[8]Anna Sophia of Hessen-Darmstadt, Abbess of Quedlinburg, *Der treue Seelenfreund Christus Jesus/mit nachdenklichen Sinn-Gemahlden* ... (Jena: Georg Sengenwald, 1658), HAB shelfmark 915.2 Theol. (3). This was reprinted in 1675 and 1689. A portion of the 1658 edition may be found in Merry Wiesner-Hanks and Joan Skocir, ed. and trans., *Convents Confront the Reformation: Catholic and Protestant Nuns in Germany* (Milwaukee: Marquette University Press, 1996). The page numbers listed in this paper refer to this translation.

serpent-treader [i.e., Adam]: "I have the man of the Lord." And, although she erred personally at the time, even so her inclination was good (Gen.4:1). Did Debora not venerate her God with the most glorious song of praise to be found (Jud. 5)? How joyful, too, was Hanna's heart that she rejoiced to honor God the Lord (1 Sam. 2). Did not Judith offer a new song to honor God when she freed the city of Bethulia from the Assyrian army encampment (Jth. 16)? Who is not moved to the same joyful heart of the exquisite Magnificat of the holy Virgin Mother of God, Mary (Luke 1:47)? How could this example not remind us to follow after her, especially since Christ enjoined us to hold fast to [the example of] the wise virgins, to be prepared when he as our heavenly soul's bridegroom will come. We must be prepared to serve him and not be locked out from the wedding house together with the foolish (Matt. 25:10). (69–71)

A similar list of Old and New Testament women publicly proclaiming the truth appears in Anna von Medum's *Geistlicher Judischer Wunderbalsam*, first published in Amsterdam in 1646 and reprinted in 1660.[9] This is an unusual two-part tract of more than two hundred pages, the first part directed to Christians urging them to give up images and other aspects of worship which have (in Medum's opinion) no biblical basis so that the Jews will convert, and the second an address to Jews laying out Old Testament prophecies that indicate Jesus is the Messiah. The work also includes a spiritual autobiography describing how Medum was called by God to preach to the Jews—she apparently preached her message orally as well—and a ten-page justification of her actions. In this Medum discusses the many women in the Old and New Testaments who preached and prophesied, noting that women even did circumcisions and that God has called "every Christian to be a house-preacher" (41). At times she stresses the gender neutrality of God's command, particularly to members of the nobility like herself, and at others uses very female metaphors, describing herself as a childless bride and widow, whom God has impregnated with spiritual seed so that she will have many "spiritual children" (87). Among these spiritual children are the Jews, for whom Medum notes she is "ready to suffer more pain than a mother in hard labor does for her child" (110) or a "mother who sees her child in a fire and puts her body and life in danger to pull the child out of the fire" (209).

[9]Anna von Medum, *Geistlicher Judischer Wunderbalsam / von den Allerheilsambsten und Herrlichen Specereyen Göttliches Worts* ... (Amsterdam, 1646). HAB shelfmark 394.74 Quod.

Though I have found no other woman who viewed the Jews as her spiritual children (and Medum's text still awaits a full analysis), a number of other noblewomen saw their subjects and servants in this light and directed various types of works to them. Emilie Juliana von Schwarzburg-Rudolstadt published a collection of hymns and prayers for "marriage and other similar matters," *Geistliches Weiber Aqua Vit,* "out of our sovereign-motherly (*Landes-mütterlichen*) heart, mouth, and hand, for the desired strengthening and edification of our subjects (*Landeskinder*)."[10] Anna Elisabeth von Schleebusch published four collections of spiritual meditations and religious quotations, one of which she directed to "the worthy members of my household as well as every Christian devoted to God" and another "not only to my children but to my grandchildren ... as Jacob before his departure blessed all of his children and also especially his son Joseph's children."[11] (She thus goes beyond comparing herself to the usual heroic *women* from the Old Testament to comparing herself to a patriarch.)

Heide Wunder and others have been exploring the new sense of responsibility toward their subjects that female regents and rulers in the small states of the empire developed in the early modern period, and these works by noblewomen fit very much into that pattern.[12] Very occasionally works by women exhibit a slightly different political consciousness, however. In 1620, Martha Salome von Belta published a political tract in the form of conversations which argued that the recent outbreak of the Thirty Years' War was the fault of the Catholics instead of the Protestants.[13] Though the work has a strong religious theme and is addressed to "the Christian reader," Belta also describes herself as "a zealous lover of her fatherland" (*ihres Vatterlands eyffrige Liebhaberin*) who has published this "for the good of her fatherland." Thus Belta, like Zell sixty years earlier, justified her speaking out and publishing not as a ruler of a state but as a member of a political community, with language implying women's inclusion in that community, a phenomenon that historians of

---

[10]Emilie Juliana von Schwarzburg-Rudolstadt, *Geistliches Weiber-Aqua-Vit/ Das ist Christliche Lieder und Gebete* ... (Rudolstadt: Fleischer, 1683). HAB shelfmark Tl 62.

[11]The first text is Anna Elisabeth von Schleebusch, *Heilige Übung Gottliebener Seelen / oder geistliche Andachten* ... (Leipzig: Andreas Zeidler, 1703), HAB shelfmark Jh 2308, and the second is *Anmuthiger Seelerquicker Würtz-garten oder auserlesenes Gebet-Buch* ... (Leipzig: Andreas Zeidler, 1702), HAB shelfmark Jh 2309. The quotations are from the unpaginated forewords.

[12]Heide Wunder, et al. "Konfession, Religiosität und Politisches Handeln von Frauen vom Ausgehenden 16. bis zum Beginn des 18. Jahrhunderts," unpublished paper.

[13]Martha Salome von Belta, *Militistogati anatomia oder Böhmischer Warsager* ... (Warnstadt: Judith Richterin, 1620). The quotations are from the full title and the unpaginated foreword.

women do not usually see developing in Europe until the English Civil War or the French Revolution.[14]

In their examinations of women's subjectivity, authorial voice, and self-understanding, most literary scholars have concentrated on diaries, memoirs and other sorts of what are in German termed *Ego-dokumente*.[15] They have explored the development of the authorial or autobiographical 'I', an 'I' that is not the person herself but both the textual double of a real person and a self-evident textual construction.[16] Though there are limitations about what she— the autobiographical 'I'— can tell us about the real woman who created her, she does (and here I am showing my colors as a historian, not a literary scholar) indicate that the real woman did not, as my students would say, put up with the garbage about female silence. Going beyond traditional *Ego-dokumente* allows us to find further evidence, as this very brief discussion of just a few of the female-authored texts held by the Herzog August Bibliothek indicates.[17] Natalie Davis' recent study of three seventeenth-century women who wrote is titled *Women on the Margins*, and I would stress in conclusion that we must also search *in* the margins for insights about women.[18] The margins of women's writings, the forewords and prefaces and afterwords which often frame women's writings or publications—whatever the genre of the actual work— can also yield surprising information about women's ideas and inner lives.

[14]For women in England see Hilda Smith, ed., *Women Writers and the Early Modern British Political Tradition* (Cambridge: Cambridge University Press, 1998), and in France see Sara E. Melzer and Leslie W. Rabine, eds., *Rebel Daughters: Women and the French Revolution* (New York: Oxford University Press, 1992).

[15]Studies of women's autobiographies which cover the early modern period include: Magdalene Heuser, ed., *Autobiographien von Frauen: Beiträge zu ihrer Geschichte* (Tübingen: Max Niemeyer, 1996); Felicity Nussbaum, *The Autobiographical Subject: Gender and Ideology in 18th-Century England* (Baltimore: Johns Hopkins, 1989); Felicity Nussbaum, Estelle C. Jelinek, eds., *The Tradition of Women's Autobiography from Antiquity to the Present* (Boston: Twayne, 1986); Domna Stanton, ed., *The Female Autograph* (New York: New York Literary Forum, 1984). To my knowledge, the only early modern German women's autobiography that has been translated into English is that of the pietist Johanna Eleonore Petersen, translated by Cornelia Niekus Moore, in Jeannine Blackwell and Susanne Zantop, eds., *Bitter Healing: German Women Writers from 1700 to 1830* (Lincoln: University of Nebraska Press, 1990), 51–78.

[16]Gisela Brinker-Gabler, "Metamorphosen des Subjekts: Autobiographie, Textualität und Erinnerung," in Heuser, *Autobiographien*, 400.

[17]The best introduction and listing of the texts by German women in this period is Jean M. Woods and Maria Fürstenwald, *Schriftstellerinnen, Künstlerinnen und gelehrte Frauen des deutschen Barock* (Stuttgart: J.B. Mezlersche, 1984), which covers the seventeenth and early eighteenth centuries and indicates the location of many of the works by women. There is, unfortunately, nothing similar for an earlier period.

[18]Natalie Zemon Davis, *Women on the Margins: Three Seventeenth-Century Lives* (Cambridge, Mass.: Harvard University Press, 1995).

ACKNOWLEDGMENT

My research on women's writings held by the Herzog August Bibliothek in
Wolfenbüttel was carried out in the summer of 1987 and was supported by the
American Council of Learned societies and the Deutsche Akademische
Austauschdienst

First edition of a famous educational work with commentary by Lucrezia Civitali of
Lucca, which may be the only classical text edited by a woman during the
Renaissance.

Appendix I

Presentation to Robert V. Schnucker at Sixteenth Century Studies Conference (1990)

Jerome Friedman for Friends of Schnucker

OVER THE YEARS ONE NAME has been more identified with the Sixteenth Century Studies Conference than any other. One person sits with the organization's books and conference schedules and sees to the day-to-day functioning of its many projects. Similarly, one person is more identified with the journal than any other. One person puts the journal to bed at night and brings it to life every day of the year, sees to its physical health, and even stuffs the envelopes and after that the mail bags. There is no individual whose cooperation more of us have enjoyed and whose help more of us have appreciated than Robert Victor Schnucker. Without exception, there is no aspect of this organization's existence, in the past or the present, and no aspect of the journal's publication, that does not bear Professor Schnucker's insignia. In a word, if something is happening, Bob is always involved and usually intimately so. Some people know Bob as the managing editor and book review editor of the journal, or as the permanent secretary of the Sixteenth Century Studies Conference, or as the editor of *Historians of Early Modern Europe*. We have all become used to his preachings to send money and to have our libraries purchase multiple copies of the journal and the monograph series.

There is a great deal more to Bob Schnucker than these few titles would indicate, though his immense personal modesty usually keeps anyone from appreciating how important he is to all aspects of this organization's existence. Indeed, it is this modesty that necessitated that this project be kept secret lest Bob feel too uncomfortable to accept an honor he knew about, and Professor Schnucker has only now learned of this award in his honor.

If the award was a secret, Bob's professional efforts surely are not. As the managing editor of the SCJ, Bob gave the journal its current format, which is, without a doubt, the best layout of any journal in European or American history. He established the book review policy which in fact covers all of early modern Europe and the "Book Reviews" section is the single best resource for publications in the field. Bob is also responsible for the economic success of the journal. Few people know work to arrange for a legal status which would be beneficial to the SCSC as well as the journal. And fewer remember how Bob engineered to move the journal to his university in Kirksville. The result was a successful operation which not only covered its own costs and the expense of several extra numbers but which could also underwrite the costs of the monograph series, which we all know about because he keeps trying to have us buy copies for every occasion. The fact is, the monograph series is of consistently high quality.

Bob is just as important as an organization official. He has served in every office in this organization and is currently the permanent secretary. At a time when organizations have become increasingly bureaucratic and removed from their membership, in academia and elsewhere, Bob provides the personal touch and the glue that holds us together. Bob actually responds to every letter he receives the day he receives it. And what letters!!! Even Erasmus did not write as much as Bob does, and Bob, unlike Erasmus, has the disadvantage of also working for a living. Whether it is giving good advice to fine new scholars wishing to get on the program and thereby arrange travel money for a first paper, or handling a problem for a senior member who feels his work has gotten stale, Bob acts, speaks, and writes to each person with sensitivity and respect. Bob's concern is for people and he treats everyone's needs as if they were his own.

If Bob did not exist, we could not create him because he is special—but we could certainly create an award for Bob in recognition of the affection, respect, and the gratitude so many of us here tonight feel for him. Bob, I am honored to present to you this award, which is engraved "in serviendo consumor." By the way, you also know the person who conceived of this dedication, but he too wishes to remain anonymous. In fact, I think it is fair to conclude these few observations with the statement, Bob, that you just do no know who your friends are!

Appendix 2

The Work of Robert V. Schnucker

Professional Organizations

Robert V. Schnucker was never simply a member of any organization to which he belonged. Often he served as chair or secretary; almost as often he was a founder and one who gave direction; always he was an active and inspiring contributor. Below is a partial list of scholarly organizations that he served in significant ways:

American Academy of Religion
American Association of University Professors
American Council of Learned Societies
American Historical Association
American Society of Church History
Center for Reformation Research
Chief Administrative Officers, ACLS
Conference of Editors of Learned Journals
Conference of Faith and History
Conference of Historical Journals
Ethics and Human Experimentation Committee of the Kirksville College of
    Osteopathic Medicine
Mediterranean Studies Association
Missouri Conference for the Humanities
Missouri Committee for the Promotion of History
Missouri Committee for Religion in Higher Education
Missouri History Conference
Renaissance Society of America
Sixteenth Century Studies Conference
Social Science Educational Consortium
Society of Biblical Literature
Society for History Education
Society for Reformation Research
Society for the Scientific Study of Religion (Fellow)

Publishing Activities

Much of Schnucker's academic life has been spent seeing to it that young scholars could share the fruits of their research with a broad academic audience. To that end he founded and led a number of publishing outlets, listed below, and was a consultant for numerous like-minded individuals and organizations.

Cofounder of Forum Press

Editor of *Network News Exchange* for ten years

Editor and publisher of *Scholars of Early Modern Europe* (formerly *Historians of Early Modern Europe*) for twelve years

Editor of *Editing History* for twelve years

Publisher for Sixteenth Century Essays and Studies series since its inception in 1982

Managing Editor of *The Sixteenth Century Journal* since its start through 1997

Book Review Editor of *The Sixteenth Century Journal* since its start through 1997

President, Sixteenth Century Journal Publishers, Inc.

Director, Thomas Jefferson University Press at Truman State University, Kirksville, Missouri

Faculty Committees

Schnucker is the consummate teacher whose students benefited from his research and publishing on learning skills. On his own campus he belonged to the following committees and organizations:

Chair, Faculty Committee on Religious Activities

Member, Council on Teacher Education

Member, Council on General Education

Chair, Day of Dialogue

Member, Faculty Senate (first member elected from the Social Science Division)

Regent's Committee for Selection of New President (twice)

Member, Faculty Constitution Committee

Chair, Instructional Services Committee

Member, Committee for Reform of the General Education Curriculum

Chair, Supervision of the Gardner Track Project Committee

Curricular Experience

Schnucker's vision of a liberal arts university manifested itself long before his institution was designated as Missouri's statewide liberal arts and sciences university, as evidenced by the following activities:

Organized first Religion and Philosophy Department to be approved by the Board of Regents

Created and taught the first auto-tutorial course

Created and ran the Human Resources Management Degree Program

Was cocreator of the Learning Skills Inventory, a copyrighted instrument that measures fifty-five discrete learning skills of an individual student so that a teaching environment can be tailored to fit to the learning skills of the student.

Robert Schnucker teaching at Truman State University, Kirksville, Missouri

COURSES TAUGHT

Schnucker's teaching interests were wide, and as a member of the faculties of both the History Department and the Philosophy and Religion Department, he taught the following courses:

American Puritanism
Asian Religions
History of American Religious
  Thought
History of the American Legal System
History of Christian Thought
Medieval History
Reformation and Renaissance History
Tudor-Stuart Studies
World Civilization

Basic Theology
Contemporary Religious Thought
Ethics for Police Officers
Religious Ethics in Contemporary
  America
Old and New Testament
Philosophers and the Law
Philosophy of Religion

Publications

Publications are listed by date, with contributions to reference works gathered at the end of the list:

"La position puritaine à l'égard de l'adultère," *Annales* 26/6 (1972).

"New Wine in Old Skins: David McClelland's Psychological Explanation for the Weber–Tawney Thesis," *Fides et Historia* (Spring 1973).

"Some Aspects of the Educational System of confucius," ERIC/ChESS (1973).

Test Booklet for the three editions of Clough, et al., *A History of the Western World,* published by D. C. Heath (1973 ff.).

"The English Puritans and Pregnancy, Delivery, and Breast Feeding," *History of Childhood Quarterly* 1/4 (1974).

"Elizabethan Knowledge of Birth Control Techniques and Puritan Attitudes Toward Them," *Journal of Interdisciplinary History* (Spring 1975).

"Individualized Self-Learning in the Teaching of western Civilization," *The History Teacher* (August 1974).

A Modular Learning Program for World History. Forum Press, 1974.

"Cognitive Mapping and History Learning," *AHA Newsletter* (1975).

"Individualized Independent Learning in the Library," *The Library-College Perimeter.*

"A Glossary of Terms for *Western Civilization.*" Little-Brown, 1975.

"Religious History of Adair County," *A Book of Adair County History,* 1976.

"What's Wrong With Teaching History," *AHA Newsletter* (January 1979); reprinted in *Australian History Newsletter* (1980).

"Observations on the Teaching of History," *Network News Exchange* (S[ring 1980).

"Improvement of Instruction or Barking Up the Wrong Tree," Proceedings of the Conference for the Improvement of Freshman Level Instructin, April 1981.

Helping the Humanities Journal Survive. SCJ Publishers, Inc., 1983.

Report on preliminarly data on a three-dimensional history test, in *The History Teacher.*

Report on electronic book reviews in *OAH Newsletter.*

Articles and reports in *Editing History* for more than ten years.

Editor of *Calviniana: The Ideas and Influence of John Calvin.* Sixteenth Century Essays & Studies, vol. 13. Kirksville, Mo.: Sixteenth Century Journal Publishers, 1988.

Numerous book reviews in scholarly journals.

DRAWING BY D. WHITESIDE, 1985

Articles in Reference Works

Ten articles in *The New Internatinal Dictionary of the Christian Church.* Grand Rapids: Zondervan, 1974.

Seven articles in *Baker's Dictionary of Theology.* Grand Rapids: Baker Book House, 1988.

Introductory article in *Lion Church History Dictionary.*

Two articles in *Evangelical Dictionary of Theology.* Baker Reference Library, vol. 1. Grand Rapids: Baker Book House, 1984.

THE CONTRIBUTORS

BRIAN G. ARMSTRONG is emeritus professor of history after thirty-one years of service at Georgia State University. He is author of *Bibliographia molinaei: An Alphabetical, Chronological, and Descriptive Bibliography of the Works of Pierre Du Moulin (1568–1658)* (1997), editor of *Probing the Reformed Tradition* (1989), and coeditor of *Calvinus sincerioris religionis vindex/Calvin as the Protector of the Purer Religion* (1997) as well as a frequent book reviewer, contributor to Festschriften, and contributor to history and church history journals. He is president elect of the International Congress for Calvin Research.

ROBIN B. BARNES is professor of history at Davidson College in North Carolina. He is the author of *Prophecy and Gnosis: Apocalypticism in the Wake of the Lutheran Reformation* (1988) as well as numerous essays on the cultural history of the Reformation and early modern religious mentalities. His recent work has focused on astrology in the Reformation era. He is associate editor of *The Sixteenth Century Journal*.

ROBERT G. CLOUSE is professor of history at Indiana State University, where he has served for more than thirty-five years. His publishing career began in 1965 with *Studying Modern Civilization*. With Bonniedell Clouse, he coedited the popular *War: Four Christian Views* (1981), translated into German as *Der Christ und Der Krieg* as well as *Women in Ministry: Four Views* (1989). He also coedited *Two Kingdoms: The Church and Culture Through the Ages* (1993), and is a frequent contributor of chapters and articles, including "A Little Victory Over Death: Reflections on Organ Transplants," *Christianity Today* 32/5 (March 1988). His most recent work includes *The Millennium Manual* (forthcoming).

RICHARD COLE is professor of history at Luther College, Decorah, Iowa. He is author of "Renaissance Humanists Discover America" in *A Humanist's Legacy: Essays in Honor of John Christian Bale* (1990). His research interests center around the dynamics of printing vis-à-vis the early decades of the Reformation in sixteenth-century Germany.

DAVID P. DANIEL is a research fellow at the Institute of Historical Studies of the Slovak Academy of Sciences and a member of the Evangelical Theology faculty of Comenius University in Bratislava, Slovakia. His recent works include *A Bibliography of the Lutheran Confessions* (1988), *Slovakia and the Slovaks: A Concise Encyclopedia* (1994), *A Guide to Historiography in Slovakia* (1995), and a translation of *Lexicon of Slovak History* by D. Skvarna et al. (in press) as well as chapters in numerous works about the Reformation in Europe.

JEROME FRIEDMAN is professor of history at Kent State University. His publications include *The Most Ancient Testimony: Sixteenth-Century Christian-Hebraican the Age of Renaissance Nostalgia* (1983) *Blasphemy, Immorality and Anarchy: The Ranters and the English Revolution* (1987), *The Battle of the Frogs and Fairford's Flies: Miracles and the Pulp Press During the English Revolution* (1993), and he is editor of *Regnum, Religio et Ratio. Essays Presented to Robert M. Kingdon*. (1987). Friedman also writes on the history of photography and camera design and serves as contributing editor to both *Camera Shopper* and *Photographical World* of London. He is an avid collector of subminiature and espionage cameras.

ROBERT M. KINGDON is emeritus professor of history at the University of Wisconsin and director of that university's Institute for Research in the Humanities. He served as senior editor of *The Sixteenth Century Journal* from its inception to his retirement from that position in 1994, and as an officer of the corporation until 1997. He has served as officer and active member of numerous academic and professional associations, and was awarded an honorary doctorate from the University of Geneva. His publications are well known to scholars of early modern studies. Recent work includes *Myths About the St. Bartholomew's Day Massacres: 1572–76* (1988), *Adultery and Divorce in Calvin's Geneva* (1995) and *Registres du Consistoire de Genève: Au temps de Calvin. Tome I, 1542-1544* (1996) "A New View of Calvin in the Light of the Registers of the Geneva Consistory," in, *Calvinus Sincerioris Religionis Vindex*, ed. Wilhelm H. Neuser and Brian G. Armstrong (1997),

ROBERT A. KOLB is mission professor and professor of systematic theology at Concordia College in St. Louis, Missouri and is director of the Institute for Mission Studies. He served as associate editor of *The Sixteenth Century Journal* from its inception until his retirement at the end of 1997. His scholarly works include *For All the Saints: Changing Perceptions of Martyrdom and Sainthood in the Lutheran Reformation* (1987), *Teaching God's Children His Teaching: A Guide for the Study of Luther's Catechism* (1992), *Speaking the Gospel Today: A Theology for Evangelism* (1995), and *Luther's Heirs Define His Legacy: Studies in Lutheran Confessionalization* (1996).

WILLIAM S. MALTBY is professor of history emeritus at the University of Missouri–St. Louis. Among his publications are *The Black Legend in England: The Development of Anti-Spanish Sentiment, 1558–1660* (1971) and *Alba: A Biography of Fernando Alvarez de Toledo, Third Duke of Alba* (1983).

JAMES V. MEHL is professor of humanities and chairperson of the Department of Communication Studies, Theatre, and Humanities at Missouri Western State College in St. Joseph. He has edited *Humanismus in Köln / Humanism in Cologne* (1991) and *In laudem*

Caroli: Renaissance and Reformation Studies for Charles G. Nauert (1998). His articles dealing mainly with German humanism, have appeared in such journals at *The Sixteenth Century Journal, Renaissance Quarterly, Journal of Medieval and Early Modern Studies, Humanistica Lovaniensia, Archive for Reformation History,* and *Publishing History.* He is also editor of *Interdisciplinary Humanities,* the journal of the National Association for Humanities Education.

RAYMOND A. MENTZER is professor of history at Montana State University. He is the author of several books, including *Blood and Belief: Family Survival and Confessional Identity among the Provincial Huguenot Nobility,* (1994) and he edited *Sin and the Calvinists: Morals Control and the Consistory in the Reformed Tradition* (1994). His current research focuses on social discipline within the French Protestant community during the sixteenth and early seventeenth centuries. He is general editor of the Sixteenth Century Essays & Studies series, now published by Thomas Jefferson University Press of Truman State University.

CHARLES G. NAUERT is professor of history at the University of Missouri–Columbia. He has worked for several years as an historical annotator for the ongoing publication of the letters and collected works of Erasmus by the University of Toronto Press and was author of the introductions and notes for volume 11 of *The Collected Works of Erasmus* (1994). His most recent book is *Humanism and the Culture of Renaissance Europe* (1995). From the late 1970s through 1996, he served as the general editor of the Sixteenth Century Essays & Studies series, then published by Sixteenth Century Journal Publishers, Inc.

PAULA L. PRESLEY is director/editor-in-chief of Thomas Jefferson University Press at Truman State University, production editor of *The Sixteenth Century Journal,* and a freelance book indexer. She is author of articles in *Editing History* (1985) and *Missouri Library World* (1996) as well as "The Library Degree and Academic Publishing," in *What Else Can You Do with a Library Degree: Career Options for the 90s and Beyond,* edited by B.-C. Sellen (1997).

PETER D. SANDLER is the owner of Peter D. Sandler Editorial Services in Glenside, Pennsylvania, is fluent in most western languages and Latin, and has been the proofreader for Sixteenth Century Publishers, Inc., and Thomas Jefferson University Press since 1991. He edits, copyedits, and indexes books, writes newspaper articles, and translates and interprets between French and English. His applies meticulous scrutiny to each and every publication of the *Sixteenth Century Journal,* and he generously donated time to proofreading this book.

Larissa Juliet Taylor is associate professor and chair in the Department of History at Colby College as well as book review editor of *The Sixteenth Century Journal*. She is the author of *Soldiers of Christ: Preaching in Late Medieval and Reformation France* (1992), *François Le Picart and the Beginnings of the Catholic Reformation* (1999), and numerous articles. She is also the recipient of the John Nicholas Brown Prize of the Medieval Academy of American.

Raymond B. Waddington, professor of English at the University of California, Davis, is senior editor of *The Sixteenth Century Journal* and series editor for Garland Studies in the Renaissance. He is the author of *The Mind's Empire* (1974) and numerous articles and reviews. He is coeditor of *The Rhetoric of Renaissance Poetry* (1974), *The Age of Milton* (1980), and *The Expulsion of the Jews* (1994). His fields of interest include Renaissance literature and art, Shakespeare, Milton, cultural and intellectual history, iconography, rhetoric, Italian and Latin.

Merry E. Wiesner-Hanks is professor and chair of the Department of History at the University of Wisconsin–Milwaukee. She is coeditor of *The Sixteenth Century Journal* and is author of *Working Women in Renaissance Germany* (1986), *Women and Gender in Early Modern Europe* (1993), *Gender, Church, and State in Early Modern Germany: Essays by Merry E. Wiesner* (1998), and more than forty articles and other publications on various aspects of women's lives and gender structures in early modern Europe, especially in Germany.

INDEX

Illustrations are indicated by *italics*. An Index of Scripture References is on page 167.

This ream marker should be returned with any comments concerning the ream immediately below.

No. 8

P. H. GLATFELTER CO.
QUALITY PAPER SINCE 1864

References

Colophon

In habent sua fata libelli is set entirely in Bembo typeface, 10.5/13 for body text, 8.5/11 for footnotes. It is the typeface used since 1985 for *The Sixteenth Century Journal*.

Bembo was modeled on typefaces cut by Francesco Griffo for Aldus Manutius' printing of *De Aetna* in 1495 in Venice, a book by classicist Pietro Bembo about his visit to Mount Etna. Griffo's design is considered one of the first of the old style typefaces, which include Garamond, that were used as staple text types in Europe for two hundred years. Stanley Morison supervised the design of Bembo for the Monotype Corporation in 1929.

Bembo is a fine text face because of its well-proportioned letterforms, functional serifs, and lack of peculiarities; the italic is modeled on the handwriting of the Renaissance scribe Giovanni Tagliente. Books and other texts set in Bembo can encompass a large variety of subjects and formats because of its quiet classical beauty and its high readability.

Cover art and title page by Teresa Wheeler, Truman State University designer. Printed in United States of America.

Littera scripta manet.
—Horace